iPad
The Missing Manual

iPad: The Missing Manual

BY J.D. BIERSDORFER

Published by O'Reilly Media, Inc., 1005 Gravenstein Highway North, Sebastopol, CA 95472.

O'Reilly books may be purchased for educational, business, or sales promotional use. Online editions are also available for most titles (*safari.oreilly.com*). For more information, contact our corporate/institutional sales department: 800.998.9938 or corporate@*oreilly.com*.

Executive Editor: Chris Nelson

Editor: Peter McKie

Production Editor: Nellie McKesson

Illustrations: Rob Romano and J. D. Biersdorfer

Indexer: Julie Hawks

Cover Designer: Karen Montgomery

Interior Designers: Ron Bilodeau and J.D. Biersdorfer

Print History:

May 2010:   First Edition.

Images on pages xviii, 3, and 29 appear courtesy of Apple, Inc. Image on page 5 appears courtesy of Logitech. Image on page 36 appears courtesy of Sprint. Images on page 278 appear courtesy Belkin (top) and Griffin Technology (bottom).

ISBN: 978-1-449-38784-6

[CK]   [11/10]

Contents

Chapter 4

Chapter 5

Chapter 6

Chapter 7
Shop the App Store

Chapter 8
iBooks & ePeriodicals

The Missing Credits

About the Author

J.D. Biersdorfer is the author of *iPod: The Missing Manual*, *Netbooks: The Missing Manual* and co-author of *The Internet: The Missing Manual*, *iPhoto '09: The Missing Manual*, and the second edition of *Google: The Missing Manual*. She's been writing the weekly computer Q&A column for *The New York Times* since 1998 and has covered everything from 17th-century Indian art to the world of female hackers for the newspaper. She's also written articles for the *AIGA Journal of Graphic Design*, *Budget Travel*, *The New York Times Book Review*, and *Rolling Stone*. She studied in the Theater & Drama program at Indiana University and spends her spare moments playing the banjo and watching BBC World News. Email: *jd.biersdorfer@gmail.com*.

About the Creative Team

Peter McKie (editor), who still has his second-generation iPhone, edited this book with a keen sense of iPad envy. He has a master's degree in journalism from Boston University and lives in New York City, where he researches the history of old houses and, every once in a while, sneaks into abandoned buildings. Email: *pmckie@oreilly.com*.

Nellie McKesson (production editor) is a graduate of St. John's College in Santa Fe, New Mexico. She lives in Brockton, Mass., and spends her spare time studying graphic design and making t-shirts (*www.endplasticdesigns.com*). Email: *nellie@oreilly.com*.

Julie Hawks (indexer) is an indexer for the Missing Manual series. Her other life includes photography, tinkering with databases, and enjoying nature. Email: *juliehawks@gmail.com*.

Acknowledgements

I would like to thank David Pogue for getting me into the book business back in 2002 and for being a terrific editor on our mutual projects over the years. Also thanks to Peter McKie for making sense of things during the mad scramble, and to Nellie McKesson and all the Missing Manual folks at O'Reilly.

Big thanks to Mac guru Alan Yacavone for his 3G help and to the gang at Niles Creative Group for their video expertise and artistic inspiration. I am also grateful to Apple for providing the iPad images and to the assorted other iPad accessory companies who made their digital photography available.

Book deadlines are detrimental to one's social life, so mad props to Tory, Deb, Linda, Barb, and Andy for understanding. And thanks to the family (especially and most importantly, Betsy Book) for putting up with me during the long hours with Steve Earle and the Carolina Chocolate Drops blasting forth.

—J.D. Biersdorfer

The Missing Manual Series

Missing Manuals are witty, superbly written guides to computer products that don't come with printed manuals (which is just about all of them). Each book features a handcrafted index and RepKover, a detached-spine binding that lets the book lie perfectly flat without the assistance of weights or cinder blocks.

Recent and upcoming titles include:

Access 2010: The Missing Manual by Matthew MacDonald

Buying a Home: The Missing Manual by Nancy Conner

CSS: The Missing Manual, Second Edition, by David Sawyer McFarland

Creating a Web Site: The Missing Manual, Second Edition, by Matthew MacDonald

David Pogue's Digital Photography: The Missing Manual by David Pogue

Dreamweaver CS5: The Missing Manual by David Sawyer McFarland

Excel 2010: The Missing Manual by Matthew MacDonald

Facebook: The Missing Manual, Second Edition by E.A. Vander Veer

FileMaker Pro 11: The Missing Manual by Susan Prosser and Stuart Gripman

Flash CS5: The Missing Manual by Chris Grover

Google Apps: The Missing Manual by Nancy Conner

iMovie '09 & iDVD: The Missing Manual by David Pogue and Aaron Miller

iPad: The Missing Manual by J.D. Biersdorfer with David Pogue

iPhone: The Missing Manual, Second Edition by David Pogue

iPhone App Development: The Missing Manual by Craig Hockenberry

iPhoto '09: The Missing Manual by David Pogue and J.D. Biersdorfer

iPod: The Missing Manual, Eighth Edition by J.D. Biersdorfer with David Pogue

JavaScript: The Missing Manual by David Sawyer McFarland

Living Green: The Missing Manual by Nancy Conner

Mac OS X: The Missing Manual, Leopard Edition by David Pogue

Mac OS X Snow Leopard: The Missing Manual by David Pogue

Microsoft Project 2010: The Missing Manual by Bonnie Biafore

Netbooks: The Missing Manual by J.D. Biersdorfer

Office 2010: The Missing Manual by Nancy Connor, Chris Grover, and Matthew MacDonald

Office 2008 for Macintosh: The Missing Manual by Jim Elferdink

Palm Pre: The Missing Manual by Ed Baig

Personal Investing: The Missing Manual by Bonnie Biafore

Photoshop CS5: The Missing Manual by Lesa Snider

Photoshop Elements 8 for Mac: The Missing Manual by Barbara Brundage

Photoshop Elements 8 for Windows: The Missing Manual by Barbara Brundage

PowerPoint 2007: The Missing Manual by E.A. Vander Veer

Premiere Elements 8: The Missing Manual by Chris Grover

QuickBase: The Missing Manual by Nancy Conner

QuickBooks 2011: The Missing Manual by Bonnie Biafore

Quicken 2009: The Missing Manual by Bonnie Biafore

Switching to the Mac: The Missing Manual, Leopard Edition by David Pogue

Switching to the Mac: The Missing Manual, Snow Leopard Edition by David Pogue

Wikipedia: The Missing Manual by John Broughton

Windows XP Home Edition: The Missing Manual, 2nd Edition by David Pogue

Windows XP Pro: The Missing Manual, 2nd Edition by David Pogue, Craig Zacker, and Linda Zacker

Windows Vista: The Missing Manual by David Pogue

Windows 7: The Missing Manual by David Pogue

Word 2007: The Missing Manual by Chris Grover

Your Body: The Missing Manual by Matthew MacDonald

Your Brain: The Missing Manual by Matthew MacDonald

Your Money: The Missing Manual by J.D. Roth

Introduction

The rumors began years ago: Apple was making a tablet computer! Technology journalists and Apple fans alike hung on every word from company CEO Steve Jobs, waiting for him to reveal the device that, for a long time, was as publicly elusive as unicorns dancing on rainbows. But then, on January 27, 2010, Mr. Jobs introduced the iPad.

Tablet computers, of course, are nothing new. Tech companies have tried the concept since the 1990s. But those flat slabs never caught on for a variety of reasons. Some required input with an easy-to-lose stylus; some had slow, unresponsive touchscreens; and some were so heavy it felt like you were hauling around a patio flagstone that happened to run Windows XP. Most of the public took one look and went: "Nah."

Then came the iPad, and the public showed much more interest, judging by the 300,000 iPads sold the day the tablet went on sale (April 3, 2010).

So why has the iPad proven so popular when the whole tablet concept hasn't exactly burned up the market? One theory: combine a growing desire for Internet access and a shift to digital music, books, and video with a sophisticated, fast, lightweight touchscreen device and you have a gadget perfectly suited to the emerging world of personal media devices. Sure, the iPhone does all that, but you don't have to squint on the iPad. The iPad is both an evolution and a solution.

And thanks to the thousands of third-party apps already available, the iPad can move beyond being just a platter that serves up media and Internet content. In fact, it can pretty much be whatever you want it to be.

You know, this tablet computer thing just may take off at last.

How to Use This Book

The thin pamphlet that Apple includes in each iPad box is enough to get your tablet up and running, charged, and ready to play on the Internet. But you probably want to know more about how the iPad works, all the great things it can do, and where to find its coolest features. This book gives you more iPad info than that wee brochure. It's pre-printed for your convenience, neatly organized by task and topic, *and* it has nice big color pictures.

About→These→Arrows

Throughout this book, and throughout the Missing Manual series, you'll find sentences like this one: "Open the View→Column Browser→On Left" menu. That's shorthand for a longer series of instructions that go something like this: "Go to the menu bar in iTunes, click the View menu, select the Column Browser submenu, and then slide over to the On Left entry." Our shorthand system keep things more snappy than these long, drawn-out instructions.

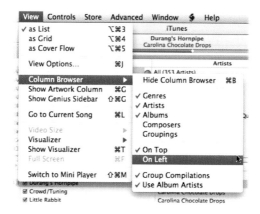

The Very Basics

To use this book, and indeed to use a computer, you need to know a few basics. This book assumes that you're familiar with a few terms and concepts:

- **Clicking.** To *click* means to point the arrow cursor at something on the screen and then to press and release the clicker button on the mouse (or laptop trackpad). To *double-click*, of course, means to click twice in rapid succession, again without moving the cursor at all. To *drag* means to move the cursor *while* pressing the button.

   When you're told to *Ctrl+click* something on a PC, or *⌘-click* something on the Mac, you click while pressing the Ctrl or ⌘ key (both of which are near the Space Bar). But this is an iPad book. You'll tap more than click.

- **Menus.** The *menus* are the words at the top of your screen or window: File, Edit, and so on. Click one to make a list of commands appear, as though they're written on a window shade you just pulled down.

- **Keyboard shortcuts.** Jumping up to menus in iTunes takes time. That's why you'll find keyboard quickies that perform the same menu functions sprinkled throughout the book—Windows shortcuts first, followed by Mac shortcuts in parentheses, like this: "To quickly summon the Preferences box, press Ctrl+comma (⌘-comma)."

If you've mastered this much information, you have all the technical background you need to enjoy *iPad: The Missing Manual*.

About MissingManuals.com

This book helps you get the most out of your iPad. As you read through it, you'll find references to websites that offer additional resources. Each reference includes the site's URL, but you can save yourself some typing by going to this book's Missing CD page at *http://missingmanuals.com/cds/ipadmm/*.

There, you'll find clickable links to the sites mentioned in this book.

The Missing CD page also offers corrections and updates to the book. To see them, click the View Errata link. You're invited to submit corrections and updates yourself by clicking "Submit your own errata" on the same page. To keep this book as up to date and accurate as possible, each time we print more copies, we'll make any confirmed corrections you've suggested.

While you're online, you can register this book at *http://tinyurl.com/yo82k3*. Registering means we can send you updates about the book, and you'll be eligible for special offers like discounts on future editions of *iPad: The Missing Manual*.

Safari® Books Online

 Safari® Books Online is an on-demand digital library that lets you search over 7,500 technology books and videos.

With a subscription, you can read any page and watch any video from our library. Access new titles before they're available in print. Copy and paste code samples, organize your favorites, download chapters, bookmark key sections, create notes, print out pages, and benefit from tons of other time-saving features.

O'Reilly Media has uploaded this book to the Safari Books Online service. To have full digital access to this book and others on similar topics from O'Reilly and other publishers, sign up for free at *http://my.safaribooksonline.com*.

1

Get to Know Your iPad

Sure, you've seen the concept of the iPad before. It's a popular prop in futuristic science-fiction shows like *Star Trek: The Next Generation*: a flat slab of a computer, wirelessly connected to a network that instantly pulls down any information you need, right then and there. (In fact, in the *Star Trek* universe, this device was called a PADD, short for Personal Access Display Device.)

But one thing those movie and TV gadgets never seemed to have is a manual so you could find out things like, say, how to turn down the sound when someone asks a question during your game of Bejeweled 2, or how to get back to the screen where your photos live.

Here on 21st-century Earth, these things may not be obvious for new iPad owners, but that's where this book—and, in particular, this chapter —comes in. In this chapter, you'll learn how to navigate your iPad so you can find the programs you want, jack it into your computer to load movies and photos, and make sure you get it charged up for a full day of fun.

The science fiction is no longer fiction; the future is now.

Turn the iPad On and Off

Think of the iPod, the iMac, and the iPhone. In addition to making products that start with "i," Apple loves to make sleek devices that have a minimum of buttons to disrupt their smooth skin. The iPad is no exception.

Run your finger along the iPad's top edge and you'll find a small black button on the right (circled). It's got a long name: On/Off, Sleep/Wake.

Here are all the things this button does:

• **It turns the iPad off and on.** To turn the iPad totally off, so it gobbles no power at all, press and hold this button for a few a seconds. If you're not going to use your 'Pad for a few days, this is the way to conserve as much battery life as possible.

When you do go for the total shutdown, the iPad presents you with an on-screen arrow to confirm your request. Touch the arrow with your finger and slide it along the screen from left to right.

To turn the iPad back on, press the button again for a second or two. After a minute or so of boot-up gyrations, you're back in business.

• **It puts the iPad to sleep and wakes it up.** To save its strength, the iPad turns off its screen and slips into Sleep (standby) mode when you tap the button. Press the button quickly to wake it up from its power nap. (If you leave your 'Pad untended for more than a minute or so, it goes to sleep then, too. To change its nod-off settings, see page 263.

Whenever you turn on the iPad or wake it up from its electronic slumber, you end up on a locked Home screen. To get to the iPad's goodies, swipe your finger along the slider in the direction of the Unlock arrow. Why is the Home screen always locking itself? Because on a touchscreen device, one unintended tap when the 'Pad's in your backpack or pocketbook can turn on a program

without you knowing it, and *poof*, there goes *that* battery charge.

Use the Volume and Lock Buttons

The buttons on the right edge of the iPad keep your screen stable and handle the audio level for movies, music, and other apps that make noise.

Here they are, from top to bottom:

❶ **Screen Rotation Lock.** The iPad senses which way you're holding it and always tries to rotate the screen orientation to match. But sometimes, like when you want to read in bed, you don't want the screen spinning as you shift around. Flip the lock button on the side of the iPad to force the screen to stay in one position until you hit the switch again to unlock it.

❷ **Volume.** Press the top half of this rocker-style switch to increase the volume through the iPad's speaker or the ear-buds you may be wearing (see page 263). Press the bottom half of the switch to lower the volume; hold it down for a second or two to mute. The iPad displays a little volume graphic on-screen so you can see where you are on the Relative Scale of Loudness.

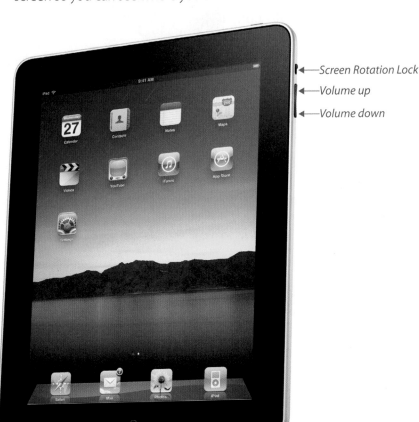

←——Screen Rotation Lock
←——Volume up
←——Volume down

Connect Through iPad Jacks and Ports

While the iPad's innards are full of state-of-the-art hardware, the outside isn't very complex at all—just four buttons (On/Off-Sleep/Wake, Volume, Screen Rotation Lock, and, discussed on page 6, the Home button). The outside of the iPad sports two jacks where you plug in cords. Here's what you do with 'em.

❶ **Headphone Jack.** Although it doesn't come with its own headphones, as iPods and iPhones do, the iPad does offer a headphone jack on its top-left edge. You can plug in any pair of earbuds or headphones that come with the standard 3.5-millimeter stereo miniplug. Page 5 has more on that.

❷ **Dock Connector.** The flat port on the iPad's bottom edge is called the Dock Connector. You plug the provided USB cable in here to connect your iPad to your computer for battery-charging, as well as for music, iBook, and video fill-ups from your iTunes library. This thin port has been a fixture on iPods since 2003, which means that certain accessories, like stereo-audio docks meant for an iPod, may work for the iPad just fine—but check the tech specs before you buy anything new. The Dock Connector snaps right into the tablet's optional external keyboard, too.

Note You may notice two other features on the iPad's outer edges (no, sadly, neither's a USB port or an SD card slot). The small hole near the headphone jack is the iPad's microphone for Voice Memos and other "listening" apps. And behind that trio of mesh-covered holes near the Dock Connector hides the iPad's external speaker.

Add Earbuds and Earphones

Want to use your iPad for private listening? Back in the old days, the only headphones you could get came with a cord attached, and those still work just fine. But if you want to free yourself from wires while you lay back, relax, and listen to a Bach cello suite, get a pair of stereo Bluetooth headphones that connect wirelessly to the Bluetooth chip inside the iPad. Your only entanglement then will be mind with music.

Here's how you get either type of headphone to work on the iPad:

- **Wired.** Pretty much any pair of headphones or earbuds with the ubiquitous 3.5mm stereo plug fits the iPad's headphone jack. (Why, yes, you *can* use the familiar white earbuds from your iPod if you want.) Just be sure to push the plug firmly into the headphone jack so it fully connects.

- **Bluetooth.** When you shop for stereo Bluetooth headphones, look for those advertised as *A2DP*; they're designed to play back music in stereo. To get them to work, you need to pair the headphones with your iPad. (*Pairing* means introducing two Bluetooth devices so they can communicate with each other; you only have to do this the first time you use the two devices together.)

The 'phone manual tells you which button to push on the headphones to pair the two. As for the iPad, start on the Home screen and tap Settings→General→Bluetooth. Turn Bluetooth on. The iPad looks around and once it finds the 'phones, it lists them by name. If the headphones require a passkey (listed in the  manual), the iPad keyboard appears so you can type in the digits. Once paired, the iPad screen says *Connected* next to the headphones icon and the sound now plays over your wireless connection.

 Tip On some Bluetooth headsets, a small transceiver plugs into the iPad jack and communicates with the 'phones. If you have one of these, you don't need to turn on the iPad's Bluetooth chip; the transceiver does the communicating for you.

Find the Home Button

There's only one button on the front of the iPad: the Home button. This round, gently indented switch sits in the bottom-center of the iPad's black picture frame (known as the bezel in geek-speak). This is the button you'll probably use most often in your iPad adventures.

Pressing the Home button does a few things. For one, it *always* takes you Home—back to the iPad's main screen, where you can get to all your program icons. Since the iPad lets you run only one application at a time, you use the Home button to switch programs, too. You could be waist-deep in a Keynote presentation (see page 158) and want to take a break with an episode of *Glee*. Just press the Home button to close Keynote (and automatically save your file, by the way) and go back to the main iPad screen, then tap open your Videos icon to get to your shows.

But the Home button has a few more tricks up its sleeve. You can program it to do specific tasks when you double-click it. To set this up, go to the Home screen and tap Settings→General→Home. Here, you have three choices for double-clickin' Home-button fun. Tap the one you want:

- **Home.** Often end up six screens of apps away from your first Home screen, with its Settings icon and other default programs? Double-click to go Home.

- **Search.** Do you find yourself summoning the Spotlight search function (page 28) constantly to find stuff on your iPad? Select Search to go there in two clicks.

- **iPod.** Is music a constant part of your iPad experience, even when you wander away from the iPod app (page 102)? Choose iPod here to summon the music playback controls with the Home button two-press.

Tour the Home Screen Icons

Even before you add a single app to the iPad, it comes with a whole bunch of programs ready to use. These include personal-organization tools like Calendar, Contacts, and Notes, a Maps app so you can find your way around, YouTube to catch up on the latest in online videos, and a Videos program to play movies you sock away on the iPad itself.

The iTunes and App Store icons take you to Apple's online stores, while the Settings icon lets you adjust the way the iPad and its programs behave. Along the bottom of the screen, you'll find icons for Safari (the iPad's web browser), Mail, Photos, and iPod—the latter's where all your iTunes music hangs out. Don't worry, you'll learn about all these apps and icons in Chapter 6.

Add More Home Screens

Once you start adding programs to the iPad, you may find your Home screen getting a little crowded. Fortunately, the iPad lets you have more than one Home screen—in fact, you can have 11 of 'em.

To navigate among them, flick your finger across the iPad's surface. The small white dots at the bottom of the screen (circled) show you how many Home screens you have and which one you're on.

Want to rearrange your icons? Press and hold any icon for a few seconds until all the icons start wiggling and jiggling. Use your finger to drag them around to new locations—or off the edge of one screen and onto the next. Press the Home button to stop the Dance of the Icons.

 Note If your Home screen looks different or your Home button won't do shortcuts, odds are your iPad is running newer software. See Page 274 for more information

Install iTunes on Your Computer

To copy the music, videos, photos, and other stuff from your Windows PC or Mac over to your iPad, you need to install Apple's iTunes multimedia, multi-function jukebox program on your computer (you'll set up iTunes on your iPad in just a sec). With iTunes, you also get Apple's QuickTime software—a video helper for iTunes. Don't worry, it's all free and just a web download away:

❶ **Fire up your computer's web browser and point it to** *www.itunes.com/downloads*.

❷ **Click the "Download Now" button.** (Turn off the "Email me…" and "Keep me up to date…" checkboxes to spare yourself future marketing missives.) Wait for the file to download.

❸ **When the file lands on your hard drive, double-click the** *iTunesSetup.exe* **file.** If you use a Mac, double-click the *iTunes.dmg* file and then open the *iTunes.mpkg* file to start the installation. If your Mac's younger than six years old, you probably already have iTunes installed. Go to Menu→Software Update and ask your Mac to see if there's a newer version of iTunes, just in case.

❹ **Follow the screens until the software installer says it's done.**

You may need to restart your computer after you install iTunes. Once that's done, you're ready to connect your new iPad to your computer.

 The hardware and operating-system requirements needed to run iTunes are listed below the Download Now button. If you have an older computer, it's worth a glance just to make sure your rig can handle the program.

Connect to Your Computer

Odds are you had that iPad out of its box about five seconds after you got it. Yeah, you've been running your hands over its smooth edges, turning it on and tapping your way around the screen. In addition to that sleek tablet, you'll find the following in the box:

❶ A white USB cable with Apple's flat 30-pin Dock Connector plug on one end and a standard flat USB plug on the other.

❷ A square-shaped 10-watt USB power adapter.

❸ A little pamphlet of basic quick-start information that's not nearly as fun or as colorful as this book.

What you want right now is the USB cable. Connect the small, narrow end to your computer's USB port and the wide, flat end to the iPad. The first time you connect your iPad to a computer, the iTunes Setup Assistant walks you through a few steps to get your iPad ready to go.

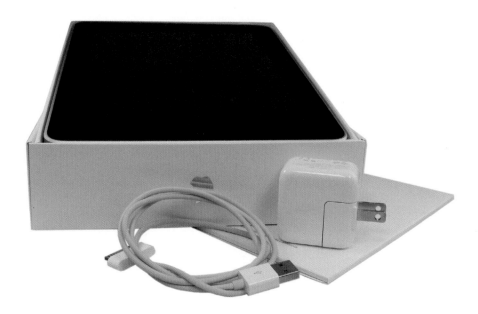

Set Up Your iPad in iTunes

The first time you plug in your new iPad (after you install iTunes, of course), the Setup Assistant leaps into action, asking you to name your iPad, and if you'd like to sync all the photos, videos, and other content on your computer to the tablet. If you use iTunes already to manage an iPod or iPhone, odds are you already have a healthy media library on your computer.

Depending on the size of your iPad's drive, you may be able to fit all your stuff on it—or maybe not, if you have more than 16, 32, or 64 gigabytes of digital treasures on your computer. If you have less than that and want to take it all with you, just click the Finish button in the Setup box. iTunes loads a copy of everything in its library that fits onto your iPad.

During this process, the Setup Assistant lets you turn on the iPad's VoiceOver feature, which is part of Apple's accessibility software for its products, described at *www.apple.com/accessibility/voiceover*. VoiceOver is a screen reader for the visually impaired that announces menu names and titles out loud. It basically narrates what's on the iPad screen, speaks up when you get new messages, and describes whatever icon you touch. (If you want to try the feature later, choose Settings→General→ Accessibility→VoiceOver→On.)

Disconnect from Your Computer

When it comes time to disconnect your iPad from the computer, you don't really have to do anything special: Just unplug the cable and take off, iPad in hand. The only time you *don't* want to unplug the cable is when the iPad screen says *Sync in Progress*. This means the iPad and computer are exchanging data and if you disconnect the USB cable, one of those devices is *not* going to get all the files you're trying to copy between the two.

 Tip You can cancel a current sync session by dragging the Cancel Sync slider on the iPad's screen.

Now, the simplicity of this disconnection process may sound scary to longtime iPod owners who remember ominous error messages and sometimes scrambled iPods if they pulled the plug. If you want to go old-school with an Eject button, iTunes gives you a couple of options:

❶ Click the little Eject icon next to the name of your iPad in the iTunes Source list (circled).

❷ If your iPad's already selected in the Source list, choose Control→Eject iPad or press Ctrl+E (⌘-E).

Now you can unplug your iPad without fear.

Work with iTunes

iTunes not only lets you decide which songs, books, and videos end up on your iPad, it also helps you keep your iPad's internal software up to date, shows you how much space you have left on your tablet, and lets you change your music, video, and podcast synchronization options.

When you connect your 'Pad to your computer, it shows up in the iTunes Source list (in the Devices area), Click the iPad icon to see your options, represented by a series of tabs at the top of the screen. Each tab lets you control a different kind of content, like music, photos, or games.

Here, on the Summary screen, iTunes tells you:

❶ The size of your iPad's storage space and its serial number.

❷ Whether your 'Pad has the latest software on it (and if you're having problems with your iPad, you get the chance to reinstall the software).

❸ Whether you set iTunes to automatically synchronize with your iPad or whether you need to update its contents manually. (Automatic means everything in iTunes ends up on your iPad—space permitting, of course; manual means you get to pick and choose what gets transferred.)

❹ The different media types filling up your iPad. This info comes in the form of a bar at the bottom of the screen. iTunes color-codes your media types (blue for Audio, yellow for Photos, and so on) and shows you how much space each takes up using the appropriate color in the bar. For even more detail, click the bar to see your media stats in terms of number of items, the amount of drive space they use, or the number of days' worth of a particular type of media you have.

❺ Your iPad's contents and playlists. Click the flippy triangle next to the iPad (circled right).

So that's what you can learn about your iPad and its contents from looking at iTunes. Later in this book, you'll learn how to transfer different types of media to the iPad and how to use them on the tablet.

For example, Chapter 13 is all about playing your favorite music on the iPad, Chapter 14 covers syncing and playing videos, while Chapter 15 explains copying your photos from computer to iPad—which makes a great handheld picture frame to show off your shots.

To learn more about iTunes and how it works, take a trip to Chapter 11 for a detailed tour through the program. And if you want to explore the virtual shelves of the iTunes App Store so you can load up your iPad, skip to Chapter 7.

 Note After this book originally went to press, Apple updated the iTunes software. Most of the images in this book show the more colorful iTunes 9, but iTunes 10 works almost identically—the most noticeable difference is iTunes 10's drab gray interface.

Charge the iPad Battery

Many Apple devices ship with enough power to run them for a short while. But as you poke and prod your new gadget, that charge won't last long, so you'll want to get the iPad connected to a power source to refill its battery properly. You can charge your 'Pad in one, or maybe two, ways:

- **Charge by AC adapter.** Look! Another charger for your collection! Your iPad comes with a square little 10-watt AC adapter ready to keep your tablet charged. It has a USB port on one side, and a plug on the other. To boost your battery, plug the flat end of the iPad's USB cable into the cube's USB port. Then plug the cube's pronged end into an electrical outlet. Hitch up the Dock  Connector side of the USB cable to the bottom of your iPad and charge away. (Older, smaller adapters from iPhones and older iPods may work if you turn the iPad screen off to direct the full stream of juice to the iPad's battery, but their low flow will likely charge the iPad much more slowly than its native adapter.)

- **Charge by computer.** Unlike iPods and iPhones, charging the iPad over your computer's USB port isn't a sure thing anymore. While USB ports on some newer computers—like late-model iMacs—have enough juice, many older ones don't. To see for sure, grab the USB cable and plug your iPad into your PC or Mac's USB port. If you see a "Not Charging" message in the top corner of your iPad, you know your port is underpowered. (The USB port will probably "trickle charge" if the iPad screen is off, but very slowly.)

It takes only a few hours to fully gas up your iPad's battery. When you plug it in, the iPad displays a translucent battery that fills up with green power. A smaller, black-and-white battery icon up in the iPad's status bar displays a lightning bolt, along with a percentage of the battery's current charge.

The iPad is fully charged when the battery icon in the menu bar shows 100%.

Apple says a full battery charge lasts up to 10 hours for web browsing, videos, and listening to music. Your results may vary.

Extend Battery Life

Apple posts various recommendations on its iPad website to ensure long battery life:

- Don't expose your iPad to extreme hot or cold temperatures—keep it between 32 and 95 degrees Fahrenheit. (In other words, don't leave it in a hot, parked car, and don't expect it to operate on Mt. Everest.)

- Use your iPad regularly (not that you wouldn't). And be sure to charge it at least once a month to keep that battery chemistry peppy.

- Put the iPad to sleep to conserve power (press the Sleep/Wake button on top).

- Take the iPad out of any heat-trapping cases before you charge it up.

- Dim the screen when you don't need it at total brightness (see page 262).

- When you see the Low Battery icon or message, plug your iPad into an electrical outlet using the AC adapter. The iPad battery indicator shows roughly how much charge the battery has left.

- Features like the music equalizer—or jumping around within your media library—can drain your battery faster, as can using big, uncompressed file formats, like AIFF (see page 188). To cut back on the equalizer, see page 267.

- That wireless chip inside the iPad saps power even if you're not trawling the Web. Save energy by turning it off when you don't need it; go to Settings→Wi-Fi and tap Off. Lower the frequency with which you check email or have data pushed to the iPad from the Internet to save some energy as well—make those adjustments at Settings→Mail, Contacts, Calendars. Bluetooth and Location Services also take their toll, and you can turn them off by visiting the Settings icon.

Keep the iPad Screen Clean

Like the iPhone and iPod Touch, the iPad's glass touchscreen is the main way you communicate with the device. Each time you surf the Web or send some email, your fingers tap, slide, and flick across this smooth surface. Do this sort of thing on a normal piece of glass and you end up with a smudged and sticky window or mirror, gunked up from finger grease, moisturizer, and whatever else you may have on your hands.

Thanks to a special coating (explained in the Note on the opposite page), the iPad's screen tries to repel fingerprints. But with enough use, even that has its limits; your screen begins to look like a small child who's eating a glazed doughnut has been touching your iPad repeatedly — with both hands. If this happens, wipe the screen gently with a soft, lint-free cloth—the kind you use to clean a flat-panel TV screen, camera lens, or pair of glasses.

Whatever you do, *don't* use products like Windex, Formula 409, stuff from spray cans, ammonia- or alcohol-based cleansers, solvents, or a scratchy cleaning pad. These types of cleaning products will only compromise the iPad's special coating, and you don't want that.

If the rest of the iPad gets schmutzed up, a quick cleaning session can return its shine. To buff it up, turn it off (page 2) and unplug it from any connected docks or USB cables. Then take a lightly water-dampened lint-free cloth and wipe down the iPad's back and sides. Be careful not to slop water into openings

 Tip Smears and screen glare got you down? A thin sheet of plastic screen-protector film from your favorite accessory dealer could be your ticket to iPad happiness— and extra protection as well. For example, there's Zagg's $40 military-grade InvisibleSHIELD at *www.zagg.com*.

like the headphone jack, Dock Connector port, or speaker grills. Then wipe your slab down with a *dry* lint-free cloth.

The iPad screen is scratch-resistant, but it could break if you accidentally bounce the tablet off a concrete floor or have some other gravity-related mishap. If disaster strikes and you crack or chip the screen, don't use the iPad or try to pry out the broken glass. Put it in a box or wrap it up to prevent glass shards from falling out, then take it to your nearest Apple Store or authorized Apple service provider for repair. Appendix B has more on iPad care and repair.

To protect your iPad as much as possible, both from accidental drops or even bouncing around in your shoulder bag alongside house keys, sunglass cases, and loose credit cards, consider a case for it. Accessory makers have already come up with a huge selection of cases, from stately leather portfolio models to neon-colored rubber shells meant to jazz up your iPad while helping you keep a firm grip on the thing.

When considering a case, think about how you plan to carry and use the iPad. If it's going to ride along in a backpack, a sturdy padded pouch may be more protective that a thin leather binder-type cover. Page 278 has some tips on the type of cases available and where to buy them.

 Apple describes the iPad's screen as having a "fingerprint-resistant *oleophobic* coating," which makes it sound like the device has some sort of psychiatric condition or a fear of butter substitutes (known as oleomargarine back in the day). Not to worry! *Oleo*, from the Latin *oleum*, just means "oil" — like the natural oils from your fingertips when you slide them around the iPad's glossy screen. The oleophobic coating is just a plastic polymer applied to the iPad's glass that's supposed to cut down on smeary pawprints.

2

Interact with Your iPad

Touchscreens are nothing new; these days you find them every-
where. They've been on automatic teller machines for years, and
dispensing New York City subway fare cards for more than a decade.
Some delis let you order up a turkey-and-swiss by pressing a touch-sensitive menu. So, in the grand scheme of things, the iPad's touchscreen interface isn't unfamiliar.

But *using* the iPad takes more than touch. You tap, you flick, you swipe, you
double-tap, you drag, you press-and-hold. *Which* motion you make and
when you make it depends on *what* you're trying to do at the time. And
that's *where* this chapter comes in.

Over the next few pages, you'll learn how to do the digit dance so your
iPad responds to your every command. You'll also pick up a few keyboard
shortcuts, and learn how to use your fingers to find stuff on your 'Pad. So
get those hands limbered up by turning the page to get started.

Finger Moves for the iPad

The "brain" behind the iPad—its operating system—is smart enough to respond to a series of very different touches. The ones you make depend on what you want to do. These are the moves:

- **Tap.** Take the tip of your finger and directly touch the icon, thumbnail, song title, or control you see on-screen. The iPad isn't a crusty old calculator, so you don't have to push down hard; a gentle press does the trick.

- **Drag.** Keep your fingertip pressed down on the glass and slide it around to scroll to different parts of the screen. This way, you can set volume sliders or pan around a photo. A *two-finger drag* scrolls a window within a window (like the floating window that pops up over your Facebook screen when you call up your Facebook Friends List).

- **Slide.** A slide is like a drag, except that you use it almost exclusively with one special control—the iPad's Unlock/Confirm button, which sits in a "track" that guides your slide  as you wake your iPad from sleep or confirm a total shut-down.

- **Flick.** Lightly and quickly whip your finger up or down your screen and watch a web page or song list whiz by in the direction of your flick. The faster you flick, the faster the screen scrolls by. In a photo album, flick side-to-side to see your images parade triumphantly across your screen.

- **Finger Spread and Pinch.** To zoom in on part of a photo, document, or web page, put your thumb and index finger together, place them on-screen where you want to zoom in, and make a spreading motion across the glass. To zoom out, put your spread fingers on-screen and pinch them together.

- **Double-Tap.** This two-steppin' tap comes into play in a couple of situations. First, it serves as a quick way to zoom in on a photo or web page. Second, if you're watching a video, tap the screen twice to toggle between aspect ratios—the full-screen view (top, right), where the edges of the frame get cropped off, or the wide-screen, letterboxed view (bottom, right), which movie lovers favor because it's what the director intended a scene to look like.

Use the iPad Keyboard

The iPad has no physical keys—unless you buy the optional keyboard (see page 29). A virtual keyboard, therefore, is the default system for entering text.

The iPad's keyboard pops up whenever you tap on an area that accepts input, like the address bar of a web browser, a blank Note page, or the text area of a new email message.

To use it, just tap the key you want. As your finger hits the glass, the light-gray target key confirms your choice by flickering to a darker gray.

The keyboard works in portrait (vertical) mode, but it's roomier when you go for the landscape (horizontal) view. The button with the keyboard icon in the bottom-right (circled above) makes the keyboard go away. The keyboard has a few other special keys. They are:

❶ **Shift (⇧).** When you tap this key, the normally clear arrow turns blue to show you it's in effect. The next letter you type appears capitalized. Once you type a letter, the ⇧ key returns to normal, signalling that the following letter will show up in lowercase.

❷ **Backspace (⌫).** This key actually has three speeds: Tap it once to delete the letter just to the left of the blinking cursor. Hold it down to "walk" backward, deleting each letter as you go. Finally, hold it down long enough, and it deletes *words* rather than letters, one chunk at a time.

❸ **.?123 .** Tap this button to insert numbers or punctuation. The keyboard changes to offer a palette of digits and symbols. Tap the same key—which now says ABC—to return to the letters keyboard. (Happily, there's a much faster way to get a number or symbol—touch and hold the **.?123** key, and then drag your finger to the number or character you want.)

When you're on the numbers/symbols pad, a new button appears, labeled **#+=** . Tapping it summons a *third* keyboard layout, containing less frequently used characters, like brackets, the # and % symbols, bullets, and math symbols.

When you type letters into a web form (or anyplace that's not a web address), the iPad adds a return key to the keyboard so you can move from one line to the next. This key morphs to say Join when you type in a WiFi password, Go when you enter a URL, and Search when you query the search box.

Cut, Copy, and Paste

The iPad's ability to move text and images around within a document (or between documents) is useful, but it's not the tablet's most intuitive feature. And no, you can't use Ctrl-C to copy something because the keyboard *has* no Control key. But never fear, here's how you move text and images from place to place—or program to program:

❶ To cut or copy text that you can edit (like an outgoing email message or a note), double-tap a word to high-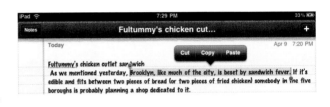
light it. A Cut | Copy | Paste | Replace box pops up. To select more words, drag the blue dots on either end of the selected word. Then tap the Cut or Copy command. (If you select more than one word, you don't see the Replace option; the next page has more on that.)

❷ For pages you *can't* edit (like incoming emails), hold your finger down until you see a magnifying glass and insertion-point cursor. Drag it to the text you want to copy. When you lift your finger, a Select or Select All box appears. Select gives you the blue dots you can drag to highlight more text or photos. Select All highlights everything on-screen. Lift your finger to get
a Copy button. Web pages work a little differently: When you lift your finger there, you go right to the Copy button, as shown above.

❸ Tap the spot where you want to paste the text or photo. You can even jump to a different program. Now, tap within it to get the Paste button.

❹ Tap that button to copy the text or pic into the new location, file, or program.

Make a mistake and wish you could undo what you just did? Give the iPad a quick shake and tap the Undo Paste or Undo Typing button that appears. Just

---

Tip Need to select a whole paragraph at once? Tap it quickly four times.

be careful when you shake that iPad—you don't want to send your $500 high-tech tablet flying across the room because you pasted the word "celery" on the wrong line of a recipe.

In addition to the Cut, Copy, and Paste options in files where you can edit text (like Notes), you can also replace a misspelled word with one that's spelled correctly. Or you can replace one word with a different word altogether. To get the Replace option, double-tap or select a word on-screen. When the Cut | Copy | Paste | Replace box appears, tap Replace. The iPad offers up a few alternate words for you. If you see the word you *meant* to type, tap it to replace the text.

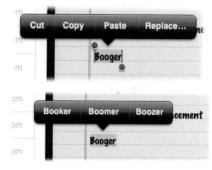

But enough about text—want to copy a photo or video into a message-in-progress or some other program? Hold your finger down on the screen until the Copy button pops up, as shown in the illustration below. Tap the Copy button, create an email, and tap the message body to get a Paste button. Tap it to insert your image or video.

If you want to copy multiple items, like pictures out of a photo album, tap the 🗗 icon in the top-right corner. Next, tap the photos you want to copy; blue checkmarks appear in the corners to indicate your selection. Tap the Copy button on the top-left side of the toolbar, switch to the program where you want to deposit your pics (like a mail message under construction), and press the glass until the Paste button appears.

Discover iPad Keyboard Shortcuts

As you've probably discovered by now, the iPad keyboard has to get a bit creative to fit all the keys you need on a small patch of glass. But let's face it, when you're trying to finish an email message, jumping around between keyboard layers to find an ampersand or apostrophe gets old fast. To help balance economy and efficiency, Apple built in a number of keyboard shortcuts and tricks to help you out.

- **Web addresses.** When you type a web address in Safari, the keyboard helpfully adds keys for commonly used characters. For example, you  get a slash, underscore, hyphen, and, best of all, a *.com* button (circled). Not going to a *.com* address? Press and hold the *.com* button to get your choice of *.edu*, *.org*, or *.net*, and slide your finger over to the one you want. When you finish, tap the Go button.

- **Bad aim.** Finger on the wrong key? If you haven't lifted your digit off the screen yet, slide it over to the correct one and let go.

- **Instant apostrophes.** The iPad fills in the apostrophe on many contractions for you, so if you type *cant*, the tablet corrects it with *can't*.

- **Accented characters.** Need an accented letter, say, an *é* instead of a plain old *e*? Press and hold the *e* character to reveal a whole bunch of accented choices. Slide your finger to select the one you need. This trick works on most letters that take accent marks.

- **Punctuation.** Apple's press-and-slide trick works in a couple of other places as well. Need an apostrophe instead of that comma key on the main keyboard? Press the comma and slide. Need an ampersand but don't want to tap all the way into the ?123 keyboard? Press the ?123 key and slide over to it without taking your finger off the keyboard—or having to switch back to the ABC keyboard.

> **Tip** If you don't look at text as you type—and don't notice the iPad's auto-corrections until after it makes them—you can have the tablet pipe up and verbally announce its word suggestions. Just tap through to Settings→General→Accessibility→ Speak Auto-text. You can turn it off here, too.

- **Auto-correction.** The iPad's dictionary tries to automatically correct typos and spelling errors as you tap along. If you want to accept the suggested correction for a word you just typed, hit the space bar and keep going. Don't agree with the iPad? Tap the word to reject the suggested correction. Proper nouns often make the iPad's dictionary overeager to help, but if you reject its suggestions enough times, it eventually learns what you want. In some programs, words the iPad is still suspicious about get underlined in red; tap them to see alternate spelling suggestions. (If the constant corrections bug you, turn them off at Settings→General→Keyboard→Auto-Correction.)

Speaking of the Settings area, the iPad tucks away several helpful shortcuts here. Just go to Settings→General→Keyboard to see them.

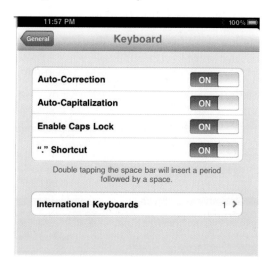

- **Auto-Capitalization.** When you turn this setting on, the iPad automatically capitalizes the first letter after a period.

- **Enable Caps Lock.** If you NEED TO TYPE LIKE THIS FOR A WHILE, flip on this setting. Now, when you double-tap the Shift (⇧) key, it turns blue and keeps capitalizing until you tap it again to turn it off.

- **"." Shortcut.** With this setting turned on, you just have to double-tap the space bar at the end of a sentence to automatically end it with a period and move one space ahead to start your next sentence with a capital letter.

When you tap the International Keyboards option, you can add foreign-language keyboards. Turn the page to find out more.

Use an International Keyboard

If American English is your only language, you can skip these next two pages. But if, over the course of your iPadding day, you find yourself communicating in French, Spanish, German, Russian, Chinese, Japanese, Dutch, Flemish, Italian, Canadian French, or British English, you can add a keyboard layout that reflects the standards of those languages.

To give your iPad some global input:

❶ Tap Settings→General→Keyboard→International Keyboard and tap Add New Keyboard.

❷ On the Add New Keyboard screen, peruse the list of languages and tap the one you want to converse in, like German to add a German-character keyboard. The iPad adds your choice to your personal list of keyboards at Settings→General→Keyboard→International Keyboard→Keyboards.

❸ You get your choice of keyboard layout, too. To pick one, tap the language name in your list of keyboards. Here, you can pick the keyboard layout (QWERTY, AZERTY, QWERTZ, and so on) for the iPad screen. If you plan to use an external keyboard as well (or instead), you can select a hardware layout, too, like the one for a Bluetooth keyboard that uses the standard German character map or one that uses the Dvorak layout.

Once you add and configure your new keyboards, call them up when you need to leap into a memo in Dutch or Japanese.

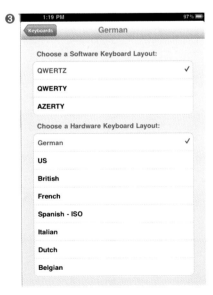

You can switch keyboards two ways:

❶ First, you can tap the key that has the globe icon (circled), just to the left of the space bar. With each tap, it cycles through your personal keyboards, briefly flashing its name on the space bar. Stop when you see the keyboard you want.

❷ Alternatively, you can press down on the globe key for a minute to pop up a list of all your keyboards, then slide your finger up to the one you want.

Type away. When you want to switch back to English or to another keyboard language, go to the globe.

Delete a Keyboard

To delete an international keyboard you no longer want, choose Settings→General→Keyboard→ International Keyboard. Tap the Edit button above the Keyboards list, then tap the ⊖ next to the one you want to lose, and then tap the Delete button that appears. To rearrange the order in which your keyboards appear in the globe menu, use the grip strip icons (≡) to drag them into the desired new world order. Then tap Done.

 Note The iPad offers several languages that use non-Western character sets, including Japanese, Chinese (Simplified) Pinyan, and Chinese (Simplified) Handwriting. "Handwriting on a keyboard?" you wonder. No problem for the iPad: when you select Chinese (Simplified) Handwriting as your keyboard option, you get a virtual touchpad on the screen to enter Chinese character strokes with the tip of your finger. The iPad sees what you're doing and offers a list of matching characters you can choose from.

Search the iPad

Once you get your iPad fully loaded, you may actually want to find something on it—a certain song in your music library, a calendar appointment you need to reference, or someone's address. If you have 64 gigabytes of stuff on a bulging iPad, you may not want to wade around looking for a nugget of information. You can, however, shine the *Spotlight* on it.

Spotlight is the iPad's built-in tool for introspection and self-searching. It lets you scan your iPad for words, apps, phrases, names, titles, and more. You can call up song files, old appointments, email messages with directions to Gettysburg, and all sorts of other things. You get to Spotlight in a few different ways:

- If you're on your first Home screen, press the Home button to call up Spotlight.

- If you're a few Home screens deep, flick backwards from left to right until you *pass* your first Home screen and arrive at the Spotlight screen, where you can flick no further.

Once you're on the Spotlight screen, type the name or words you're looking for ("Doctor Lee" or "Owen" or "Gettysburg"). Spotlight begins to search even before you finish typing, and narrows the list as you continue. On the search results screen, tap any item to open it.

You can even launch an app from the list of results—which is a great way to fire up programs after you fill up your 11 Home screens with icons and don't have any place to display app links anymore.

> **Tip** The iOS 4.2 iPad update allows multitasking—you can keep one app running while you switch to another. To do that, when you're in the first app, press the Home button twice, and then pick your next app from the on-screen list. Page 274 has more on updating to iOS 4.2.

Add an External Keyboard

It's okay, you can admit it. You've tried and tried and tried, but you just can't deal with that flat glass typing surface. Your fingers long for the tactile feel of softly clicking Chiclet keys beneath them, especially for huge documents or programs that require lots of text entry.

If this describes you, fear not. You can get the comfort of a physical keyboard, and you even have a couple of options.

Bluetooth Keyboard

The iPad conveniently has a Bluetooth chip tucked inside it, so you can use the slab with a Bluetooth-enabled wireless keyboard, like the stylish $69 model Apple makes (shown here). To get the iPad ready for the wireless keyboard, choose  Settings→General→Bluetooth→On. Then follow the instructions that come with your particular keyboard to put it into Bluetooth pairing mode—this usually means holding down a button until something blinks.

The iPad looks around for nearby devices, and should find the keyboard singing its Bluetooth siren song. When you see the keyboard in the Devices list, select it and type in any passkey numbers it requests (check your keyboard manual for them) to complete the connection. The Bluetooth icon (✳) and keyboard name appear on-screen to announce their pairing. To go back to the virtual keyboard, choose Settings→General→Bluetooth→Off or press the Eject key on the Bluetooth keyboard.

iPad Keyboard Dock

If you want to simultaneously power your 'Pad while you type, consider Apple's combination iPad Keyboard Dock. It's a full-size keyboard sitting atop a charging dock. You plug the power cord into the wall, stick the iPad in its little charger booster seat and peck away with the screen tilted at a comfortable viewing angle.

You can also connect the iPad Keyboard Dock USB cable to our computer to do some syncing. With even more optional cables, you can connect the dock to your TV, stereo, or video projector. Visit *store.apple.com* to see the iPad Keyboard Dock and other accessories, like the plain iPad Dock, the Component and Composite AV cables, or the Dock Connector to VGA Adapter.

3

Get Online

You can get content onto your iPad in two ways: by pulling it down from the sky—or rather, the Internet—and by synchronizing it with your computer to copy over music, videos, books, and other files through iTunes. This chapter tells you how to get your iPad set up for that first option. (If you want to read up on the second one because you just can't wait, jump ahead to Chapter 11.)

Every iPad can connect to the Internet over a Wi-Fi connection. You can get online from your home wireless network or from a Wi-Fi hot spot at the local technology-friendly coffee shop. But some iPads don't need to be anchored to a stationary Wi-Fi network to get to the ether. Wi-Fi + 3G iPads can reach out and connect to the Web over AT&T's 3G data network—which covers a large part of the country.

This chapter explains the difference between Wi-Fi and 3G, how to set up each type of connection, and how to stay safe online while using either. So if you're ready to fire up that wireless chip and get your iPad out on the Internet, read on.

Should You Use Wi-Fi or 3G?

If you bought the Wi-Fi iPad, you don't have much of a decision to make here—you get your Internet access by jumping onto your nearest wireless network or *hot spot*. (A hot spot is a wireless network like the one you may have at home, but it's in a public place, like an airport or coffee shop; it's sometimes free, but more likely you'll pay a fee to use it, as page 34 explains).

If you have your own Wi-Fi network, say at home, you can pop your iPad onto it with just a couple of taps—see the next page for instructions. If you don't have your own network, you need to set one up or find a nearby Wi-Fi hot spot you can legally use if you want to download email, web pages, and iTunes Store content out of thin air. (The iPad doesn't have an Ethernet jack for those old-fashioned wired network connections, by the way.)

But if you bought the 3G-enabled iPad, you have a choice of connections. You're not limited to a Wi-Fi network because you can use AT&T's mostly nationwide 3G data network—the same one iPhones use for email, web surfing, and telephone calls.

So if you have a choice, which should you use, and when? In general, stick with Wi-Fi when you can. It's likely going to be faster. And remember, AT&T charges you to use its 3G network. You may not care if you're grandfathered into the old $30 unlimited access deal, but if you have the budget $15-a-month plan for 250 megabytes of data, you may be surprised at how quickly that 250 megs adds up (it's less than two hours of streaming mediocre-quality web video).

That said, if there's no Wi-Fi hot spot in range, let 'er rip with the 3G. You now have a link to the Internet pretty much wherever you go—so long as you're under AT&T's network umbrella.

 Tip If you haven't yet bought an iPad and are torn between the Wi-Fi and Wi-Fi + 3G models, take a quick look at AT&T's 3G network map at *www.att.com/wireless* to make sure you live in an area that actually *has* 3G coverage. It's a nationwide network, but there are some gaps in less-populated areas.

Get Your Wi-Fi Connection

No matter which iPad you have, you can connect to the Internet over a working *Wi-Fi* network, known to geeks as an 802.11 or *Wireless Fidelity* network. It's the same technology that lets laptops, handheld game consoles, and portable media players get online at high speed. In fact, when you first turn on your iPad and try to use an Internet-focused app like Safari, the iPad may pop up a box with a bunch of network names and suggest you join one. Just find your network in the list and enter your password.

If you're not prompted to join a network, here's how to set up the iPad on your home wireless network for the first time:

❶ On the iPad's Home screen, tap Settings→Wi-Fi. This brings you to the wireless settings area. Next to Wi-Fi, tap the On button.

❷ In the "Choose a Network" box, do just that. The iPad sniffs around the air and displays the names of all the Wi-Fi networks it finds nearby (which, if you live in a crowded apartment building, could be a lot). Locate the name of your own home network in the list and tap its name to join it.

❸ Type in the network's password if asked. Secure networks—those that require passwords to keep freeloaders and intruders from glomming onto them and sucking up bandwidth—are marked with a lock icon (🔒). You need to enter a password to get onto the Internet from locked-up networks.

Once you type in your network password, the Wi-Fi icon (📶) in the iPad's top menu bar should bloom, indicating that yes, you are on the Internet. Fire up Safari or YouTube and enjoy the ride.

If you're not getting the happy Wi-Fi icon, repeat the steps above and carefully retype your network password. You should also make sure that your home network is indeed up and running.

You should only have to run through this setup process the first time you join a network. The iPad is savvy enough to remember your network password after you successfully connect once.

Use Public Wi-Fi Hot Spots

Your iPad isn't confined to connecting via your home network. It can jump onto any other Wi-Fi pipeline within range: the wireless network at your office or on campus, free public wireless networks in city parks, or any other place the iPad picks up the sweet scent of 802.11. When it finds networks in the area and you're not currently connected to one, it lists the available networks you can tap and join. Most public-access networks don't even require passwords.

Along with free networks, you can find *commercial* hot spots out there for the joining, but you need a little something extra with one of these: money—as in your credit-card number. You usually find these types of networks in airports, large megabookstore chains, hotel rooms, and other places that dispense Wi-Fi access for an hourly or daily fee.

To join one of these pay networks, tap its name (probably something official-sounding) in the list presented by your hot spot-sniffing iPad. Next, tap open Safari. The network will be there, squatting on your browser's home page with a request for your plastic digits before you can engage in any Web activity.

If you do a lot of traveling and don't have the Wi-Fi + 3G iPad, you may want to consider signing up for a service plan with a commercial hot-spot provider like T-Mobile (*hotspot.t-mobile.com*), Gogo Inflight (*www.gogoinflight.com*), or Boingo (*www.boingo.com*). AT&T has a side gig in the hot spot business as well (*www.wireless.att.com/sbusiness/wifi*) and 3G users get to hop on for free, thanks to their monthly deal with the company.

Tip Need a list of hot spots around the country? Check out JWire at *http://v4.jiwire.com/ search-hotspot-locations.htm*.

Stay Secure: Wi-Fi Network Safety Tips

The word "wireless" brings with it a sense of freedom: no wires, no cords, no strings attached. But with all that freedom comes the potential for danger, because your personal information isn't humming along inside an Ethernet cable from Point A to Point B—it's flying around in the air.

Most of the time, this isn't a problem. That is, unless you have someone evil lurking nearby who knows how to snatch data out of the air. Then you could be at risk of identity theft or other ills if, say, someone gets hold of the credit-card number you just typed in to buy a pair of shoes.

To make things as safe as possible, keep these few basic tips in mind when you ride the airwaves:

- **Make sure your home network is protected by a password.** Yes, it may be an extra step when you set up your wireless home network, and it may make the connection a tad slower overall. But it keeps intruders and squatters off your network where, at the least, they hog your bandwidth and, at worst, they infiltrate all your connected computers and devices and steal personal information.

- **Don't do any financial business on public wireless networks.** Since you didn't set up this Wi-Fi network yourself, you don't truly know how secure it is—or who else is lurking on it. So save the online banking or stock-trading chores for home. Use the iPad to check the score on the Saints game or catch up on the headlines while you sip your mocha latte.

- **Use a VPN for business on the road.** If you *do* have to take care of company business on your iPad while traveling, get the folks in your corporate systems department to set you up with *virtual private network* (VPN) access so you can safely surf the Web using your company's secure network as your portal to the Web.

Remember, the Internet is a wonderful, glorious, scary, intense, and sometimes dark place. Be careful out there.

Use a Mobile Broadband Hot Spot

So you didn't buy the Wi-Fi + 3G iPad and now you're regretting it. So what do you do—slap the Wi-Fi iPad up on eBay and use the proceeds for your Wi-Fi + 3G iPad Upgrade Fund? Lurch from hot spot to hot spot all over town? Sit on the couch and complain?

If trading up to a 3G model isn't in your future, you have another option: a *mobile broadband hot spot* device. This portable hot spot pulls down a cellular-data network signal from a carrier—probably Verizon or Sprint here in the U.S.—and divvies it up into a mini Wi-Fi network so that four to five wireless devices (laptops, Portable PlayStations, iPads, etc.) can get onto the Internet. Novatel's *MiFi* and the *Overdrive* from Sierra Wireless are two models.

Sounds great, doesn't it? Having a Wi-Fi network wherever you go has its advantages, but there's a downside: cost. First, you have to pay for the hardware itself, which costs around $100 to $250. Then you have to sign up for a service plan, which adds at least $40 a month and involves a contract.

If you do math, this is obviously more than the $15, $25, or $30 you'd shell out for 3G service from AT&T. And the Wi-Fi + 3G iPad doesn't require any additional hardware (though the 3G capability itself adds $130 to the iPad's cost).

But here's where the pocket network *does* make sense: using it to get *multiple* devices online wherever you go. This could be a family of three Wi-Fi iPads, an iPad and two laptops, and so on. The $40 monthly service fee covers everyone and is cheaper than buying individual 3G 'Pads and 3G service plans. (If you haven't bought your iPad yet, Verizon offers a special deal that includes an iPad, a MiFi, and lower data rates, starting at $20 a month for a gig of wireless data.)

If this sort of thing fits into your personal picture, you can investigate the mobile 3G broadband hot spot option further at Verizon Wireless (*www.verizonwireless.com/b2c/mobilebroadband*) or Sprint (*www.sprint.com*).

Use Skype to Make Internet Calls

The iPad is not an iPhone, but that doesn't mean you can't make telephone calls with it. Well, certain kinds of calls, specifically *VoIP* calls. VoIP stands for *Voice over Internet Protocol*. It's a technology that basically turns Internet wires into telephone wires.

With special software and a microphone, VoIP lets you place calls from computer-to-computer or even from computer-to-regular-phone. And with programs like Skype, you can place calls from iPad-to-iPad, iPad-to-computer, or iPad-to-phone. Best of all, you can get Skype for free in the App Store.

To use Skype, you need to set up an account with the service. It's sort of like setting up an instant-messaging program. During the process, you pick a user name and password that appears in the Contacts list of people you make Skype calls with.

To make a call from Skype, just tap the name of a person (who also needs to be online) in your Contacts list. To call a regular phone line, tap the little blue phone icon (circled), enter the number on the keypad, and hit the green Call button.

Skype calls themselves can be free if they're going from computer or iPad to computer or iPad, but Skype charges a bit of coin to jump off the Internet and call real phone numbers. The rates are low compared to standard phone services, and it's a popular way to make cheap overseas calls. For instance, for $6 a month you can make unlimited calls to landlines in the country of your choice (and more than 40 countries offer Skype calling). You can find prices for Skype's various calling plans at *www.skype.com/prices*.

Skype can be a great way to keep up with the folks back in the Old Country on the cheap, but call quality can vary. The Internet can be a very busy network, which can affect the fidelity of the voice signals traveling across it.

 Tip Using Skype with a headset-microphone combo can help calls sound better and cut out some of the echo between you and your chat pals.

Pick an AT&T 3G Service Plan

If you paid a little bit extra for the Wi-Fi + 3G iPad model, you don't have to worry about going from Wi-Fi hot spot to Wi-Fi hot spot to stay connected to your email. You have a connection wherever your iPad and AT&T's 3G network happen to be in range of each other. The iPad's Wi-Fi works right out of the box, but before you can start using AT&T's nationwide network, you first need to sign up for a cellular data account.

You have your choice of two monthly plans here:

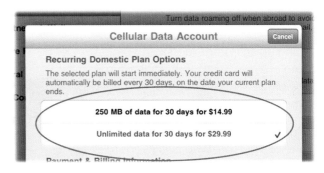

- **250 Megabytes.** This $14.99 plan gives you 250 megabytes of data coming and going off your iPad every 30 days. The iPad warns you when you get close to the limit and you can buy more, but how much data is that realistically? *PC Magazine* estimates 250 megabytes equals about 500 medium-to-large web pages. So that 250 megs will add up fast, especially if you send and receive a lot of big email attachments, like photos.

- **2 Gigabytes/Unlimited.** New iPad owners can download two gigabytes of data a month for $25 each month. But if you bought your iPad before June 7, 2010, you had the option of a $30-a-month unlimited data plan (see the note on page 40).

There are three other things to know about the plans:

❶ You can cancel your service at any time because there's no contract lashing you to the mast of the AT&T ship for one or two years.

❷ If you don't plan to use your 3G service regularly (maybe you just signed up for one month for that cross-country trip), you need to remember to *cancel* your account. It automatically renews itself every month and bills your credit card until you manually put an end to it. See page 42.

❸ With any plan, you also get unlimited free access to any of AT&T's Wi-Fi hot spots, which you can often find in places like major airports, Starbucks coffee shops, McDonald's hamburger emporiums, and Barnes & Noble bookstores. This could be helpful for people watching the meter on the 250-megabyte plan, because you can switch off the 3G chip and cozy up to some free Wi-Fi from AT&T.

Sign Up for AT&T 3G Service

Once you've decided which plan you want—or to start out with, anyway—it's time to unleash your credit card and open a 3G data account. Keep in mind, this is a brand-new account that has nothing to do with any other AT&T or iTunes Store accounts you may already have. The monthly charges are billed directly to your Visa, MasterCard, Discover, or American Express card.

You can sign up for 3G service right on the iPad:

❶ From the Home screen, tap Settings→Cellular Data→View Account.

❷ Once you tap that View Account button, a window pops up. Here, you fill in your name, phone number, email address, and 3G account password; you use your email address and 3G password later to log in and make any account changes. You also choose which plan you want and type in your credit card infor- mation. Tap Next when you're done.

❸ AT&T's Terms of Service agreement, always delightful beach read- ing, appears on-screen. Read it for the fine print (so you know what you're in for) or skip it, but tap Agree to move on.

❹ On the next screen, verify your billing information and plan choice. Tap the Submit button.

A box appears telling you that AT&T is now activating your iPad's 3G account. In a few minutes, you should see an alert box on-screen telling you your data plan has been activated. Now you're ready to iPad all over the place.

Use the AT&T Data Network

When there's a Wi-Fi network within range, the iPad will automatically join (or ask you if you want to join) it so you can enjoy a speedier connection than what you get with the 3G network. When you're out of range, however, the iPad maintains its link to the Internet with its 3G chip.

When the iPad is using the cellular network, you see the AT&T signal bars (◾◾◾▮▮) in the upper-left corner of the screen. AT&T's cellular data network isn't all high speeds and roses, however. Depending on your location, the tablet's connection speed may drop. The icons in the top left corner tell you which network you're on:

- **Wi-Fi.** (🛜) You're connected to a Wi-Fi hot spot, most likely the fastest of all the connections, but this can vary by individual network—some overloaded coffee-shop or hotel networks can feel like dial-up.

- **3G** (🄌) The second fastest in potential network options, the 3G (which stands for the *third generation* of data networks) is available in most urban areas. *This* is what you're paying for with your monthly bill.

- **EDGE** (🄴) The EDGE network is slower than 3G, but can handle most data transfers if you wait around long enough. The name, in case you were wondering, stands for Enhanced Data rates for GSM (or Global) Evolution.

- **GPRS** (°) The slowest of all network options, the General Packet Radio Service network has been letting mobile phones send and receive data for years.

Even though your iPad may drop to turtle speed when you're out in the thinner coverage areas of AT&T's network, just remember: a trickle of data is still *some* data, and better than no data at all.

> **Note** In early June 2010, AT&T suddenly changed its service offerings for iPads and iPhones to remove the Unlimited plan for monthly data use. While the 250 megabyte plan for iPad stayed the same, "Unlimited" was replaced by a very limited 2 gigabytes-a-month plan for $25. This move lead to at least one class-action lawsuit and a whole bunch of unhappy Netflix users with 3G iPads. AT&T also introduced a $20 *tethering* plan, which lets an iPhone act as a broadband modem for laptops and other devices. Alas, it doesn't currently work with iPads — unless there's some unauthorized hacking around on the gadgets.

Turn 3G Service Off or On

Always having an Internet connection around is quite convenient in today's data-munching world. You never have to worry about missing an important email message or sudden news development.

But there are times when you want to turn off your 3G service, such as when you're getting perilously close to your 250 megabytes of monthly data and don't want to give AT&T any more money, or when you're traveling overseas and want to avoid monster charges for inadvertently roaming onto a different network (page 261).

In times like these, tap Settings→Cellular Data→Cellular Data→Off. You can also turn off Data Roaming by tapping through Settings→Cellular Data→Data Roaming→Off. And if you need to turn off all your iPad's wireless powers, choose Settings→Airplane Mode→On. When it's safe to start surfing again, come back to these screens to turn everything back on.

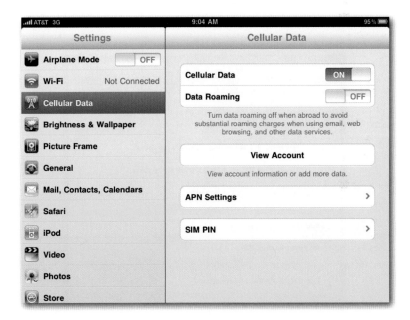

 Note The APN (*access point name*) Settings shown above control the iPad's cellular connection. You shouldn't have to mess with them for a regular AT&T account, but you'll need to adjust them if you use the iPad with a different wireless carrier, perhaps overseas. And that other wireless carrier should provide you with its own micro-SIM card and network info that you need to type into the APN Settings box.

Change or Cancel Data Plans

If you need to upgrade your data plan from 250 megabytes to 2 gigabytes, add another 250 megs of data, see how much data your iPad has gobbled this month, cancel your monthly plan, or change the credit-card number AT&T charges every month, there's one place to go: the AT&T Account settings on the iPad.

To get there, tap Settings→Cellular Data→View Account. Since your account settings contain billing and personal information, you need to type in the same email address and account password you used when you originally set up your cellular account on the iPad. (If you forgot your password, click the *Forgot Password?* link in the box.)

Once you get to the Cellular Data Account settings, your options are laid out before you. Tap Add Data or Change Plan if you want to add on another 250 megabytes of data after your monthly allowance runs out, upgrade to the Unlimited plan, or outright cancel your plan. If you plan to travel overseas, you can also sign up for AT&T's International plan, explained on the next page.

Tip You can also see your iPad's data meter by tapping Settings→General→Usage.

Travel Internationally with the iPad

If you and your iPad have to pop across the pond for a trip to London or attend a business meeting in Tokyo, you may want to get a data plan and micro-SIM card from a local wireless carrier in the country you plan to visit. If this is too much to bother with, AT&T does offer its own international data plans to keep you connected. Be warned, however, that prices are astronomical compared to the company's relatively low, low U.S. network prices.

For example, a mere 20 megabytes of international data within a 30-day billing period is $24.99. There's no unlimited plan, so if you're a heavy Internet user, the maximum plan is 200 megabytes of data for the month—at a whopping 200 bucks. (And you thought the currency exchange rates were crazy.)

Still, if you must, you must. Tap Settings→Cellular Data→View Account and tap Add International Plan to see a list of countries and plans available.

4

Surf the Web

Sure, you can surf the Web on a smartphone. Many phones have their own browsers that show scaled-down versions of websites. But odds are you strain your neck and squint your eyes to read the tiny screen, even when you zoom in for a closer look. For most people, microbrowsing is fine on a train or waiting in line at the cineplex. But who wants to do that in a coffee shop, campus library, or on the couch?

Browsing the Web on the iPad eliminates the old strain 'n' squint. It uses a touch-sensitive version of Apple's Safari browser that shows you pretty much a whole web page at once. Forget mouse-clicking—your fingers do the walking around the Web on the iPad; you jump from link to link with a tap and zoom in on pages with a two-finger spread.

From the basics of tablet-style browsing to general tips about security, this chapter gives you the grand tour of Safari on the iPad, your wide-open window to the World Wide Web.

Take a Safari Tour

You get onto the Web by tapping the Safari icon on the Home screen (circled); the very first time you do so, a blank browser window appears, ready for your instructions. To type a web address into the browser, tap the address bar so the iPad keyboard pops up, ready for your input.

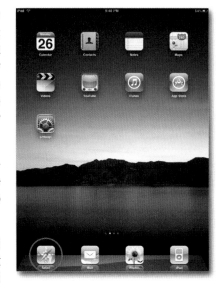

Safari has most of the features of a desktop browser: bookmarks, autocomplete (for web addresses), cookies, a pop-up blocker, and so on.

When you go to a web page, 'Pad-Safari behaves just like a desktop browser. It highlights the address bar as it loads all the elements on the page, and gives you Apple's circular "Wait! Wait! I'm load-ing the page!" animated icon at the top of the screen.

Here's a quick tour of the main screen elements, starting from the upper-left:

- ◄, ► **(Back, Forward).** Tap the ◄ button to revisit the page you were just on.

    Once you tap ◄, you can then tap the ► button to return to the page you were on *before* you tapped the ◄ button.

- ▢ **(Page Juggler).** Safari can keep multiple web pages open, just like any other browser. You can have up to nine pages open at one time.

- ▢ **(Bookmarks).** This button brings up your list of saved bookmarks (skip ahead a few pages to read more about bookmarks).

- **✛ (Add Bookmark).** When you're on a page you might want to visit again, bookmark it by tapping this button.

- **Address bar.** This empty white box is where you enter the *URL* (web address) for a page you want to visit. (URL is short for Uniform Resource Locator, which makes it sound like a search service for military supplies.)

- **✖, ↻ (Stop, Reload).** Click the ✖ button on the address bar to interrupt the download of a web page you just requested (if you made a mistake, for instance, or if it's taking too long).

Once a page finishes loading, the ✖ button turns into a ¢ button. Click this circular arrow if a page doesn't look right, or if you want to see the updated version of a web page that changes constantly (such as a breaking-news site). Safari re-downloads the page.

- **Search box.** Safari has a separate little box for typing in search terms. Tap here and the keyboard pops up. Type in your keywords and tap the Search button that replaces the Return key on the keyboard.

Zoom and Scroll Through Web Pages

These two gestures—zooming in on web pages and then scrolling around them—have probably sold more people on Apple's multitouch operating system for the iPod-iPhone-iPad than any other feature. It all happens with fluid animation and a responsiveness to your finger taps that's positively addicting. New owners often spend time just zooming in and out of web pages simply because they can.

When you first open a web page, you get to *see* the entire thing. After the iPhone and iPod Touch, this isn't particularly new. But unlike your experience on the smaller devices, when you open a web page on the iPad, you can actually *read* the entire thing. Really!

But say you want to zoom in on a picture or take a closer look at something. The next step is to magnify that *part* of the page.

The iPad offers three ways to do that:

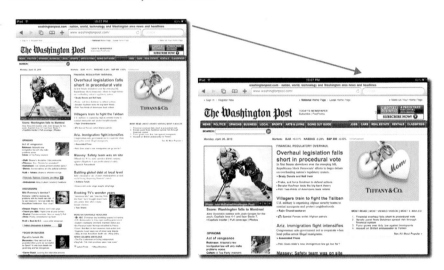

- **Rotate an iPad in Portrait Mode.** Turn the device 90 degrees in either direction. The iPad rotates and magnifies the image to fill the wider view.

- **Do the two-finger spread.** Put two fingers together on the glass and then spread them apart. The web page stretches before your very eyes, growing larger. Then pinch to shrink the page back down again. (Most people do several spreads or several pinches in a row to achieve the degree of zoom they want.)

Double-tap

- **Double-tap.** Safari is intelligent enough to recognize different *chunks* of a web page. One article might represent a chunk, for example, and a photograph another chunk. When you double-tap a chunk, Safari magnifies *just that chunk* front and center on the screen. It's smart and useful—and great for iPad readers who need a lot of magnification.

  Double-tap again to zoom back out.

Once you zoom out to the proper degree, you can scroll around the page by dragging or flicking with your finger. You don't have to worry about clicking a link by accident; if your finger's in motion, Safari ignores the tapping action, even if you happen to land on a link.

To go ahead and actually click a link, simply tap it with your finger.

Tip Every so often, you'll find, on certain web pages, a *frame* (a column of text) with its own scroll bar—an area of content that scrolls independently of the main page. (If you have a MobileMe account, the Messages list is such a frame.) The iPad offers its own way to scroll one of these frames without scrolling the whole page: it's the *two-finger drag*. To scroll within a frame, use two fingers instead of the usual one.

Create and Use Safari Bookmarks

Did you set up your syncing preferences 'twixt iPad and computer when you first got your tablet? If so, you'll find Safari already stuffed with a whole batch of bookmarks (Favorites)—that is, a list of websites you want to re-visit without having to remember and type in their URLs.

If you ripped your iPad out of its box as soon as you got it and haven't yet introduced it to your PC or Mac, you can easily copy your existing desktop computer's browser bookmarks from Internet Explorer (Windows) or Safari (Macintosh and Windows). Page 178 has instructions.

To see all your bookmarks, tap the ⌑ button at the top of the screen. The Bookmarks box appears on-screen. Some may be "loose," and many more are probably organized into folders, or even folders *within* folders. Tapping a folder shows you what's inside, and tapping a bookmark immediately begins opening the corresponding website.

Add New Bookmarks on the iPad

You can add new bookmarks right on your tablet. Any work you do here is copied *back* to your computer the next time you sync the two machines.

When you find a web page you might like to visit again, tap the **+** button (top left of the screen). Tap the Add Bookmark option to call up the Add Bookmark screen. You have two tasks:

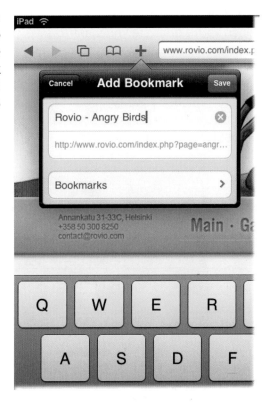

- **Type in a better name.** In the top box, you can type in a shorter or clearer name for the page than the one it comes with. Instead of "Bass, Trout, & Tackle—the Web's Premiere Resource for the Avid Outdoorsman," you can just call it "Fish."

  The box below this one identifies the underlying URL, which is totally independent of what you've *called* your bookmark. You can't edit this one.

  Click Save and you're done; the bookmark shows up in Safari's "loose" list.

- **Specify where to file this bookmark.** If you want to save a bookmark in a more organized way, tap the button that says Bookmarks >. You open Safari's hierarchical list of bookmark folders. Tap the folder where you want to file the new bookmark.

Tip If you make a mistake as you tap in a URL and don't notice it right away, you don't have to backspace all the way to the typo. Press your finger down on the text until a magnifying glass and a flashing insertion cursor appear, then drag your finger to the error, lift your finger, and correct the mistake. Then go back to where you were.

Make Home Screen Bookmarks

Are you one of those people who has shortcuts to your absolute favorite web-sites on your computer's desktop? If so, would you like to continue the tradition and put icons for your top sites on your iPad's Home screen?

Not a problem.

When you're on a site you want to save, tap the ✚ button at the top of your browser and choose "Add to Home Screen" from the menu box. The site's icon now sits right on your iPad's main screen. And don't worry about filling up your Home screen pages—you can have up to 11 of 'em and finger-flick among them.

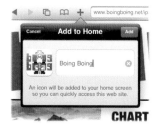

Jump to Other Web Pages

You may find yourself so mesmerized by navigating the iPad with a series of finger moves that you completely forget about the concept of clicking links, especially since you've probably been using a computer mouse to do that for the past 15 years or so.

Here's how you handle links on the iPad: Tap them with your finger.

Yes, just tap the links on the screen, much the way you'd click them if you *did* have a mouse. As you know from desktop-computer browsing, not all links are blue and underlined. Sometimes, in fact, they're graphics.

Tip If you hold your finger on a link for a moment—touch it rather than tap it—a box pops up identifying the link's full web address and offering three buttons: you can open the linked page, open it in a new browser page, or copy it to the iPad's clipboard to paste it elsewhere. Chapter 2 has more on moving text around.

Edit and Organize Bookmarks and Folders

It's easy enough to prune and groom your Bookmarks list—to delete favorites that aren't so favorite any more, to make new folders, to rearrange the list, to rename a folder or a bookmark, and so on.

The techniques are the same for editing bookmark folders as they are for editing the bookmarks themselves—after the first step. To edit a *folder* list, start by opening the Bookmarks list (tap the 🕮 button), and then tap Edit. (You can't edit, delete, or move the History, Bookmarks Menu, or Bookmarks Bar folders themselves, but you can edit the bookmarks inside them.)

To edit the *bookmarks* themselves, tap the 🕮 button, tap a folder, and *then* tap Edit.

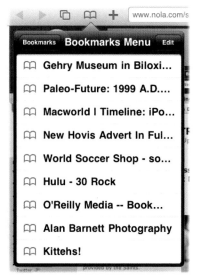

Tip If you're a newshound, there's one thing definitely worth bookmarking: the *RSS feed* of your favorite site—or all the RSS feeds from all your top sites. RSS feeds are subscriptions to story summaries from a site; the abbreviation itself stands for Really Simple Syndication. Subscribe, and you spare yourself the tediousness of checking sites for updated news and information manually, plus you get to read short summaries of new articles without ads and blinking animations. If you want to read a full article, you just tap its headline.

Safari, as it turns out, doubles as a handy RSS reader. Whenever you tap an "RSS Feed" link on a web page, or whenever you type the address of an RSS feed into the Address bar (it often begins with *feed://*), Safari automatically displays a handy table-of-contents view that lists all the news blurbs on that page.

Now you can:

- **Delete something.** Tap the 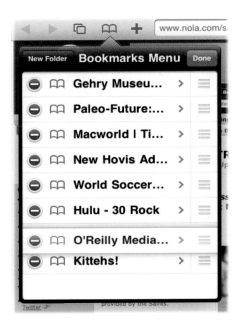 button next to a folder or bookmark, and then tap Delete to confirm.

- **Rearrange the list.** Drag the grip strip (≣) up or down in the list to move the folders or bookmarks up or down.

- **Edit a name and location.** Tap a folder or bookmark name. If you tap a folder, you arrive at the Edit Folder screen, which lets you edit the folder's name and, if this folder's *inside* another folder, you can reassign it. If you tap a bookmark, you see the Edit Bookmark screen, where you can edit the link's name and the URL it points to.

  Tap the Back button (upper-left corner) when you finish.

- **Create a folder.** Tap the New Folder button in the upper-left corner of the Edit Bookmarks mini-screen. You're offered the chance to type a name for it and whether you want to file it inside another folder.

  Tap Done when you finish.

Sync Your Bookmarks

Bookmarks—those helpful little point-and-click shortcuts that have saved you countless hours of mistyping website addresses—are a reflection of your personality, because they tend to be sites that are important to you. Fortunately, you can copy any bookmarks you have on your computer to your iPad. In fact, it's a two-way street: any bookmarks you create on your iPad can make the trip back to your computer, too.

iTunes can transfer your bookmarks from Internet Explorer or Safari. Just plug in your tablet, click its icon in iTunes, and click the Info tab. Scroll down past Contacts, Calendars, and Mail Accounts until you get to the section called Other. Then:

- **In Windows,** turn on *Sync bookmarks from:*, and then choose either *Safari* or *Internet Explorer* from the pop-up menu. Click Apply or Sync.

- **On the Mac,** turn on *Sync Safari bookmarks* and click Apply or Sync.

If you ever want to blow away all the bookmarks on your iPad and start over with a fresh set from your computer, scroll down to the Advanced area of the Info screen (where it says "Replace information on this iPad"). Then put a check in the box next to Bookmarks before you sync again.

Special Instructions for Firefox Fans

If Mozilla's Firefox browser is your preferred window to the Web, you can still move those foxy favorites over to your iPad, but you'll have to do it the long way—by first importing bookmarks from Firefox into Safari. And while this setup will get your bookmarks onto your tablet, it won't establish a *two-way* sync; new bookmarks you add on the iPad won't get synced back to Firefox.

- **Windows.** Download a free copy of Safari (*www.apple.com/safari*), start it up, and let it import your Firefox bookmarks during the setup process. Press Ctrl+Shift+B to see all your bookmarks, weed out the ones you don't want, and then set the iPad to sync with your desktop's Safari.

- **Macintosh.** You already have Safari. If you have your whole bookmarked life in Firefox, grit your teeth and open that dusty Safari anyway, then choose File→Import Bookmarks. Navigate to your Firefox bookmarks file, which is usually in your Home folder, and go to Library→Application Support→Firefox→Profiles→*weird scrambled-named folder like e9v01wmx. default* folder. Inside, double-click the file called bookmarks.html.

You've just imported your Firefox bookmarks. Now, in Safari, press ⌘-Shift-B to show all your bookmarks on-screen. Delete the ones you don't want on the tablet, and then set the iPad to sync with Safari.

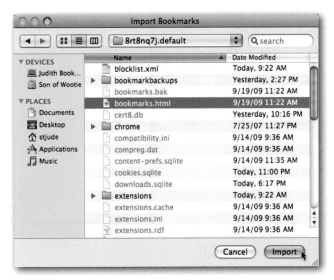

Actually, *most* other browsers can export their bookmarks. You can use that option to export your bookmarks file to your desktop, and then use Safari's File→Import Bookmarks menu to pull it in from there.

Call Up Your History List

Behind the scenes, Safari keeps track of the websites you've visited in the last week or so, neatly organized in subfolders like "Earlier Today" or dated folders from your last few days of browsing. It's a great feature when you can't recall the URL for a site you visited recently—or when you remember that it had a long, complicated address and you just can't face pecking it into the iPad keyboard all over again.

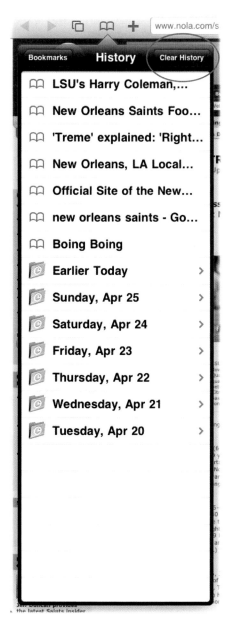

To see the list of recent sites, tap the ⊞ button, and then tap the History folder, whose icon bears a little clock to make sure you know that it's special. Once the History list appears, just tap a bookmark (or a folder name and *then* a bookmark) to revisit a web page.

Erase the History List

Some people find it creepy to have Safari maintain a list of every website they've recently seen, right there in plain view of any family member or co-worker who wanders by. They'd just as soon not have their roommate/wife/husband/boss/parent/kid know what they've been up to, Web-wise.

You can't delete just one particularly incriminating History list. You can, however, delete the *entire* History list, thus erasing all your tracks. To do that, tap Clear History (circled) in the top right corner and confirm it.

Congratulations! You've just rewritten History.

Save Images From the Web (and Mail)

Every once in awhile, you come across an image on a web page that you just have to have on your computer. It could be a cool sports photo of your favorite ball player, an image of a house on a real-estate site, or a wacky picture of a disgruntled cat. Now, on a regular system, you just have to right-click (Control-click) the image with your mouse and choose Save Image to Desktop. But how do you do that on the iPad, where there's no mouse, trackpad, or obvious way to right-click on anything?

Easy: Just press the desired photo or graphic with your finger. A box pops up with a whole bunch of options like Open, Open in New Page, Save Image, and Copy. Tap the Save Image button to download a copy of the picture to your iPad's Photo Library (page 239). From there, you can look at it any time you want, or email it to someone (page 243).

> **Tip** Speaking of email (which is covered in the next chapter), you can also use the ol' press-and-save move with photo attachments to messages. And if you have a message with multiple photo attachments, the iPad's smart enough to offer you a button to save all the images as well.

Stream Web Audio and Video

When the iPad was announced, there was much grumbling about the fact that it wouldn't play files in the Adobe Flash format—which is a large portion of the videos out there on the Web, as well as the code behind of many browser-based videogames. In fact, some people thought the lack of Flash would be a crippling blow to the iPad's chances of success.

But guess what? A lot of people bought the iPad anyway. Sure, it doesn't recognize Flash, RealPlayer, or Windows Media file formats. But the iPad isn't *utterly* clueless about streaming online goodies. After all, it has that whole YouTube app (page 94) that plays plenty of videos. It can also play some QuickTime movies, like movie trailers, as long as they've been encoded (prepared) in certain formats (like H.264). It can also play MP3 and WAV audio files right off the Web. Here are a few sites to sample:

- **BBC News.** The Beeb's podcasts stream nicely and you can search shows by radio station, genre, or get an A to Zed list; the company also has a fine iPad app mentioned in Chapter 8. *http://www.bbc.co.uk/podcasts/*

- **"Meet the Press" audio stream.** You can find an MP3 edition of the venerable Sunday-morning talk show here: *http://podcast.msnbc.com/audio/podcast/MSNBC-MTP.xml*

- **National Public Radio.** NPR has many of its signature programs, like "All Things Considered" and "World Café," plus "Morning Edition" and its other newscasts, online and ready to stream through your iPad's speaker at *m.npr.org*. (NPR also has a news-focused iPad app in the App Store, too.)

- **New York Times podcasts.** Check out a whole page of different news shows that start streaming when you tap the MP3 link. *www.nytimes.com/podcasts*

Actually, any old MP3 file plays fine right in Safari. If you already played through your 16, 32, or 64 gigabytes of music synced from your computer, you can always do a web search for *free mp3 music*.

As for video, you have more to watch on the Web than just 'Pad-friendly streaming videos at Home→YouTube. Apple, in addition to making iPods and Macs, hosts a huge collection of movie trailers on its site at *trailers.apple.com*. Tap a movie poster to get started.

Work With Online Apps

With the rise of mobile Internet-connected devices came the increased popularity of *cloud computing*—using programs that reside and store files online, up in the clouds, where you can get to them from any Web-enabled machine. This means you don't have to drag around a seven-pound laptop stuffed with business software just to update a spreadsheet, because you can edit it *online* with a two-pound netbook. Or an iPad.

Not every cloud-computing site works with the iPad—Adobe's Flash-based Photoshop.com site, which lets you edit pictures online, for example. Others may have limited functionality, like the ability to read files, but not edit them. Still, if you need to quickly look up something in a document stored online or check the status of an ongoing project, pointing your iPad toward the cloud works.

Google Docs is probably one of the most popular cloud-computing apps, partly because it's free, partly because it can handle Microsoft Office documents, and partly because it belongs to the growing Google Empire. To use it, you just need a Gmail or Google account (also free at *www.google.com*). Once you sign up, you can create, edit, and share files right in your computer's Web browser—including word-processing documents, spreadsheets, and basic presentations.

Since all those files are online anyway, you can also get to them from the Safari browser on the iPad. There are some limitations, though. For one, you currently can't edit documents or presentations on the iPad, so these files are pretty much read-only copies for reference when you're on the road. You can, however, do basic editing on your spreadsheet files.

And unlike Google Docs on a standard computer, you can't use the "offline" feature that lets you edit and save files even when you don't have an Internet connection. (That's because a piece of necessary software, called Google Gears, doesn't work with the iPad's operating system.)

Another cloud-computing company, Zoho (*www.zoho.com*), has a whole slew of business and productivity apps that work through your computer's browser. Many of them are free for personal use; you just need to sign up for an account. Zoho Writer, Sheet, and Show roughly correspond to Microsoft Word, Excel, and PowerPoint, and can open and edit files in those formats. The company also has a front door for mobile devices at *mobile.zoho.com*; you can log in through the iPad if you need to refer to your file stored online in a less-cluttered interface.

If you're a big fan of cloud computing and already use services like the Basecamp project management site (*basecamphq.com*) or DropBox for file-sharing (*www.dropbox.com*), take a run through the Productivity section of the App Store for iPad-friendly programs that work specifically with those sites. For example, the free QuickOffice Connect app gives you a convenient portal to your files stored on Dropbox, Box.net, Google Docs, and MobileMe (Chapter 16).

Dedicated Basecampers have several App Store choices as well. Programs like Satchel ($10) Groundwork ($8), Insight ($10), and Outpost ($13) let you keep tabs on ongoing projects, tasks, and deadlines by checking in with your iPad.

Social Networking on the iPad

With your iPad, you can keep connected to all your favorite social networking sites whenever you hop onto a wireless network—because, after all, a large part of many people's day is spent keeping up with events on Facebook, MySpace, Twitter, and the like. Some sites even have their own iPad apps.

Chapter 7 has info about the Store and instructions on how to install iPad apps. Once you're ready, here's some of what's out there:

- **Facebook** and **MySpace.** Both mega-popular destinations have free applications, right there in the App Store—but they're made for the iPhone. They do scale up to iPad size with a tap of the 2x button, but it's a trade-off between a smaller workspace and a blotchy display. Although the app versions are more streamlined for a touchscreen, if you don't want to bother, there's *www.facebook.com* and *www.myspace.com* in Safari.

- **Twitter.** Using this widely popular micro-blogging service is much easier on the iPad than trying to text out pithy thoughts on a tiny mobile phone keypad (unless, of course, it's an iPhone). Most Twitter apps are still iPhone-oriented, but *Twitterific for iPad*, free and shown below, does an excellent job of turning your tablet into an easy-to-tweet dashboard for all your thoughts of 140 characters or less.

- **AIM.** You can't get more social or networked than with instant messaging, which keeps you in touch with all your online pals through real-time, typed conversations. *AIM for iPad* works just like its computer and smartphone counterparts: pick a friend off your Buddy List and shoot over a message to start a conversation. But the iPad edition doesn't end with AIM—you can also pull in updates from Facebook, MySpace, Foursquare, Twitter, YouTube, and other social sites.

- **Flickr.** Several apps are available for browsing pictures on this massive photo-sharing site, but most are for the iPhone. Perhaps the best way to experience Flickr is to just point Safari at *www.flickr.com*.

- **Photobucket.** If the Photobucket site is where you choose to share your pictures online, check out the free *Photobucket for iPad* app. You can download any Photobucket image to the tablet, easily search the entire site, and create albums right on the iPad.

- **Loopt Pulse.** Loopt uses location services to put you on the map and show you restaurant reviews and concert listings right in your area. The free *Loopt for iPad* app makes it all more readable.

Use Autofill to Save Time

Some people will love the iPad's simple virtual keyboard, and some will hate it because it feels like typing on a glass coffee table. And some will use it only when buying things online while relaxing in a hammock out back. No matter how you feel about the keyboard, there's one feature built into Safari that's bound to please everybody: *Autofill*.

Autofill, as its name suggests, automatically fills in your name, address, and phone number on web forms—saving you the drudgery of typing in the same information all the time. It's convenient, reduces your keyboard time, and speeds up purchases for power shoppers.

Along with your contact info, Autofill can remember passwords for websites that require them, but be careful with this. If you accidentally lose your iPad or someone steals it, the thief can waltz right into your password-protected accounts and steal even more from you.

To turn on Autofill, start on the iPad's Home screen and tap Settings→ Safari→Autofill. On the Autofill screen, tap the On button next to Use Contact Info. Tap the My Info line below it and choose your own name and address out of your Contacts list. (See page 90 if you don't have a contact file for yourself.) Now, when you come to a web form that wants your info, you get an Autofill button on the iPad keyboard to tap instead of typing.

If you want to go ahead and use the password-supplying part of Autofill, tap the button on the Settings screen to On. Now, whenever you hit a site that requires your password, Safari gives you three choices: *Yes*, *Never for this Website*, and *Not Now* (the latter means you'll get pestered again on your next visit). Say Yes and the browser logs you into the site automatically from then on.

To play it safe, it's a good idea to only say Yes to non-money-related sites like an online newspaper and tap Never for this Website for any bank, stock-trading, e-commerce, or other site that involves money and credit-card numbers.

Manipulate Multiple Pages

Like any self-respecting browser, Safari can keep multiple pages open at once, making it easy for you to switch among them. You can think of it as an alternate version of *tabbed browsing*, the feature you find on desktop Safari, Internet Explorer, and Firefox, which keeps a bunch of web pages open simultaneously—in a single, neat window.

The beauty of this arrangement is that you can start reading one web page while the others load into their own tabs in the background. On the iPad, it works like this:

- **To open a new window,** tap the ◻ button on the top-left side of the menu bar. The current web page shrinks into a mini version. Tap New Page to open a new, untitled browser page; now you can enter an address.

- **To switch back to the first window,** tap ◻ again. You see a grid of up to nine open pages, looking sort of like baseball-card versions of their larger selves. Find the page you want to see again and tap it to open it full-screen.

You can open a third window, and a fourth, and so on, and jump among them, using these two techniques.

- **To close a window,** tap ◻. In the collection of shrunken pages, locate the miniature window you want to close, and then tap the ✖ button at its top-left corner.

 Note Touchscreen Safari can handle nine open web pages at once. If you try to go for that tenth one, it starts replacing an older open page with the new one.

Pop-up Blockers, Cookies, and Security

Internet criminals will try to rip you off no matter what browser you use. Phishing—when a devious website masquerades as a legitimate site to dupe people into entering personal information—has long been a problem. 'Pad-Safari has a Fraud Warning setting, which alerts you when you *might* be on a fishy, phishy site. You can turn it on in Settings→Safari.

And the world's smarmiest advertisers have been inundating us with pop-up and pop-under ads for years—nasty little windows that appear in front of a browser window or, worse, behind it, waiting to bug you when you close the front window. They're often deceptive, masquerading as alert or dialog boxes, and they'll do absolutely anything to get you to click them.

Fortunately for you, Safari comes set to block those pop-ups so you don't see them. It's a war out there—but at least you have some ammunition.

The thing is, though, pop-ups are sometimes legitimate—notices of new banking features, seating charts on ticket-sales sites, and so on. Safari can't tell these pop-ups from ads—and so it stifles those pages, too.

What to do? If a site you trust says "Please turn off pop-up blockers and reload this page," you know you're probably missing out on a *useful* pop-up message. In those situations, you can turn off Safari's universal pop-up blocker. From the Home screen, tap Settings→Safari. Where it says "Block Pop-ups," tap the On/Off switch.

Cookies

Cookies are something like web page preference files. Certain websites—particularly commercial ones like Amazon.com—deposit them on your hard drive like little bookmarks, so the site remembers you the next time you visit. Ever notice how Amazon.com greets you with "Welcome, Leroy" (or whatever your name is)? It's reading its own cookie, left behind on your hard drive (or in this case, on your iPad).

Most cookies are perfectly innocuous—and, in fact, are extremely helpful, because they help websites remember your tastes. Cookies also spare you the effort of having to type in your name, address, and so on, every time you visit these sites.

But fear is widespread, and the media fans the flames with tales of sinister cookies that track your movement on the Web. If you're worried about invasions of privacy, Safari is ready to protect you.

To check all this cookie security out, from the Home screen, tap Settings→Safari. The options here are like a paranoia gauge. If you click Never, you create an acrylic shield around your iPad. No cookies can come in, and no cookie information can go out. You'll probably find the Web a very inconvenient place; you'll have to re-enter your information upon every visit to the site, and some websites may not work properly at all. The Always option means, "Oh, what the heck—just gimme all of them.""

A good compromise is From Visited, which accepts cookies from sites you *want* to visit, but blocks cookies deposited on your iPad by sites you're not actually visiting—cookies you get, say, from an especially evil banner ad that a hacker has planted on a page. There are quite a few of those these days.

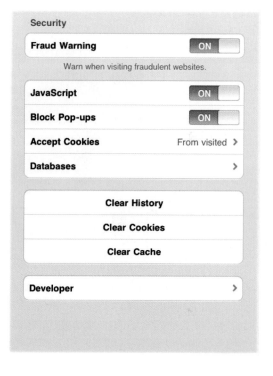

The Safari settings screen also offers a Clear Cookies button (it deletes all the cookies you've accumulated so far), as well as Clear History and Clear Cache buttons.

A *cache* is a little patch of the iPad's storage area where your iPad retains bits and pieces of web pages you visit—the page's graphics, for example. The idea is that the next time you visit the same page, the iPad won't have to download those bits again. It's already got them on board, so the page appears much faster.

If you worry that your cache eats up space, poses a security risk, or is confounding a page (by preventing the most recent version of the page from appearing), tap this button to erase it and start over.

5

Keep in Touch with Email

Email has become a part of daily life for most of us. You wake up and check it, you go to work and check it all day, and you probably come home after work and check it once more before bed to make sure you haven't missed anything. The ability to compose, send, and receive email messages on a mobile phone redistributes some of the time spent parked in front of a computer. But still, there you are—hunched over, peering and pecking into a tiny screen.

The iPad changes all this. Now you can lean back on the couch, flip on the tablet with the press of a button, and have *room* to deal with your mail on its spacious 9.7-inch screen. No more terse, abbreviated messages inspired by a cramped little keypad, either. With the iPad's full-sized onscreen keyboard, you can compose your thoughts in full without having to drag the laptop out of the home office and wait for it to boot up.

This chapter gives you a tour of the iPad's email program, from setting up your mail accounts to hitting the Send button on that first message. And just remember, when you're done checking your email, movies, music, and that new best seller are just a tap away—and you don't even have to get off the couch.

Set Up an Email Account (or Two)

Thanks to its Wi-Fi or 3G connectivity, the iPad can reach out and grab your email out of thin air. Using it, you can read, write, and send messages to stay in the loop of your digital life.

But to get your messages flowing into the 'Pad's Mail program, you need to supply the slab with your email account settings so it knows where on the Internet to look for your mailbox. You can do this is a couple of ways:

Sync mail settings with iTunes

You get email on your computer, right? If you're using a dedicated program like Apple Mail or Microsoft Outlook, you can copy those account settings over to your iPad and not have to fiddle with server addresses and other arcane tech settings.

To do it this way, connect the iPad to your computer, click its icon in iTunes, and then click the Info tab. Scroll down to Sync Mail Accounts and put a check in the box next to "Sync selected mail accounts." Pick the accounts you want to tote around on your iPad. Click Sync or Apply to copy the settings—but not your computer-based messages—over to the iPad, where you can check mail on the tablet.

Set up mail accounts on the iPad

Tap the Mail icon. If you use Exchange, MobileMe, Gmail, Yahoo, or AOL, tap the appropriate icon. If you don't use any of those, tap Other.

On the next screen, type in your name, email address, password, and a short description ("Personal Gmail", say). If you tapped Other, be prepared to type in the settings you got from your Internet provider when you signed up for your account. This includes things like your email account user name, password, and the addresses of your ISP's incoming and outgoing mail servers (which look something like *mail.myserver.com* and *smtp.myserver.com*, respectively).

If you don't happen to know this information off the top of your head and can't find the paperwork from your ISP, check the technical support area of its website for "email configuration settings" or "email server addresses." Or just peek at the account information in the mail program on your regular computer.

Click Save and the Mail program goes out and gets your new messages. Repeat the process if you have more than one email account.

 Need help sorting through email geekery like the difference between IMAP and POP? Flip to the last two pages in this chapter for an explanation.

Tour the iPad's Mail Program

Once you get it set up, the iPad's email program works pretty much like any other postal program: You read messages, you write messages, you send messages. But instead of popping open overlapping multiple windows for the In box, a message you're reading, and a message you're composing, the iPad keeps things in tight formation.

You don't have to click a thing to see your Inbox along the left side of the screen and an open message displayed alongside it: Just hold the iPad *horizontally*. Your In box appears as a vertical list, showing the sender's name, the message subject, and a two-line preview of each message. A Search box lets you scan mail for specific keywords. A blue dot next to the message means you haven't read it yet. Tap a message preview in the Inbox to see it open up and fill the rest of the screen—message header, text, and attachments.

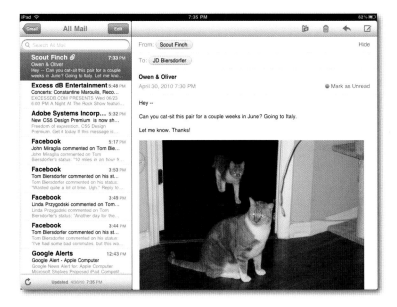

When you want to reply to a message (or forward it on to somebody else), tap the ← icon. This brings you a fresh copy of the message on-screen, ready for you to write back—or fill out a new address to forward along. It also brings up the iPad's virtual keyboard for the heavy fingerwork.

> **Tip** Don't care for the iPad's built-in mail program or want programs that make it work more to your liking? Just pop into the App Store and browse through the Utilities and Productivity sections to see what may work for you.

If you find the screen a little too busy with all these window panes, hold the iPad *vertically*. This 90-degree move takes away all the background boxes and brings the one message you need to deal with front and center, filling the screen.

But with its streamlined tool-bar, iPad Mail doesn't have a lot of room for labels that tell you what all the buttons do. If you need a translator for all those cryptic little Dan Brownish symbols, here's a handy guide, generally moving from left to right along the screen:

- **▲,▼ (Previous Message, Next Message).** When you have a message open on-screen, you don't have to switch back to the In box view to go on to the next one (or back to the one before). Just tap the ▲ button to revisit the message you were previously reading—or tap the ▼ icon to move on to the next one in the box.

- **Ċ (Check Mail).** Tap the Ċ button to have the iPad check for new messages and reload your Inbox with the fresh arrivals.

- **🗀 (Move to Folder).** Want to save an open message to a different folder within that account? Tap this icon and pick the new folder.

- **🗑 (Delete).** Tap here when you're done with this message for good—or if it was an annoying piece of spam to begin with.

- **↩ (Forward, Reply).** When you want to respond to a message or send it along to another recipient, tap the ↩ button and selection its destination from the menu that pops up.

- **☑ Compose New Message.** Need to fire off a fresh note to somebody? Tap here to get started with a brand-new blank message form.

Read Mail

So how do you get started reading your messages once you get your mail accounts all set up? Like this:

❶ In the iPad Home screen, tap the Mail icon. Its default position is in the bottom row of icons, between Safari and Photos.

❷ If you're connected to the Internet, the iPad checks all the email accounts you set up and downloads any new messages it finds.

❸ If you're holding the iPad horizontally (landscape mode), your Inbox sits along the left side of the screen. Tap a message preview to see it displayed in full in the middle of the screen. If you're holding the iPad in its vertical position (portrait mode), the first or currently selected message fills the window; tap the Inbox button in the upper-left corner to see what else awaits you. If you're in another mailbox like All Mail, tap the mail account name in the left corner to retrace your steps to your mailboxes.

❹ Work your way up and down the mailbox, either by tapping the message previews in the Inbox list or by using the ▲ and ▼ buttons (page 75) to scoot up or down the list from the main screen. Tap the Mark as Unread button on the message if you want it to appear as new mail again so you can deal with it later.

File Attachments

Email messages often come with attached files from other programs. The iPad can open and display Microsoft Office and iWork files. It can also handle PDF, RTF, .vcf, and text files, as well as several photo and graphics files. Some types of video and audio files, too, as long as the files aren't copy-protected.

File attachments like photos usually appear open and visible in the message, so if someone sends you a few snaps from their vacation on Italy's Almafi Coast, you don't have to hunt around for icons at the bottom of the mess to tap them open—you can instantly be envious without any extra effort.

Some attachments—things like word-processing documents, spreadsheets, and presentations—typically appear as icons at the bottom of a message. Tap that Excel chart icon and the whole file pops open to fill the iPad's screen.

Use Information in Messages

Ever notice how a lot of email messages involve setting up dinner dates, appointments, meetings, and other gatherings that use addresses and other people's contact info? The iPad's mail program knows this—and is ready to do something about it.

For example, say you get a message suggesting dinner at a new restaurant—with the address helpfully pasted in the message. If it's an unfamiliar location, press down on it. The iPad, which has already recognized that there's a street address in the message, pops up a box offering four options—including the ability to open the address in its Maps program. Now *that's* service!

The other options in the pop-up box include:

- **Create New Contact.** If your sender includes personal information like a name, address, and phone number in a message, you can add it to your Contacts list with a tap

- **Add to Existing Contact.** If you have the name—but not the number—in your Contacts file already, you can add in the new info.

- **Copy.** Need to move this information into another message or program? Select Copy and when you get to the destination file, hold your finger down and select Paste.

Once you master reading email, turn the page to find out how to write and send messages of your own on the iPad.

Write and Send Email

When you're ready to write—or write back—the iPad is there for you. If you're starting from scratch with a new message, tap the ☑ icon at the top of the screen. If you're replying to (or forwarding) a message you previously received, tap the ← icon and select Reply, Reply All, or Forward. Either way, you get a new message form.

❶ If this is a brand-new message, tap the To: field at the top. The iPad keyboard appears for your text-entry pleasure. If the recipient is in your Contacts list (page 90) or you've written to the person before the person before, the iPad cheerfully suggests addresses and fills in the To: line on your tap. Filling in the Cc: (carbon copy) field works the same way. If you're replying to an older message, the address or addresses of your correspondents are already there for you.

❷ Tap the Subject line and type in whatever this message is about. Even if you're replying to someone, you can tap in and edit the Subject line using the handy delete key on the iPad keyboard.

❸ Tap the message body area and type your missive.

❹ If you have multiple mail accounts, tap the From: field and choose the account you want to use here.

❺ When you finish, tap the Send button in the top-right corner of the message to fire off your note. Hit Cancel if you change your mind.

> **Tip** Want to email a photo? Bop into the Photos app from the Home screen and tap open the album containing the image or images you want to send. Tap the ☛ icon at the bottom of the screen and then tap the photos you want to mail. The tap the Share button to create a new message with the images already attached. If you already have the message started, you can also paste in a pic from the Photos app.

Take Control of Your Email

Messages can quickly pile up, especially if you have several accounts funneling mail into your tablet. If you find yourself splashing around in a rising tide of mailbox flotsam, here are a few quick things you can do to get things back under control:

- **File messages in different folders.** Some mail providers, like Yahoo and AOL, let you create your own folders to sort messages the way you prefer, like by topic or sender. If you had your own folders set up with the service before you got the iPad, the folders should be there after you add that account to the tablet. To file a message into one of these personal folders, tap the 📁 icon and choose the folder you want to use as the message's new home.

- **Delete all the junk at once.** Zapping unwanted messages out of your Inbox one by one with a finger swipe is tedious, but there's a faster way. Just tap the Edit button at the top of the Inbox pane. Buttons for Delete (🗑) and Move (📁) appear at the bottom of the screen. In the message list, tap the ones you want to either nuke or refile. Each message you select slides out into a "pile" next to the Inbox list—these are readable versions, so you can make sure you aren't dumping messages you still need. Once you

make your selections, tap the appropriate button below to send all those messages to the same place at once: either the trash or a different folder.

- **Scan for spam.** Want to see the messages that are personally addressed to you either in the To: or Cc: fields—and not mail addressed to you and 500 other people from bulk mailing lists or junk-mail dealers? The iPad can identify your personal messages by sticking a distinct little **To** or **Cc** tag on them. To turn on the tags, choose Settings→Mail, Contacts, Calendars and flip the On switch next to "Show To/Cc Label." Messages without these tags stand out and make more obvious targets for the mass-deletion method described above. The next page has more adjustments you can make to the Mail program's settings.

Adjust Mail Settings

Like most programs, the iPad's mail app comes with certain default set-tings for things like the size of the type that appears on screen. If you don't like the way text looks or want to make other tweaks to the program (like how many lines of a message appear in the Inbox preview list), take a trip to Home→Settings→Mail, Contacts, Calendars.

From here, you can:

- **Change the minimum font size.** Unlike paper mail, you can easily make the print bigger or smaller for more comfortable reading. Size choices range from Small to Giant.

- **Add a custom signature.** As with a regular mail program, you can add a personalized tag at the bottom of each outgoing message. Popular signatures include your contact information or quotes from *The Matrix*.

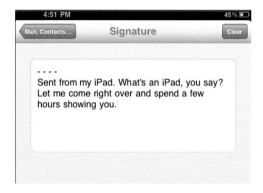

- **Show more (or less) preview in your message list.** By default, the iPad's mail program shows you a two-line preview of each message so you have some idea what it contains. You can change this from one to five lines, or select None to turn off the preview entirely.

- **Set a default mail account.** If you have multiple email accounts set up on your iPad, you can use this setting to designate one of them as your default account for all outgoing messages (and for messages you create by tapping mail links in other programs). Remember, you can always tap the From: field in a message to switch to a different account.

- **Delete unwanted mail accounts.** Need to ditch an account because it's become too spam-laden or you need to streamline things? Flick up to the Accounts section, tap the name of the doomed account to get to its settings, and tap the Delete Account button.

Webmail on the iPad

Despite the fact that you can get your messages on the iPad through its dedicated Mail app, that's not the only way to monitor your Inbox. As you may remember from the last chapter, the iPad has a nice sturdy web browser. With it, you can check your accounts from webmail services (Yahoo, Gmail, Hotmail, AOL, and so on) by logging in through Safari. Doing it this way can be helpful if you just want to deal with your mail on the website it belongs to, no matter what device you're using.

Depending on the service you use, you may find that it offers a streamlined mobile version of your mailbox when you log in through the iPad's browser. Bigger services like Yahoo and Google even have their own free apps in the App Store designed to make it easier to check mail, news, and other features on your iPad. So, however you prefer to get your mail, the iPad gives you plenty of options.

POP3 and IMAP Accounts on the iPad

Those freebie, web-based accounts are super-easy to set up. But they're not the whole ball of wax. Millions of people have a more generic email account, perhaps supplied by their employers or Internet providers. They're generally one of two types:

- **POP accounts** are the oldest, most compatible, and most common type on the Internet. (POP stands for Post Office Protocol, but this won't be on the test.) But a POP account can make life miserable if you check your mail on more than one machine (say, a PC and an iPad), as you'll discover shortly.

    Unless you are allowed by your ISP to save mail on the server, a POP server transfers incoming mail to your computer (or iPad) before you read it, which works fine as long as you're using only *that machine* to access your email.

- **IMAP accounts** (Internet Message Access Protocol) are newer and have more features than POP servers, and have caught up in popularity. IMAP servers keep all of your mail online, rather than making you store it on your computer; as a result, you can access the same mail from any computer (or iPad). IMAP servers remember which messages you've read and sent, and even keep track of how you've filed messages into mail folders. (Those free Yahoo email accounts are IMAP accounts, and so are Apple's MobileMe accounts and corporate Exchange accounts. Gmail accounts *can* be IMAP, too, which is awesome.)

    There's really only one downside to this approach: If you don't conscientiously delete mail after you've read it, your online mailbox eventually overflows. On IMAP accounts that don't come with a lot of storage, the system sooner or later starts bouncing new messages, annoying your friends. Fortunately, even the free mail places offer at least 10 megabytes of storage these days, which helps cut down on the overflow

The iPad can communicate with both kinds of accounts, with varying degrees of completeness.

 Tip The iPad generally copies your IMAP messages onto the iPad itself, so you can work on your email even when you're not online. You can, in fact, control where these messages are stored (in which mail folder). To see this, open Settings→Mail, Contacts, Calendars→your IMAP account name→Account Info→Advanced. See? You can specify where your Drafts, Sent messages, and Deleted messages wind up on the iPad.

If you haven't opted to have your account-setup information transferred automatically to the iPad from your PC or Mac through the Info tab in iTunes, you can set it up manually right on the tablet.

From the iPad's Home screen, tap Settings→Mail, Contacts, Calendars→Add Account. Tap Other, and then enter your name, email address, password, and an optional description. Tap Save.

Apple's software attempts to figure out which kind of account you have (POP or IMAP) by the email address. If it can't make that determination, you arrive at a second screen now, where you're asked for such juicy details as the Host Name for Incoming and Outgoing Mail servers. (This is also where you tap either IMAP or POP, to tell the iPad what sort of account it's dealing with.)

If you don't know this stuff offhand, you'll have to ask your Internet provider, corporate tech-support person, or next-door teenager to help you.

When you're finished, tap Save.

6

Use the iPad's Built-In Apps

Apps, also known as "programs that run on the iPad" (and iPhone and iPod Touch), make Apple's tablet a versatile device, beyond its role as a Web window and portable email reader. As mentioned back in Chapter 1, the iPad gives you a few of its own apps right on the Home screen, alongside the previously discussed Safari and Mail apps.

Three of these apps handle personal organization tasks: Calendar (for keeping your appointments), Contacts (your address book), and Notes (for jotting bits of text to yourself). One app, Maps, helps you find yourself and chart your course, and two other apps (iTunes and App Store) point the way to shopping Apple's online stores. Aside from the Settings app (Appendix A), the rest of the Home screen icons are there to entertain you: Videos, YouTube, Photos, and iPod. This chapter gives you a tour of the 'Pad's native apps.

And remember, these are just the apps that come *with* the iPad. Once you get to know these built-in apps, you'll be ready to tackle any of the gajillion other goodies in the App Store. But that's for another chapter.

Set Up Your Calendar

Just as iTunes can sync bookmarks and mail settings from your computer to your slab, so it can snag and display a copy of your daily or monthly schedule on your iPad—*if* you happen to use Outlook on your PC or iCal on your Mac. You can also use Entourage 2004 or later by choosing, in Entourage, Preferences→Sync Services and checking the option to have Entourage share its event info with iCal. (You can sync without wires, too; see the Tip below.)

To get your life in sync between computer and iPad, fire up iTunes and then:

❶ Connect your iPad to your computer and click the iPad's icon when it shows up in the Source list.

❷ In the main part of the iTunes window, click the Info tab. Scroll down past Contacts to Calendars.

❸ Turn on the checkbox next to "Sync Calendars with Outlook" (Windows) or "Sync iCal Calendars" (Mac). If you have multiple calendars—like for Work, Home, and School—select the ones you want to copy to your 'Pad.

❹ In the lower-right corner of the iTunes window, click the Apply button.

❺ If your iPad doesn't automatically start updating itself with your date book, choose File→Sync iPad. If you haven't changed any settings but want to update your info, the Apply button in the corner of iTunes changes to Sync, and you can click that instead of going up to Menuville.

Tip If you prefer to sync wirelessly and have a MobileMe account—or are forever linked to your office with a Microsoft Exchange account—you can update your schedule over the airwaves. Just choose Settings→Mail, Contacts, Calendars and tap your account name. Tap the Calendars button to On to keep your calendar current across your devices configured to work with MobileMe or Exchange.

On the iPad, tap the Calendar icon on the Home screen to see your schedule unfold in glorious color. If you have multiple calendars, tap the Calendars button to select one and see its events—or you can consolidate your appointments into one uber-calendar. Use the Search box to find specific events.

Along the top of the screen, tap List, Day, Week, or Month to see your schedule for the short or long term, color-coded by calendar (Home, Work, School, and so on). Tap the Today button to see what's in your immediate future. List view displays your scheduled events one after the other. No matter which view you choose, the iPad shows the year's months in a bar below the calendar. Tap the triangles on either side of the bar to go forward or backward in time.

Use the iPad Calendar

The iPad isn't a static version of your calendar. You can add events to and delete them from it and sync them back to your computer (or to your MobileMe or Exchange accounts). The iPad's calendar also lets you subscribe to online calendars to keep you apprised of events on Web-based Google and Yahoo calendars—or even your favorite sports team's schedule.

Add a Calendar Event

To punch in a new appointment or event, tap the ✚ button in the lower-right corner of the calendar screen. In the box that pops up, fill in all the necessary information, like the name of the event, location, and starting and ending times. (There's also an All-Day option for those outdoor rock festivals and softball tournaments). Tap Alert if you need to be reminded about your appointment in advance—from five minutes to two days beforehand.

If you need a standing appointment, like a weekly banjo lesson or staff meeting, you have the option to repeat the event every day, every week, every other week, every month, or every year (like for your wedding anniversary or spouse's birthday). There's also a little Notes field in the Add Event box in case you need to remember some additional information about the appointment, like "Bring Q3 report" or "Take cat-allergy meds before leaving."

Edit or Delete an Event

Schedules change, especially if you work in the high-powered corporate world or have teenage children—or both. To change the time of an event, find it on the calendar, tap the event, and then tap the Edit button. If you need to cancel an appointment completely, flick down to the bottom of the box and tap the red Delete Event button.

Set Up an iPad Alert

To make the iPad pipe up with a text and audio alert for a looming event, tap Settings→General→Sounds and flip Calendar Alerts to On. At the predetermined nag time, a reminder box flashes on-screen, accompanied by an R2-D2-like booping noise. If the iPad is off, the message appears when you turn it on, but the audio alert doesn't play.

Subscribe to an Online Calendar

To see a shared calendar or one you subscribe to, add it to the iPad. If it's a specific calendar on the Web, choose Settings→Mail, Contacts, Calendars→Add Account→Other. Select the Add CalDAV Account option (when you want to add a datebook like a Google calendar; see *http://bit.ly/iYvA5* for instructions) or Add Subscribed Calendar. Enter the calendar's URL and any other account information you need to subscribe, like your user name and password.

Want to instantly add online calendars for all sorts of topics, including religious holidays, schedules of your favorite sports teams, movie release dates, and more—right on your iPad? Crank up the Safari browser and visit iCalShare.com (*http://icalshare.com*). When you find a calendar you want to add to your iPad's collection, tap the Subscribe to Calendar button on the page, and then confirm your decision in the box that pops up.

The new calendar gets added and you see its events on your schedule. Tap the Calendars button and select it to show (or hide) those dates.

Calendars you add by subscription over the Internet are read-only, so you can't add your own events to them. If you want to delete a calendar subscription, tap Settings→Mail, Contacts, Calendars. In the Accounts list, tap the name of the calendar and tap the red Delete Account button.

Tip If you have an iPad calendar set up to sync with an Exchange account, you can respond to Outlook or Entourage meeting invitations that your colleagues send you. When you get a new invite, it lands on the scheduled date and time in your calendar with a dotted line around the event. You respond to it by tapping it on the calendar or by tapping ▣ to see pending invites. Select the one you wish to reply to. Tap Invitation From to get all the details, like who called the meeting and who else got invited. When you get an invitation, you can tap Accept, Maybe, or Decline to send off your RSVP. And if you get your meeting invitations by email instead, tap the Invite icon attachment on the message to open it up and respond to the sender. If you accept, the iPad adds the event to your calendar.

If you get a lot of meeting invitations and want to know as soon as they arrive, tap Settings→Mail, Contacts, Calendars. In the Calendars area of the screen, tap the On button next to New Invitation Alert.

Maintain Contacts

Putting a copy of your contacts file—also known as your electronic address book—on your iPad is quite easy, as long as you use up-to-date software. Windows users need to have their contacts stored in Outlook Express, Outlook 2003 or later, Windows Contacts, or the Windows Address Book (used by Outlook Express and some other email programs).

Mac folks need to use at least Mac OS X 10.5 and the Mac OS X Address Book, which Apple's Mail program uses to stash addresses. You can also use Entourage 2004 or later, but you first have to *link* before you *sync*: in Entourage, choose Preferences and click Sync Services. Then turn on the checkboxes for sharing contacts (and calendars) with Address Book and iCal (Apple's calendar program). Entourage shares the info, and Address Book and iCal sync it up.

To turn your iPad into a big glass address book, follow these steps:

❶ Connect your iPad to your computer and click its icon when it shows up in iTunes' Source list. (If you use Outlook or Outlook Express, launch that now, too.)

❷ In the main part of the iTunes window, click the Info tab.

❸ Windows owners: Turn on the checkbox next to "Sync Contacts with" and then use the drop-down menu to choose the program whose contacts you want to copy. Mac owners: turn on the "Sync Address Book contacts" checkbox. If you want to sync contact groups, select them from the "Selected groups" box. You can also choose to import the photos in your contacts files.

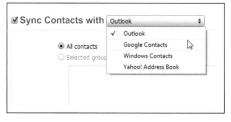

❹ Click the Apply button in the lower-right corner of the iTunes window.

The iPad updates itself with the contact information stored in your address book. If you add new contacts while you have your iPad plugged in, choose File→Update iPad or click the Sync button in iTunes to manually move the new data over to your tablet.

> **Tip** You can add contacts right on the iPad as well—tap the **+** button at the bottom of the screen and type the person's information into the form. If you're on a synced Exchange server, tap Settings→Mail, Contacts, Calendars, tap your account name, and tap the Contacts button to On to pull new addresses into the iPad over the air.

To look up a pal on the iPad, tap the Home screen's Contacts icon. Use the Search box or, on the Contacts list, flick to the person on the left side of the screen; take a shortcut by tapping the letter tab on the outer edge. Tap the name to see the person's details. Here are some of things you can do now:

- **Change the information.** Need to update an address or change a phone number? Tap the Edit button at the bottom of the contact screen.

- **Add a photo.** If you have pictures of your contacts in your desktop con-tacts program, the same photos should be here on the iPad. You can also add a picture to a contact from your iPad's Photos app. Open the contact file, tap Edit, then tap Add Photo. Find the picture you want to use. Pinch and zoom to crop it to size for the address book.

- **Find it on the map.** Tap the address to open the Maps app and see where the place is located.

- **Send a message.** Tap the person's email address to open up a new pre-addressed Mail message

- **Pass along the information.** Tap the Share Contact button on the contact's page to attach the information as a *.vcf* file (the format most computer address books use) and attach it to a new message.

To delete a contact, whack it from your computer's address book and the per-son will disappear from your iPad the next time you sync it to your computer. To delete a contact directly on the iPad, tap it open, tap Edit, flick to the bot-tom of the file, and tap the Delete Contact button.

Take Notes

Need a piece of virtual scratch paper to jot down a few thoughts? Have to type up a memo to email to colleagues, but don't own the Pages app described in Chapter 10? Want to copy a recipe off a web page and save it for future reference, when you may not have online access? The iPad's Notes program is here to serve. To get started, return to your Home screen and tap Notes. The program opens, and here's where Apple's designers got really creative.

When you hold the iPad in portrait mode, it looks like one of those yellow lined pads of paper you used to use to scribble lecture notes in school. But hold the iPad in landscape mode, as shown above, and the yellow pad shrinks down to size and shares the screen with a virtual slip of index paper, all tucked inside a faux leather folio, the kind made to sit on top of your desk and look fancy. You can even see stitches in the digital leather.

Tip If you use the Notes feature in Microsoft Outlook or Apple's Mail program, you can get your thoughts from computer and iPad. After you connect the tablet to the computer, click the iPad's icon in the iTunes Source list, click the Info tab, and scroll down to turn on the checkbox next to Sync Notes. Click the Apply or Sync button. Notes you take on the iPad get synced back to your computer as well.

When you hold the iPad in portrait mode, you can see the same index of all your stored notes by tapping the Notes button in the upper-right corner of the screen. Tap any entry in the list to jump to that particular note and open it so you can read it—or add more text to it. All of the Cut | Copy | Paste | Replace functions described back in Chapter 2 work in Notes, so you can paste in gobs of text you copy from web pages and elsewhere. You can't, however, paste picture files—you just get a string of text with the image file's name and location.

To start a new note, tap the **✚** icon in the upper-right corner to generate a blank sheet of "paper." Tap the yellow Note itself to summon the iPad's keyboard for a little good-old-fashioned text entry.

If you're looking for a certain word or words, type them into the Search box to call up a list of all the notes where the words appear. To flip forward or backward through your collected notes, tap the arrow keys at the bottom of the screen. You can even email the contents of a note by tapping the ✉ icon down below. (Hey, it costs the price of a stamp to do that with a paper note nowadays, so you just saved a little cash.)

Watch YouTube Clips

While YouTube videos on the Web usually come in the Flash format, a technology foreign to the iPad, Apple convinced the site to re-encode its millions of videos into H.264 format, a *much* higher-quality rendering than Flash—*and* one you can play via the iPad's YouTube app.

Finding a Video to Play

If you have an idea of what topic or video you want to see, tap the Search box and enter your keywords. If you're just browsing for fun times, tap one of the icons at the bottom of the screen to find videos in any of these ways:

- **Featured.** A flickable list of videos hand-picked by YouTube's editors. You see the name, length, star rating, and popularity (viewership) of each one.

- **Top Rated.** When someone watches a video on YouTube, they can give it a star rating. This list rounds up the highest-rated videos. Beware, though—you may be disappointed in the taste of the masses.

- **Most Viewed.** A popularity contest. Tap the buttons at the top to look over the most-viewed videos *Today*, *This Week*, or *All* (meaning "of all time"). Tap the Load More panel to see the next chunk of the list.

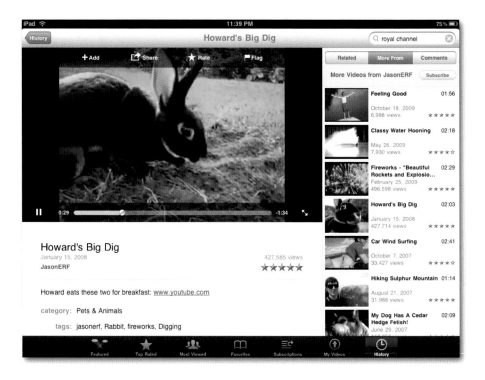

- **Favorites.** A list of videos you've flagged as your own personal faves, as described in a moment.

- **Subscriptions.** If you have a YouTube account (available free at *youtube. com*), you can subscribe to specific "channels" (themed collections) of videos and see them here. (Even the Queen of England has her own piece of YouTube bandwidth, called The Royal Channel.)

- **My Videos.** If you've used your YouTube account on your computer or iPhone to upload videos, tap here to see them once you log in.

- **History.** This is a list of videos you viewed recently on the iPad. If you want to nuke the list, hit the Clear button in the upper-left corner.

Tap any video thumbnail to open a Details screen for that video, featuring a description, date, category name, tags (keywords), the uploader's name, play length, number of views, links to related videos, and so on.

That same Details screen offers an Add button so you can add a video to your list of Favorites. Tap the Share button to send a link to the clip by email. You can also Rate and Flag selected videos.

Playing YouTube Videos

To play a video, tap its thumbnail. You can watch it in portrait or landscape mode. Tap the ▣ button to expand the clip to the screen's width in either mode.

When you first start playing a video in full-screen view, you get the usual video controls, like ▶▶|, |◀◀, ||, the volume slider, and the progress bar that lets you move to a different spot in the movie. Double-tap the screen to magnify the video, just enough to eliminate the black bars on the sides of the screen (or tap the square button in the top-right corner to do the same).

The controls fade away after a moment, so they don't block your view. You can make them appear and disappear with a single tap on the screen. Tap the Done button in the top-left corner when you finish watching. .

When you're in full-screen mode, two other icons join the playback controls: The first is the ⌒ button, which adds the video you're watching to your Favorites list. The second is the ▣ button, which lets you shrink the video down from full-screen size so you can see its Details page.

If you have the right kind of AV cable for your iPad, you can play YouTube videos on your television set as well. See Chapter 14 for more on videos and playing them on the TV screen.

Find Your Way with Maps

The iPad's Maps app makes you forget all about those folded paper roadmaps that always end up stained and crumpled in the back seat of the car. Tap open the Maps app on the Home screen. Type any address into the Maps app—and you instantly see it on the screen, its location marked with a virtual red pin. All your usual iPad finger moves work on the maps, so you can zoom, scroll, pinch, and flick your way around the world.

Like Safari, though, Maps needs an Internet connection to pull its data down from the Web, so it's not the best thing in the world for emergency directions when you're lost in a bad part of town with only a Wi-Fi iPad. (If you ponied up the big bucks for a Wi-Fi + 3G model, you don't have to worry about lack of an Internet connection, but you may still have to worry about getting mugged.)

To plot your course, tap the Maps icon on the Home screen. Here are some of the things you can do with Maps and a network connection:

- **Find an address.** Tap the Search button. In the Address box at the top of the screen, type in an address—or tap the ⌘ icon to call up your Bookmarks list. Here, you can tap places you've previously marked, see your recent locations, or map an address from the Contacts list. When the red pushpin drop onto the map, tap your ❶ in the bar above it to get an info box for that address, like the one shown on the next page.

- **Mark the spot.** Press and hold any spot on the map to drop a marker pin on it. If you miss slightly, press and drag the pin to the right address. Tap the ⓘ to see the full address, get directions (to or from there), or remove the pin. You can also add the location to your contacts or bookmarked places, or share the address by email—very handy when you set up

a group dinner at a new restaurant. If the pin's infobar has an orange and white icon of a faceless person, tap it to see a photo of the location from Google Street View that you can zoom, pan, and rotate 360 degrees; tap the map inset in the bottom-right corner to go back to the regular view. You can plant a pin the long way by tapping the bottom-right corner of the screen (where it looks like the map is peeling away), tapping the Drop Pin button, and then dragging the pin around the map to the right location.

- **Pick a view.** The Maps app doesn't skimp on the scenery. Tap the bottom-right corner to see your available map styles: Classic (traditional cartography), Satellite (a high-quality photo from a camera high in the sky), Hybrid (street labels overlaid on the photo), and Terrain (shaded elevations of the area). Tap Show Traffic if you want to see current road congestion and maybe take that antacid *before* you leave the house.

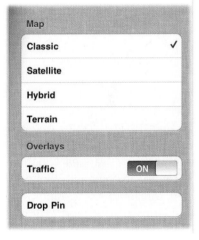

 Note Ever wonder what those green, yellow, and red lines actually mean when you look at a map of traffic conditions? The color-coding is all about the need for speed—or the lack of it. Green means traffic is moving at a rate of 50 miles an hour or more, and yellow means slower going, at 25 to 50 m.p.h. Red means traffic is creeping along at less than 25 m.p.h., so you may find some very crabby cabbies out there.

Locate Your Position with GPS

Ever look at a map and wonder exactly where you are in relation to the place you're trying to get to? Unless that map has one of those You Are Here arrows, you usually have to guess—but not if you have an iPad.

Just make sure you have an Internet connection and your Location Services turned on (page 263), too. Then tap the Current Location icon (circled) at the top of the Maps screen. The iPad drops a blue dot on the map to mark your posi-

tion to within a few hundred yards. While the Wi-Fi iPad doesn't have a GPS chip inside it like the 3G 'Pad does, it does have software that calculates your position based on a big database of Wi-Fi hot spots and cell towers.

You can even combine the ability to instantly find your current location with getting directions to someplace else. Just tap the Directions button at the top of the screen. Unless you're offline, the iPad usually starts with your current location in the first box. In the second box, type in an address or tap the ⊞ button to get to your contact addresses. Once it has the starting and ending points of your journey, the iPad pops up a blue bar offering driving, mass transit, or walking directions. The next page has more on getting them.

If you want to use your current position and navigate your way Boy Scout-style, the iPad includes a built-in digital compass. To use it, tap the Current

Location icon once to get your position, and then tap it again to activate the digital compass, which appears on the iPad screen. To rotate the compass-point north, hold the iPad parallel to the ground. To get back to regular map view, tap the compass icon in the toolbar.

If a message with a Figure 8-type symbol appears on the screen as shown here, you need to calibrate the compass, which is normal the first time you use it. Firmly grip the iPad and wave it in an "air Figure 8" pattern to fine-tune its sense of direction.

Get Directions on the Map

Need to find your way from Point A to Point B, or at least from Albany to Boston? To map your route, tap the Directions button at the top of the screen. A two-field box appears. If you don't want to use your current location, tap the ⊗ in the Start box and type in a point of origin. In the End box, type in the destination address or tap the ☐ icon and choose one from your list of bookmarked sites, recent visits, or contacts.

Once the iPad gets the starting and ending points, it calculates how to get there by car, mass transit (like train or bus), or foot. Tap the car, bus, or Walking Person icon to get a set of step-by-step directions. If you're in the middle of

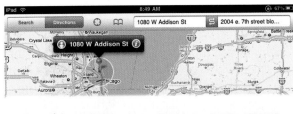

nowhere, driving directions may be all you see here. (If you need to reverse the starting and ending points of the trip, tap the S icon to flip the coordinates.)

The iPad delivers your directions in the blue bar. Tap the Start button to get going. You can see each step of your journey in one of two ways:

❶ To see all the turns in a list, tap the ▤ icon and flick down the Route Overview directions; tap the square icon to close the box.

❷ To see one turn at a time in the blue bar, tap the ← and → buttons to get each new direction displayed on the map as you go.

Unless you chose the mass-transit directions, you also get an approximate travel time for the trip. (If you did ask for mass-transit directions, tap the clock icon to get a list of transit schedules.) If you have an Internet connection as you go, the route can also update current traffic conditions.

View Photos

All the photos you sync to the iPad from your computer, save from email messages, web pages, and iPad screenshots (see the Tip on page 241), all live in
the Photos app. Tap the Photos app icon (represented by a happy sunflower)
to open it up and see what's there.

After you get some photos on the iPad, this app takes care of the sorting for
you. Photos that were in albums on your computer are in the same albums
on your iPad. You can also see all your pictures in a loose collection by tapping
the Photos button at the top of the screen.

Tap any photo thumbnail to open an album or the photo itself to full-screen
size. Chapter 15 has all the information about getting pictures on your iPad,
showing them off, making slideshows, and more. So if you're a photography
enthusiast and want flip ahead right now, this chapter *understands*.

Watch Videos

Tap open the Videos icon to find all the movies, TV shows, video podcasts, and music videos you have on your iPad. If you don't have any yet, you can get video content in a couple of ways—download it directly to the iPad from the iTunes Store (Chapter 11), or sync compatible clips from your computer to your iPad (Chapter 14). And for the record, the Videos app is where your downloaded content lives; the YouTube app (mentioned earlier in this chapter) is for streaming cool clips from YouTube's perch on the Internet.

Once you have videos on your iPad, tap the Home screen's Videos icon (it looks like one of those classic Hollywood film slates). The iPad sorts your collection by type: Movies, TV Shows, Podcasts, or Music Videos. Tap an icon to play the video. In the case of TV Shows, where you have multiple episodes, tap the show's icon and, on the following screen, tap the episode you want to see.

The iPad's high-resolution screen shows off high-quality video files quite nicely. With a folding case or an extra pillow propped up on your stomach, you have a whole new way to watch TV in bed now—without having to dig around under the blankets for the remote control.

Use the iPad as an iPod

The original boxy white-and-chrome iPod from 2001 is one of Apple's greatest success stories, and its legacy lives on with the iPad. To listen to music or see what tunes you have on your tablet, tap the orange-and-white iPod icon on the iPad's Home screen.

The iPad's iPod is an elegantly designed and organized app, made to help you find your music quickly, sorted by Songs, Artists, Albums, Genres, or Composers. The items in your library (music, spoken-word podcasts, audio-books, and custom-made playlists) appear in a neat vertical list along the left side of the screen, all awaiting your tap.

If this all sounds perfectly fine but you don't actually have any music loaded on your iPad, take a stroll to Chapter 13 for further instructions. You can also download music directly to your iPad, right from the iTunes Store, as the next page explains.

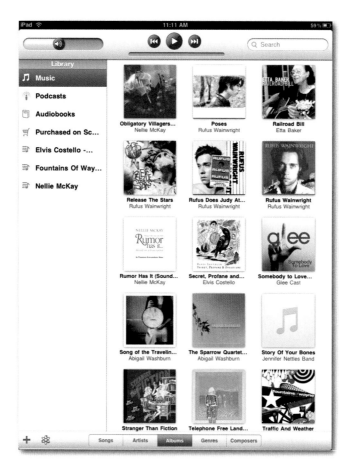

Shop iTunes and the App Store

The purple iTunes icon and the blue App Store icon on the Home Screen are all about *shopping*. Some people will find this very exciting, the chance to buy fresh new things directly on the iPad, with no cables, cars, or crankiness involved. All you need is a live Internet connection and a working credit-card number.

Much more information about each app is waiting for you in other parts of this book. For more on the iTunes Store—where you can buy music, audiobooks, movies, TV shows, and download free audio and video podcasts— take a stroll to Chapter 11.

If apps are your thing and you want to find new programs to run on your iPad, you don't have as far to go. Just turn the page to leave this chapter and move on to Chapter 7, which is all about the App Store.

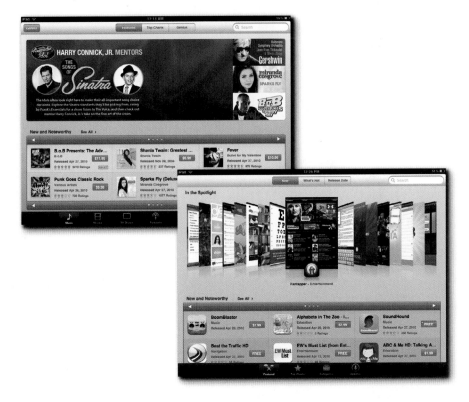

 Note "Hey," you say, "there's another icon on the Home screen that wasn't mentioned! What about Settings?" Settings is a collection of iPad set-up screens, and it gets an entire index all to itself. See Appendix A if you just can't wait.

7

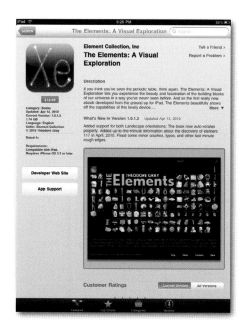

Shop the App Store

In the beginning, 2003 to be exact, there was the iTunes Music Store. Apple's perfectly legal online emporium sold songs for 99 cents a pop and quickly became a hit itself. The premise and the promise were simple: inexpensive entertainment you could instantly download and use. Just a few years later, the renamed iTunes Store added (and still sells) TV shows, movies, and simple arcade-style video games for iPods. And then in 2008, iTunes added the App Store for the iPod Touch and iPhone.

The App Store is the place to download *apps*, or programs, that run on your iPod Touch, iPhone, and now, iPad. Thousands of apps, including foreign-language tutors, electronic newspapers, restaurant guides, hurricane trackers, tiny word processors, and sophisticated handheld videogames can all be found in the App Store, with developers writing new programs every week. It's a hugely popular part of the Apple empire. Even before the iPad came out in April 2010, the App Store had sold three billion apps to eager iPod and iPhone owners.

And now that the iPad has arrived, there are more apps than ever. This chapter shows you how to get shopping by setting up an account in the store, buying and installing your first apps, and keeping them organized once you start loading up your tablet.

Go to the App Store

Remember when computer stores displayed shelves and shelves worth of software in colorful shrinkwrapped cardboard boxes? The App Store ditches the physical racks and crowds of people but still offers thousands of programs, neatly organized into 20 categories right on the other side of your Internet connection. Once you're online, you can either:

❶ Click the iTunes Store icon in the Source list and click the App Store link at the top of the screen. Or, if you're looking for a specific category of program, like, say, an expense tracker, click the small triangle that pops up in the App Store tab to open a categories submenu and go right to the Financial section. Chapter 11 has more about the Music and Video side of the iTunes Store.

❷ Click the App Store icon on the iPad's Home screen.

Either action gets you to the App Store. If you choose the iTunes path from the comfort of your laptop or desktop computer, you may have a bigger screen and an easier time browsing the store's selections—but you do have the extra step of syncing your purchases over to the iPad later (page 181).

Tour the App Store

No matter how you get there, the App Store has plenty to offer your iPad. In most cases, you land right on the store's home page, where Apple employees regularly spotlight new, timely, or interesting apps and games. Here, you can see the list of top apps, both in the budget-friendly Free Apps section and the more feature-friendly Paid Apps department.

If you click or tap any app's name or icon , you go to the program's App Store page, where you can find out more about what it does. You can also view sample screenshots, read reviews from others who have purchased the app, and see its system requirements to make sure it's iPad-compatible. For apps intended for both the iPhone and the iPad, some developers give you a choice of screenshots to inspect. Next to Screenshots, click the iPad button (circled) to see just the iPad images.

Many games include an age rating to help parents decide if a game is appropriate (or not) for children. There's also a Free Link button to download the apps that are gratis, or a Buy App link if you have to shell out some simoleons. (If you buy an app, it gets billed to your credit card. Turn the page for instructions on setting up an account with Apple.)

Across the top of each app's page, you'll see a category listed, like Weather, Sports, Games, Photography, Music, and so on. You can click the category name to see similar apps if the one you're looking at doesn't quite fit the bill.

Set Up an iTunes/App Store Account

Before you can buy any of the cool stuff you see in the Store, you need to set up an account with Apple. If you already have one from previous purchases from the iTunes Store, you can use the same name and password here—it all goes to the credit card you have on file with Apple.

If you've never bought any of Apple's online products, like iTunes movies or prints from iPhoto, you need to set up an account before you can buy anything. To do so, click the "Sign In" button in the upper-right corner of the iTunes window. If you've never had an Apple ID, click Create New Account. (If you're on the iPad, scroll down to the bottom of the screen, then tap Sign In→Create New Account.)

The iTunes Store Welcome presents you with the three steps to follow:

❶ Agree to the terms for using the Store and buying music.

❷ Create an Apple Account.

❸ Supply a credit card or PayPal account number and billing address.

As your first step in creating an Apple Account, you must read and agree to the long scrolling legal document on the first screen. The 27-page statement informs you of your rights and responsibilities as an iTunes Store and App Store customer. It boils down to two core points: *Thou shalt not download an album, burn it to CD, and then sell bootleg copies of it at your local convenience store*, and *Third-party crashware apps are not our fault*.

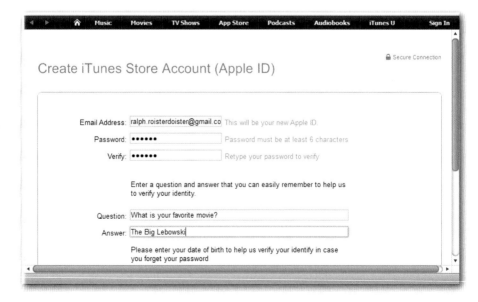

Click the Agree button to move on to step 2. Here, you create an Apple ID, password, and secret question and answer. If you later have to click the "Forgot Password?" button in the Store sign-in box, this is the question you'll have to answer to prove that you're you. Apple requests that you type in your birthday to help verify your identity. (You must be over 13 to get an account here.)

On the third and final screen, provide a valid credit card number with a billing address. You can also use a PayPal account.

Click Done. You've got yourself an Apple Account. From now on, you can log into the App Store by clicking the "Sign In" button in the upper-right corner of the iTunes window.

Sign Up Without a Credit Card

But what if you just want to download free apps from the App Store? You don't have to cough up a credit-card number. The main restriction is that you must make sure you're in the App Store, and not the main iTunes Store (where only the podcasts are regularly free). In iTunes, click the App Store link on the main iTunes Store page. Once you're in the App Store:

❶ Find a free program you want and click the Free App button.

❷ When the Sign In box pops up, click the Create a New Account button.

❸ Agree to the Terms and Conditions document and then fill out your account name, password, and birthday information.

❹ On the screen for payment options, click the payment option for None.

❺ Fill out the other required fields for name and email address, and then click the link to verify your new account.

❻ When you get the confirmation email message from the Store, click the link supplied to verify your account.

Once you finish up step 6, you get prompted to log into your account with your new user name and password. When you do, you land back in the App Store, ready to gobble up free apps for your 'Pad.

 Tip Need to change billing or other information in your iTunes/App Store Account? Sign into the store, and then click on your account name. In the box that pops up, retype your password and click the View Account button. On the account settings screen, click either the Edit Account Info or Edit Payment Information button.

Buy, Download, and Install Apps

Okay, you've found the App Store, maybe even created an Apple account ahead of time: Now you're ready to start loading up your iPad with all the cool programs, games, and utilities you can fit on it.

- **Get apps in the iTunes Store.** Click the App Store link on the main Store page and browse away. When you find an app you want, click the Free App or Buy App button to download a copy of the program to iTunes. You can see all the apps you've purchased by clicking the Applications icon in the iTunes Source list. When you finish shopping, connect the iPad to your computer, and sync 'em up, as Chapter 11 explains.

- **Get apps on the iPad.** When you've got a Wi-Fi or 3G connection, tap the blue App Store icon on the Home screen and browse away. At the top of the Featured screen, you can see what's new and hot—or what the iTunes Genius thinks you might like. At the bottom of the screen, you see a list of the most downloaded apps (Top Charts) and apps listed by category. When you find an app you want, tap the Free App or price button; the latter turns into a Buy Now button, so hit that. Type in your Store name and password (even if it's a free application), and the download begins. After the program finishes loading and installing, tap its icon to launch it. Download times vary by app size. For example, the beautiful interactive textbook pictured here, *The Elements: A Visual Exploration*, is a honking 1.74 gigabytes—so give it time.

Uninstall Apps

Not every app is a 5-star winner. One may turn out to be different from what you envisioned when you bought it, or not live up to your expectations in other ways. Or maybe some of those bigger games and programs are just taking up too much of your limited iPad real estate. And some apps may even be buggy and crashy, and perhaps you want to just remove them instead of waiting for the developer to post an update (page 117).

Here are two ways to uninstall an app:

- **Remove apps in iTunes.** Connect the iPad to your computer, and then click its icon in the iTunes Source list. In the main iTunes window, click the Applications tab. In the list, turn off the check-boxes next to the apps you want to remove and then click Sync to uninstall them. The removed apps stay in your iTunes library, but you won't be carting them around on the iPad until you select them here and resync. Page 181 has pictures.

- **Remove apps on the iPad.** As shown here on the Home screen, press and hold the unwanted application's icon until it wiggles and an X appears in the corner. Tap the X, confirm your intention to delete, and wave goodbye to that app. Press the Home button to return to business as usual.

> **Tip** While all App Store sales are final, you may be able to get a refund if an app is mislabeled or seriously doesn't perform as advertised. It's certainly not a sure thing, and you need to make your case to the iTunes Support folks calmly and clearly about why the app fails for technical reasons ("I just don't like it" is not a valid excuse). Contact customer service at *www.apple.com/support/itunes*.

Search for Apps

Just as you can buy apps on either your computer or tablet, so you can search for apps or specific types of programs with iTunes or the iPad. This function comes in handy if you don't know the exact name of the app you seek, or want to throw a few keywords into the Search box and see what comes up.

Here's how to search:

- **On the computer.** The upper right corner of the iTunes window has a nice little Search box. When you're in your library, typing keywords into the box brings up results from your own collection. But when you search with the iTunes Store selected in the Source list, your results come from the apps, games, music, and other items for sale in the online store. If you don't immediately see what you want, click the Power Search button in the top left corner to get a set of search boxes that let you narrow your results even further.

- **On the iPad.** Tap the Search icon (Q) at the bottom of the App Store screen to summon the virtual keyboard. Type in the keywords for the app you seek and tap the Search button in the keyboard. The iPad matches what you type as you go and presents a list before you finish.

In any of these situations, just click or tap the app name to get more information about the program from its page in the App Store.

Scale Up iPhone Apps

Even before the iPad was officially announced in January 2010, the App Store already had more than 100,000 programs in stock for iPhone and iPod Touch users. According to Apple, just about all of these programs can run on the iPad, so there's no software shortage for the slab here.

But while these apps can run on the iPad, most of them weren't *designed* for it. They may seem a little sparse on the bigger screen. Still, you have two ways to run those older iPhone and iPod Touch apps on the iPad:

- **Run the apps at actual size.** While this maintains the original look of the app, it looks kind of silly floating there in the middle of the iPad, like a tiny island with an ocean of dark screen surrounding it on all four sides. You have to reach in much farther across the iPad to tap the screen buttons.

- **Run the apps at twice the size.** If you don't want to squint, you can super-size that old iPhone app—just tap the 2X button in the bottom-right corner of the iPad screen (circled). The iPad then doubles each pixel on the screen to scale up the app. Depending on the program, though, Hulk-ing up your apps with the 2X button can make them look a little blotchy and weird compared to running them at the size they were intended. But you do make use of your iPad's expansive vista.

The longer the iPad is available, though, the more apps will appear written (or rewritten) expressly to fill its big glorious screen. In a year or so, the 2X feature may seem quaint little kludge.

Organize Apps

Back in Chapter 1, you learned how to rearrange the icons on the Home screen of your iPad. And after reading the first few pages of this chapter, you may now have a *ton* of groovy new app icons all over your iPad—but not in the order you'd like them. Sure, you can drag wiggling icons all over your 11 pages of Home screen, but that can get a little confusing and frustrating when you accidentally drop an icon on the wrong page. Plus, that iPad screen is awfully large and you could throw your shoulder out dragging those apps such a long distance.

If you want an easier way to fine-tune your iPad's Home screens, iTunes lets you arrange all your app icons from your big-screen computer:

❶ Connect the iPad to your computer. Click its icon in the Source list.

❷ Click the Applications tab. You now see all your applications—a complete list on the left, a giant version of the current screen in the middle, and individual pages to the right-hand side of or below the Big Screen.

❸ Select the icons you want to move. Click an icon you want to move on the JumboTron and drag it to the desired page thumbnail—iTunes re-creates both iPad screen orientations so you can fine-tune the look of your screens: landscape mode pages appear along the bottom, portrait mode screens stacked vertically on the far right. Hold down the Ctrl or

⌘ keys and click to select multiple apps. It's much easier to group similar apps on a page this way—you can have, say, a page of games or a page of online newspapers. You can even swap out the four permanent application icons in the gray bar on the bottom of the iPad screen (either here or on the tablet itself) with other apps—and squeeze in two more for a total of six apps in the permanent row.

❹ Click Apply or Sync. Wait just a moment as iTunes rearranges the icons on your iPad so they mirror the setup in iTunes.

But what if you have too many apps for the iPad's limit of 11 Home screens? Even if an app's not visible, you can find it on the tablet by flicking your finger from left to right on the first Home screen and typing in the app name in the search box that appears.

Tip Just as you can on the iPad itself, you can whack an app in iTunes by clicking it to select it and then clicking the black-circled X that appears in the app icon's upper-left corner. This just deletes the app from the iPad—not from your overall iTunes library.

Adjust App Preferences

Many apps have all their functions and controls within each program; you can get to them by tapping Setup or Options (or something similarly named) while you run the app. Some apps, however, have a separate set of preferences kept in the iPad's Settings area.

For example, your nifty little weather program may include the option to display temperatures in either Fahrenheit or Celsius and wind speeds in either miles per hour or kilometers per hour, depending on the measuring standards of your country. You can set these preferences for the application by choosing Home→Settings and flicking all the way down the screen to the collection of settings for individual apps. Tap the name of the app you want to adjust to get to its settings.

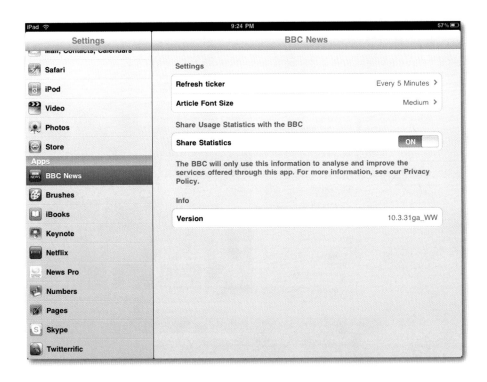

Update Apps

When you see a red circled number on the App Store icon, you know you have some updatin' to do. The number in the red circle represents the number of apps that have updates waiting for you to download and install. Updates usually contain bug fixes and programming improvements that may help wobbly apps stop crashing. Some might include new features. All updates for a particular version of an app are free.

To see which apps have updates ready, tap the App Store icon to see the list. Tap the name of the program you want to update, tap the Price button, and then tap Install. If you have multiple programs with updates ready, you can install them all in one fell swoop by tapping the Update All button. The program updates after you type in your Store password.

You can also check for app updates in iTunes. Click the Applications icon in the iTunes Source list to display all your downloaded apps, then click the "Check for Updates" link at the bottom of the window. If you have updates, iTunes alerts you with a box and gives you a button to click to see which apps are involved. (The number in the gray circle next to Apps in the Source list also gives you the total number of updates available.)

When you view a list of the updates, iTunes gives you a button in the top-right corner to install all the updates at once, but you can also update programs individually by clicking the Get Update button next to each app's name. Once you download the updates to iTunes, you need to sync the iPad with the computer to install them.

Troubleshoot Apps

Most App Store programs work perfectly fine at what they were designed to do, but things can occasionally go wrong. Maybe there was a little bug that made it through the testing process. Or maybe an iPad software update changed the way the operating system interacts with the app.

In any case, you have a few basic troubleshooting steps to try for apps that aren't playing nice with the iPad:

- **Restart the iPad.** If you just installed an elaborate videogame like *Star Wars: Trench Run* or some other complex application, it's a good idea to restart the iPad (page 270 has the steps) to get all this new software off to a fresh start with the operating system—sort of like how it's a fine notion to restart your computer after you install new programs.

- **Check for updates.** Some apps may have been sold just a tad too soon. The developer, facing bad reviews in the App Store and cranky users, quickly posts an updated version of the app that fixes the problem. Flip back a page for information on updating apps. (It's also a good idea to plug the tablet into the computer and check for iPad software updates every once in a while; see page 274 to learn how.)

 Some apps were designed to work with 3G service or the GPS. Before you tear your hair out trying to figure out why this brand-new app just won't do what it's supposed to, revisit its App Store page and recheck the system requirements to make sure it's actually *supposed* to run on the iPad, W-Fi + 3G model or otherwise.

- **Remove and reinstall the app.** Perhaps something tripped up the installation process when you first bought the app or a little piece of it somehow got damaged during a crash. If a certain app is wigging out on you, try uninstalling it (page 111), restarting the iPad (page 270), and then downloading it again from the App Store (page 110) so you can install a fresh copy of the program. Even if it's a paid app, if you previously purchased it, you can download a new copy of the same version for free. (Just to be sure, the App Store displays an alert box that points out that you've already downloaded this app before and asks you to tap the OK button to confirm your desire to download it again.) But a clean install with a new copy of the software just may do the trick if, say, your Facebook app bombs out every time you try to upload a photo.

Other steps to try include deauthorizing (page 172) and re-authorizing (page 171) your computer for using purchases from the iTunes and App Stores, or reinstalling the whole iTunes program on your computer (page 272). Sometimes, just logging out of your Store account and logging back in can resolve an issue.

If all that fails, it's probably the app's fault. You can, however, report your problem. If you're on the iPad, tap the App Store icon, find the app's page in the Store, and flick down to the bottom of the page to where the Report a Problem button lives. Tap it to get a form you can fill out and send directly to Apple.

If you're logged into your iTunes Store account on the computer, click your user name in the top right corner. In the Sign In box, click the View Account button, sign in again, and click the Purchase History button on the account settings page. Click the Report a Problem button at the bottom of the page, then click the arrow next to the problem program in your list of recent purchases. Now you get an electronic form you can fill out and send off to Apple.

> **Tip** If you need help from a human at Apple, you can either call (800) 275-2273 or email them. From the iTunes Store's main page, click the Support link. Your web browser presents you with the main iTunes service and support page; click any link in the Customer Service area and then, at the bottom of the page that appears, fill out the Email Support form. Live online chat is also available for some issues.

8

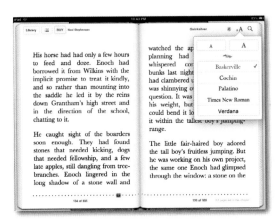

His horse had only a few hours to feed and doze. Enoch had borrowed it from Wilkins with the implicit promise to treat it kindly, and so rather than mounting into the saddle he led it by the reins down Grantham's high street and in the direction of the school, chatting to it.

He caught sight of the boarders soon enough. They had found stones that needed kicking, dogs that needed fellowship, and a few late apples, still dangling from tree-branches. Enoch lingered in the long shadow of a stone wall and

watched the ap
planning had
whispered   con
bunks last night
had clambered u
was shinnying o
question. It was
his weight, but
could bend it lo
it within the tallest boy's jumping-
range.

The little fair-haired boy adored the tall boy's fruitless jumping. But he was working on his own project, the same one Enoch had glimpsed through the window: a stone on the

iBooks & ePeriodicals

Books in their current, easy-to-use, page-turning form have been around since the second century A.D. or so. After a few years of false starts and dashed hopes, *electronic* books are beginning to woo some people away from the world of ink, paper, and tiny little clip-on book lights for reading in the dark. And as the eBook goes, so go eBook readers. The Amazon Kindle, the Barnes & Noble Nook, and the Sony Reader are among the big names on the eBook reader playground, but they all have one thing in common: drab gray-and-black text.

Enter the iPad.

With its glorious, high-resolution color touchscreen, the iPad takes the eBook experience to a new level. Instead of the blotchy grayscale images typical of electronic magazines, you see the bold, bright, original layouts of newsstand magazines. Turning the page of an eBook isn't the flash of a monochrome screen anymore, it's a fully animated re-creation of the page-flip on a real book. And the books themselves have evolved into interactive creations, with built-in dictionaries, searchable text, hyper-linked footnotes, and embedded bookmarks that make the whole reading process more efficient and engaging. So flip *this* page to see how much fun you can have reading books in the 21st century on the iPad.

Download the iBooks App

Before you can buy and read eBooks on your iPad, you have to do two things: recalibrate your brain, because Apple calls its eBooks *iBooks*, and then pop into the iTunes App Store to download Apple's free iBooks app. You have your choice of how to get there.

- **On the iPad.** You can grab the iBooks app by tapping the App Store icon on the iPad's Home screen. If you don't get an invitation to download iBooks right off the bat, as shown here, you can always find it yourself. You might see an iBooks icon on the App Store's main page, or you can tap the Search box at the top of the screen, type in *iBooks*, and wait for the app to pop up. Then tap the Install App button.

- **On the computer.** If your iPad's out of network range or you prefer to get all your apps via the desktop, you can get the iBooks app through iTunes. Fire up iTunes, click the iTunes Store link, tap the App Store tab, and search for the iBooks app there. Once you download it, you need to sync your iPad with iTunes to install it. You can only get the iBooks app in iTunes—the iBookstore itself is only available by way of the tablet for now.

Once you have iBooks installed, tap its icon on the iPad home screen to launch it and see what electronic books look like on an iPad.

 Note Did you jump right to this chapter because you really wanted to learn more about Apple's approach to the whole eBook thing? If you're feeling lost, flip back to Chapter 7. It gives you the lowdown on this App Store business and shows you how to open an iTunes account—which you need to buy books.

Go to the iBookstore

To get to all the electronic books Apple has to offer in its iBookstore, you first have to open the iBooks app. Find it on your Home screen and tap it open. You see a virtual rendition of a handsome wooden bookshelf. This is where all your downloaded book purchases eventually come to live.

For now, it likely holds a single electronic volume that came with the iBooks app: *Winnie-the-Pooh*, the illustrated children's classic by A.A. Milne. (Surely you remember the story? Honey-loving bear hangs out in the woods and learns life's lessons with his pals, who include a hyperactive tiger and a depressed donkey.)

Apple has thoughtfully included this free title so you can see an iBook for yourself before you go tapping off to buy books of your own choosing. If you want to stay and play with Pooh, there's no rush. Just tap the cover to open the book. Page 130 explains how to further navigate through the bright electronic pages of an iBook.

If you feel you've moved beyond the Hundred-Acre Wood and want to get to the Malcolm Gladwell and Doris Kearns Goodwin tomes, tap the Store button in the upper-left corner of the bookshelf. As long as you've got an Internet connection, you land in the iBookstore. Turn the page to find out what happens next.

> **Tip** If you delete your free *Pooh* accidentally or on purpose (to save space), you can usually get it back by downloading it again from the Children's & Teens section of the iBookstore. And don't sweat the file size. Compared to music and video files, most books are rather small—about 2 megabytes per title.

Browse and Search for Books

Once you tap the Store icon, you're transported into the iBookstore—which looks quite a bit like the iTunes Store and the App Store, but with book titles instead of music, videos, and TV programs. But like those other iStores, browsing and searching works pretty much the same way.

The main storefront features new best sellers, popular titles, and books the iBookstore staff finds interesting. If you're browsing for books on a specific subject, tap the Categories button (circled) and select from the pop-up menu.

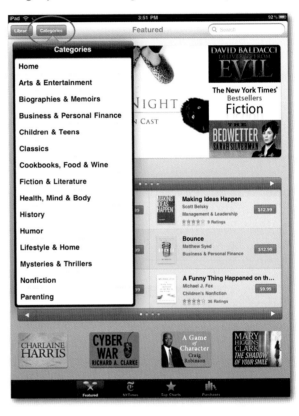

A row of four icons at the bottom of the screen sort the books into groups:

- **Featured.** The main storefront displays new and notable titles and spotlighted genres. Flick to the bottom of the screen for links to books on sale, books made into movies, books Apple's staff thinks you should read, books so enticing people are pre-ordering them, free books, and books Oprah likes. Buttons at the bottom of every Store screen let you log in or out of your Apple account, redeem iTunes gift cards, or get technical support with an iBookstore problem.

- **NYTimes.** This button reveals the weekly rankings of books on the venerable *New York Times* Best Sellers list, which has been charting books since 1942 (the author is an employee of the *New York Times*). The iBookstore's version gets updated each week, in tandem with the *Times* list.

- **Top Charts.** Tap Top Charts to see a list of the most popular books people buy though their iPads, as well as a list of the most popular *free* books (page 127) readers are snapping up.

- **Purchased.** Can't remember what you've bought? Tap here to see a list of your previous purchases. If you delete a purchased book, find it in the list here and tap the Redownload button. You don't have to pay again.

To search for a title or author, tap the Search box at the top of the Store screen. When the keyboard pops up, start typing in the title or name. A suggestions box appears to help complete your search. If Apple has titles that match your criteria, you see them listed. Tap the Cancel button to quit the search.

Tap any book cover to get more information about the title—the cover spins around to reveal a book description, star ratings, reviews from other readers, and even a button to download a free sample of the work. (Isn't this easier than leaning against hard wooden shelves and getting jostled by other customers or unleashed toddlers when you browse in a regular bookstore?) You can also tap the price button to buy the book right away.

After you read the book, you can go back to its info page and offer your own $.02 about the story or writing. Tap the stars to give it a wordless ranking or tap the "Write a Review" link to give it a more thoughtful critique. You need to log into your Store account to rank and review books, so it's not an anonymous undertaking.

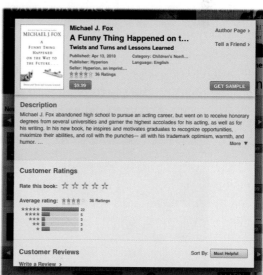

Buy and Download a Book

When you find a book you simply must have in your digital library, tap the price button next to the title. This turns into a Buy Book button. Tap that, type in your iTunes/App Store/iBookstore account name and password so Apple has a credit-card number to charge, and let the download begin.

Back in your iPad's Library—which you can always get to by tapping the Library button in the top-left corner of the Store screen—the book cover appears on your Library shelf. A blue progress bar (circled below) creeps across the cover to indicate how much of the file has downloaded.

Most books take just a couple minutes to arrive on the iPad, but this can vary with network congestion and other factors. When the book download is complete, it appears on the Library shelf with a sassy blue "New" ribbon on the cover. (Free-sample chapters get a red "Sample" ribbon.)

Find Free iBooks

Most iBook titles cost between $6 and $15, significantly cheaper than the $25 to $30 you pay for the brand-new hardcover treeware versions. But the iBookstore isn't all about the money, all the time. It offers more than a hundred eBooks on its virtual shelves, *absolutely free*.

To find this Treasure Chest of Free Literature, tap the Featured button at the bottom of the iBooks screen and flick down to the Quick Links section. Tap the Free Books link (circled). All the free titles are listed here. Tap a cover and get the description box to read the synopsis and find out what other people think of the book. Tap the Get Book button to download it; you can also get a sample, but the book itself is free, so just go for it.

Most of these free titles tend to be classic works of literature that have fallen out of copyright and into the public domain. In fact, you may have read some of them in school (or at least the Cliffs Notes guides). The offerings include *Middlemarch* by George Eliot, *The Art of War* by Sun Tzu, *Washington Square* by Henry James, *The Adventures of Sherlock Holmes* by Arthur Conan Doyle and many of Shakespeare's plays.

You can also download *Ulysses* by James Joyce. Even though the iPad weighs a pound and a half, it's still probably lighter than paperback copies of this epic Irish novel of more than 700 old-fashioned printed pages.

Free books aren't the fanciest ones on the shelf—on the outside, anyway. But while you don't get colorfully designed mini book covers (they all sort of look like they're covered in plain brown wrappers), you sure can't beat the price.

Sync Books with iTunes

As Chapter 11 explains, iTunes is your conduit to moving files between the iPad and your computer. True, you buy iBooks from the iBookstore on the iPad—but you back them up to your computer by syncing them with iTunes. Once you've synced—and therefore backed up—your iPad's contents, it's much less of a stomach-churning event if you have to restore your iPad's software (page 276) or you accidentally delete books you weren't quite done with.

To sync the iPad with iTunes, connect the tablet to the computer with its USB cable. If you previously purchased some iBooks, choose File→Transfer Purchases from iPad to copy them into iTunes for safe-keeping.

Since your computer probably has more hard drive space than your iPad does, you can also use iTunes to sync books on and off the tablet as you need them. To do so, click the iPad's icon in the iTunes Source list, then click the Books tab in the middle of the screen. Turn on the checkbox next to Sync Books. If you want to selectively sync titles, click "Selected books" and turn on the checkboxes next to the relevant books. Click Apply and then the Sync button to make it happen. (You can sync audiobooks this way, too.)

The iBooks app handles PDF files as well, like those that arrive as email attachments (tap the attachment and choose "Open in iBooks" at the top of the screen) or those you sync to your 'Pad by dragging them into your iTunes library.

Add Other eBooks to the iPad

The iBookstore isn't the only place you can get electronic books for your iPad. Since the iBooks app uses the popular ePub format for digital books, you can add those types of files as well—as long as the ePub books don't have any fun-killing, copy-protecting DRM (digital-rights management) code built in that demands a password before you can read it.

As e-readers have become more common, ePub book sites have blossomed on the Web. One place to get unprotected ePub files is the Project Gutenberg site. Founded in 1971, Project Gutenberg is a volunteer effort to collect and freely distribute great works of literature. The site has long been a resource for people who want to read the digitized classics on computers, cellphones, iPods, and more—and it has a ton of ePub books that work quite well on the iPad.

To browse and download books from the collection, visit *gutenberg.org*. You can search the site for specific books, which are often available in several electronic formats. Find a book in ePub format as highlighted here (it'll have the extension *.epub*) and download it to your computer. To get the book onto your iPad, choose File→Add to Library in iTunes. Once you get the file in iTunes, sync it to the iPad as described on the previous page. Once it's on the iPad, it looks just like a regular iBook.

> **Tip** The App Store has plenty of book-related apps as well—just click the triangle on the App Store tab and select Books from the drop-down menu. Among the notable items here are the Amazon Kindle app, which lets you read eBooks you buy from Amazon's hefty 450,000-title e-bookstore (yes, that's way more than the iBookstore has) on the iPad. The app is free, but you pay for the books you get from Amazon. Another fun app is Alice for iPad, a hyperkinetic version of Lewis Carroll's famous Wonderland tale that incorporates the iPad's accelerometer and touchscreen into the action. The full version is $9, but the Lite sampler is free.

Read an iBook

Of course, reading an iBook isn't the same as cracking open the spine of a leather-bound volume and relaxing in an English club chair with a snifter of brandy by the fire. But really—who reads books that way any more (except for the impossibly wealthy and characters on *Masterpiece Mystery*)? Aside from visiting a bookstore or library, reading books in the 21st century can involve anything from squinting through Boswell's *Life of Johnson* on a mobile phone to gobbling down the latest Danielle Steel romantic epic on the oversized Kindle DX e-reader.

Then there's the iPad way. Tap the screen to see these iBook controls:

❶ **Library.** Tap here to leave your current book and go back to the bookshelf.

❷ **Contents.** Tap this button to see the book's chapter titles and tap one to jump to that point in the book. You can also see your list of bookmarks (page 135).

❸ **Buy.** Reading a sample chapter? If you like what you read, tap the Buy button for a near-instant library acquisition.

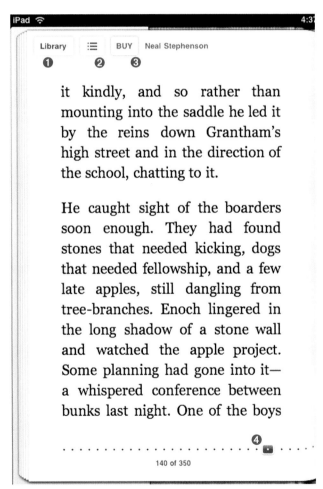

❹ **Page Navigator.** Drag the little brown slider along the bottom of the page to quickly advance or retreat through a book's pages. Keywords and page numbers flash on-screen as you drag.

The iPad can display books in either portrait mode or landscape view (shown here across these two pages). When you tap the screen, the iBook controls appear in either view. Reading iBooks is probably the reason most people use the iPad's Screen Rotation Lock button (page 3). Turning on Rotation Lock (on the right side of the iPad) prevents the screen from automatically reorienting itself (and giving you motion sickness) when you're trying to read in bed.

To turn the page in an iBook, tap the right margin on the page to go forward. Tap the left margin to go back. And you can always drag the page corner with your finger for that dramatic looks-like-a-real-page-turning animated effect.

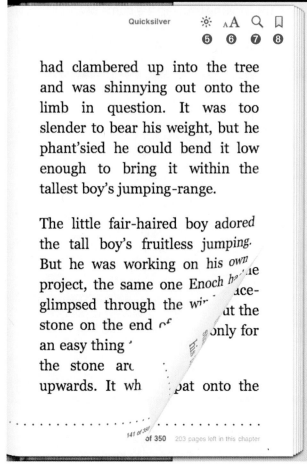

⑤ Screen Brightness. The iPad's color display is bright—too bright, sometimes. To dim the screen, tap the Sun icon and drag the slider (this move affects iBooks only).

⑥ Type. Is the font and size not to your liking? Tap here to fix it; page 132 has more.

⑦ Search. Tap the magnifying-glass icon (Q) to get a box where you can type in keywords to find mentions of a word. Page 133 has details.

⑧ Bookmark. Tap here to save your place in the book you're reading. Page 135 has more, along with info on making notes in the margins.

Change the Type in an iBook

One thing you can't really do with a printed book is make the type size bigger or smaller to suit the needs of your eyes, not the book designer's. And if you don't care for a book's typeface, you're stuck with that, too—in a printed book, that is.

But not on the iPad. Thanks to the iBooks software, you can make book type bigger or smaller, or change the look altogether. Just tap the Type icon (aA) at the top of the page. A box like the one shown below appears. Tap the little a to make the text on-screen smaller, or tap the big A to make it bigger. The size changes as you tap, so you can immediately see which size works best for you. Hate reading on white pages? Tap the Sepia button to give the page a brownish tint.

To change the typeface (font) used for the text, tap the name of another typeface in the list. The font the name appears in previews what it will look like on-screen. Tap the page when you're done resetting the book's type.

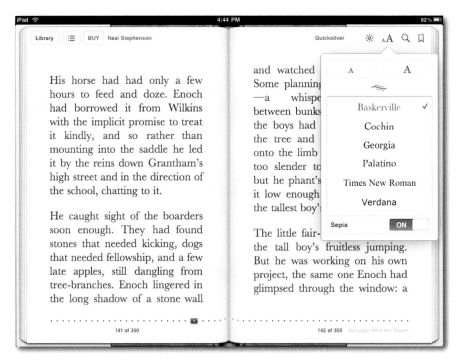

 Some of these typeface names may seem odd, but several are named after the typographers who designed or inspired the font. Baskerville, for example, was created by John Baskerville in 18th-century England. Cochin (designed by Georges Peignot in 1912) is named after the French engraver Charles Nicolas Cochin. Little did they know they'd show up in a book about the iPad.

Search an iBook

Need to pinpoint a certain word or phrase in a book to find a particular passage—or to see how many times the word appears? The iPad helps you out here, too. And if you want more information about that searched word, the iPad even offers buttons to bring up search results from Google or Wikipedia. Let's see that hardback copy of *Abraham Lincoln: Vampire Hunter* do *that*.

You have two ways to start up a search.

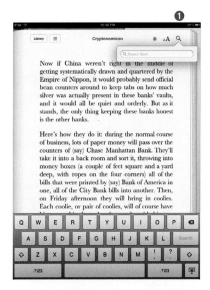

❶ Tap the 🔍 icon on the top of the book page. When the keyboard slides into view, type in your keywords and hit the Search key. Your results arrive quickly.

❷ When you're in the middle of a book page, press and hold your finger down on the word you want to search on. A box appears on-screen over the selected word with four choices: Dictionary | Highlight | Note | Search. Tap Search and let the iPad bring you a list of results—in context.

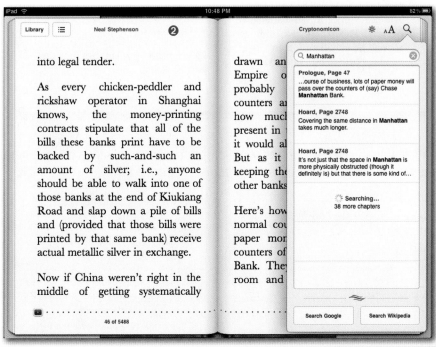

Use the Dictionary

Reading a book on the iPad means you don't need Webster's Dictionary riding shotgun to look up word definitions. This sort of thing can happen when reading scientific or historical texts, or if vocabulary was never your strong suit in high-school English class.

To see the meaning of a word you don't recognize, double-tap it (or press and hold it for a second) until the Dictionary | Highlight | Note | Search box appears. (If you want information about a full name or a phrase, drag the blue selection dots around all the words.) Tap Dictionary to see the definition.

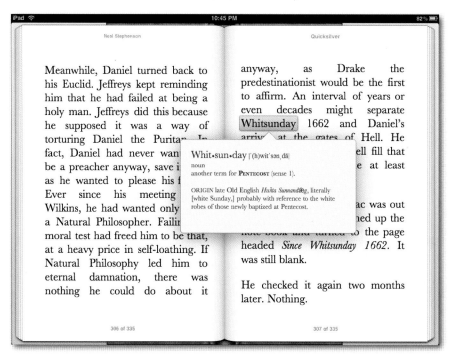

The dictionary also recognizes some proper names, but as you can see here, the results can be a bit mixed—and sometimes quite funny.

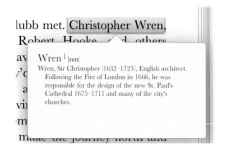

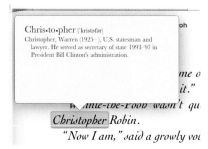

Make Bookmarks and Notes

Even if you abruptly bail out of the iBooks app and jump to another program, the iPad remembers what book you were reading and what page you were on. If you happen to be reading a dense, brain-burning book and want to remember *exactly* where you left off (or you want to mark a passage for later reference), you can set digital bookmarks or highlight text right on the page.

Tap the bookmark icon in the upper-right corner to save your place. To mark a specific spot in the text, double-tap a word to select it (or drag the blue selection dots around more words). When the Dictionary | Highlight | Note | Search box pops up, tap Highlight to swipe

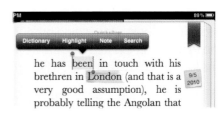

color across the selected text. Choose Note to make a digital Post-It note that you can leave in the margins. (You can also select, copy, and paste text in and out of notes when you tap them open.)

To see the places you've marked within an iBook, tap the Contents icon (▤) and then tap the Bookmarks button (circled). You see the list of bookmarks, highlights, and notes—and *when* you created them. Tap a bookmark to jump to

it or tap Resume to go to the page you left, bookmarked or not. Swipe a bookmark or note and tap Delete to remove it.

Hate the hue or want to get rid of the highlight? Tap to select it and in the box that pops up, choose a different color of the rainbow by tapping Colors or tap Remove Highlight.

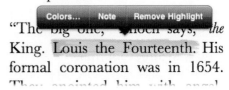

Note Have an iBook with certain words printing in blue? Those are hyperlinks that jump to the book's endnotes section so you can see the documented source for the hyperlinked material; tap the note's linked number to go back to where you were. You see this sort of thing more often in history and science books than in novels.

Use Newspaper and Magazine Apps

It's safe to say that the iPad got a huge share of media attention from the time Steve Jobs announced it in January 2010 until early April, when the tablet arrived in stores. This isn't unusual for an Apple product—remember that little cellphone Apple unleashed in 2007?

But to some observers, that Tidal Wave of Media Coverage had a few Surfers of Self-Interest riding along. That's because, in addition to changing how people consume books, videos, and other content, the interactive iPad was supposed to reinvigorate printed magazines and newspapers—a business that has seen its fortunes plummet since a little thing called the Internet came along.

Here's the good news: the iPad has inspired many news organizations to create beautiful apps to show off their content. Some are free (for now, anyway), some charge a fee just for the content, and some charge for the app *and* the content. You can find all the iPad-worthy news apps at App Store→Categories→News, but here are a few of the big ones:

- **The New York Times.** It's the full daily paper, but only free for a short time (the paper plans to charge for access in 2011). The app offers up the day's top stories in several categories, like Technology and Opinion. Tap a story summary to see it expand to the full screen.

- **Time.** An iPad-enhanced version of this newsmagazine's weekly issue is available each Friday for $4.99. You have to download the app each week to get the new issue, but it doesn't replace the content of your last issue.

- **USA Today.** Just as colorful as its print counterpart, the Nation's Newspaper is hoping to be the Nation's iPad App. Automatically updating headlines, sports scores, and the local weather forecast greet you when you open the app. Tap the section name in the top-left corner to jump to the separate Money, Sports, and Life pages.

- **The Wall Street Journal.** Since the early days of the Internet, the WSJ has been one of the few news sites on the Web to charge for full access, and its app continues the tradition. The app is free, and you can get a limited selection of stories when you register with the company. You can sign up for a full-content paid subscription ($4 a week) with the Subscribe Now link in the bottom-left corner.

- **Zinio Magazine Newsstand.** Want to browse a whole bunch of magazines and flip through a few before you buy? Try the Zinio app, which offers full-color sample pages from many printed mags (like *The Economist*, *National Geographic*, *The Sporting News*, and *Cosmopolitan*), all digitized and zoomable for your reading pleasure. The app is free, but the magazine content costs money. For example, one issue of *Us* magazine is $3.99, while a yearly subscription is $67.08.

In addition to newsstand publications, news services—which often supply stories to some of those publications—also have great apps. All of the ones mentioned below include video clips of news events as well as text stories.

- **AP News.** The Associated Press compiles the day's top stories into a free-form flow of little news bars on the screen in this no-cost app (shown on the right). Tap one to get the scoop. Photos and videos of the day are also here.

- **BBC News.** The British Broadcasting Corporation's beautifully designed app neatly organizes the day's stories in an easy-to-read, easy-to-navigate grid on the screen (shown here). Along with video clips, the Beeb—once and still a radio broadcaster—gives you a live radio stream with a tap on the Live Radio button at the top of the screen.

- **Reuters News Pro.** With its quick access to the world stock-market charts and a built-in currency converter, this free app from the Thomson Reuters service is great for the financially minded. The app also showcases the top stories and photographs of the news day.

Love news? The App Store also has apps from National Public Radio and international newspapers like *Le Monde*. You can also find apps that aggregate (collect) headlines from around the world.

Subscribe to ePublications

As mentioned on the previous page, some big news organizations don't give content away for free. To get all the publication's stories (and not just a Whitman's sampler of summaries or selected articles), some ask that you pay for them in the form of a subscription. (Information may want to be free, as the old

hacker credo goes, but professionally produced news and magazines cost money to produce—and they should therefore cost money to *consume* in the eyes of many organizations.)

Prices vary by the publication, but even if you're using a free or "lite" version of an iPad news app, most companies aren't shy about the Subscribe button. Tap it to sign up, supply your credit card number, and then wait for your new issues to download on a daily, weekly, or monthly basis when you launch the app on the iPad.

Some apps, like the Marvel Comics reader, don't offer regular subscriptions for new issues. Instead, Marvel regularly uploads digital editions of older comics to its online store for iPad fankids to browse and buy *a la carte*. You can, however, sign up for email notifications when new material arrives in the Marvel store.

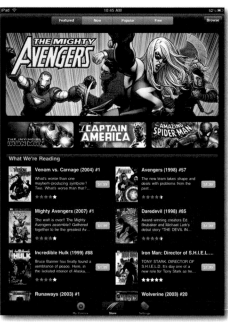

If you're not getting notifications from an app that claims to alert you when you have new issues, check the app's settings (back in the iPad's Settings area) to make sure you enabled Notifications.

Delete an iBook

Bibliophiles know how easy it is to amass piles and piles of books and magazines. Magazines are usually emotionally easier to toss out since they don't have the feeling of permanence that a book does. (On the iPad, you typically delete old issues from within the newsstand or magazine apps.) But with books—some books you want to keep forever, while others, well, not so much. So let's get some iPad drive space back now.

If a book has to go, here are some ways to do it:

❶ On the Bookshelf screen, tap the Edit button in the top right corner. When the ✖ icons appear, tap those on the books you want to delete and then confirm your choice.

❷ Connect the iPad to your computer, click the Books tab, turn off the checkbox next to the unwanted titles, and click Apply or Sync. The book is removed from the iPad, but left behind in iTunes for future reference.

❸ You can not only delete books from the iBooks List view screen, but rearrange the order of the ones left on the shelf. Tap the List View icon (circled) and then tap the Edit button. Tap the Bookshelf button at the bottom of the screen, then use the ⊖ icon to delete unwanted titles. Use the grip strip (≡) to drag existing titles into a new order.

Tip If you have a huge multiscreen list of books, the Search box at the top of the List View screen lets you find titles and author names across your iLibrary.

9

Play Games

With digital music and videos tucked inside its slim glass-and-metal form, the iPad offers plenty of entertainment choices. But if you want to *play* (instead of just sitting back and *pushing* Play), the tablet makes for a nice high-def game console as well. After a visit to the App Store, you can zap zombies or run across the tops of buildings. You can also relive those glory days at the mall, feeding quarters into a machine the size of a phone booth in your quest to chomp pesky ghosts.

You're not stuck with fuzzy little iPhone games blown up to fit the iPad, either. Many game-makers have taken popular titles back into the shop to super-size them for the iPad's big 9.7-inch screen. As a result, you get richer graphics and more precise gameplay, with plenty of room to move around. And that bigger screen makes it easier for two people to play against each other, just like the golden days of chess and checkers.

The iPad can handle everything from basic low-speed card games like euchre, all the way up to high-speed shooters with detailed 3D avatars and a pulsating soundtrack. This chapter shows you how to find the games that appeal to you and get them on your iPad. It doesn't tell you how to win, though—you have to figure *that* out for yourself.

Find iPad Games

To start your big-game hunt, hit the App Store. Tap any game icon to see its Store page, which shows you system requirements, age ratings, sample screen shots, and reviews. When you check out a game, make sure it's made for the iPad and not just for the iPhone and iPod Touch—unless you *liked* those days of pixelated graphics. Many iPad games have an HD tag on them (as in *Plants vs. Zombies HD*) or title themselves appropriately: *PAC-MAN for iPad*.

You can buy and download games in iTunes and then sync them to the iPad, or you can buy them directly on the 'Pad itself. To find games in the App Store:

- Tap Categories→Games and flick through the collection of sample screens that flow across the In the Spotlight section until you see one that's visually appealing. Tap it to learn more.

- Tap through the New & Noteworthy titles to see what's recently arrived.

- Tap the Top Charts button at the bottom of the screen. Tap the Categories button in the menu bar and choose Games to see the best-selling titles—and most popular free games. (Games, being a popular pasttime, are often the top-sellers for all the apps in the App Store).

- Tap the Search box in the upper-right corner and type in keywords for a specific type of game ("cards") or game title ("Table Poker").

When you find a game that piques your interest, buying it just takes a couple taps on the price button.

Play Games

Once you download your game, it appears on your iPad's Home screen, just like any other app. Tap it open when you're ready to play. Don't know how to play? Look for a "How to Play" or "Info" or "Rules" button somewhere on the opening screen. Some games even have a link right on the first screen to take you to a YouTube demo video or trailer explaining the game's backstory.

You don't have an Xbox or PlayStation-style game controller with the iPad, and it certainly doesn't have one of those motion-sensitive magic wands that come with the Nintendo Wii. But with its accelerometer, sensitive touch moves, and high-resolution screen to show off more realistic graphics, the iPad offers developers a variety of ways to build in gameplay controls.

In some driving games, like *Real Racing HD* (shown here), you hold the iPad like a steering wheel as you zoom around a course—just be careful not to drop it mid-race. Other games are just as creative. As its name suggests, *Flick Fishing HD* lets you cast a virtual line into the water with the flick of your wrist.

Old-school joystick games like *PAC-MAN* put a virtual version of the familiar red-handled knob in the corner of the screen, but you can lead the munching yellow disc with your finger as well. *Flight Control HD* works by letting you guide an increasing number of incoming planes into their landing zones a with finger drag along the runway.

 Tip Stuck on a certain level of a game or having trouble figuring it out? A quick web search for the name of the game and "cheat codes" can return links to tips, tricks, and hints for moving forward. Cheaters may never win, but they can level up.

Play Multiplayer Games

In the beginning of gaming history, most games were social; you played against at least one other person—chess, checkers, backgammon, tic-tac-toe, and poker, for example. Sure, solitaire was always a solo act, but most games were fun because you were competing against someone else.

Then computers arrived, and with them, games that let you play against the machine and skip the whole human-contact-and-interaction thing. Many games on the iPad are still like that, but the tablet's size and processor have encouraged developers to make titles that two people can play on two different iPads over a Wi-Fi or Bluetooth connection, as well as games that two people can play on the very same iPad—face-to-face, just like in the old days, when you played board games like Scrabble around the kitchen table.

Speaking of *Scrabble*, it's one game that takes multiplayer into the modern age, with a whole new level of creativity. The $10 version for the iPad has several modes of play, including one where friends can compete against each other by passing the tablet back and forth. If everyone at your Scabble party is an Apple hardware fan, there's also a free sidekick app that lets iPod Touch and iPhone owners turn their devices into very expensive Scrabble tile racks— while the iPad serves as the game board. (You keep your letters to yourself on the handheld until it's time to magically flip them onto the iPad over the wireless connection.

Many of the App Store's multiplayer games are electronic versions of popular tabletop games like air hockey, poker, Uno, and mahjong, which basically turn the iPad into an exquisitely designed game board. Dig deep enough, though, and you'll find all sorts of games meant for group play, including *Monster Ball HD* and the over-punctuated *Call of Duty: World at War: Zombies for iPad*. So, how to find all these games? Search for *multiplayer* in the App Store.

> **Tip** If you love social gaming, be sure to snag the iOS 4.2 update for iPad when it arrives in November 2010. The update includes the Game Center app that matches you up with new online opponents, compares high scores, and more.

Troubleshoot Games

Some games work flawlessly, never crashing and keeping you engaged for hours. Others may be a little more unstable, acting erratically, bombing out on you, and generally being annoying (especially if you paid good money for them). If that happens, first shut down and then re-start your iPad. If that doesn't help, return to the App Store to see if there are any updates for the game—many developers quickly issue fixes if enough people complain.

In general, if a game begins to crash on you, uninstall it (press down on its Home screen icon until a ⊗ appears, tap the ⊗, and press the Home button again) and then return to the App Store to download it again may help clear things up. And don't worry, you won't have to pay for the game again.

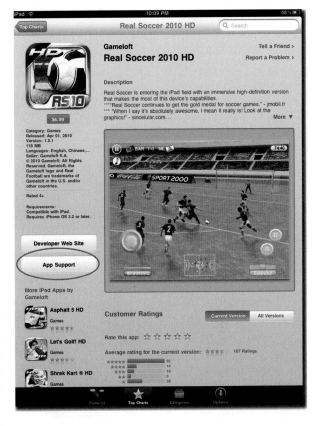

If you're still having trouble with a game or need more information about why it acts the way it does, one source for answers could be the game's creator itself. Most major developers have support and troubleshooting information on their websites. (Apple just sells the games in the App Store, so complaining to them probably won't help much, although every game's Store page has a Report a Problem link.)

Need to track down an app's support page? If you don't want to wade around in the wrong part of a developer's site, revisit the game's page in the App Store and tap the App Support button (circled). And if you really like a certain game and want to see more titles from its creator, the App Store page may also show you other games the company has created for the iPad.

An iPad Games Gallery

The App Store has just about every type of game you can think of: casual games, action games, shooting games, goofy games, mind-numbingly-repetitious-but-still-better-than-working games, and old favorites. Apple adds new games to the store every week, so if you're serious about gaming, it's worth a regular visit to keep an eye on things. If you're looking for a few games to get started with, here are the ones that proved popular with iPad owners right off the bat:

- **Angry Birds.** On the surface, its starts out as a straightforward tale about a band of kamikaze birds trying to take revenge on a herd of ugly chartreuse swine who raided their nest. But this $5 green-ham-and-eggs story teaches a few lessons about physics—you have to figure out the right 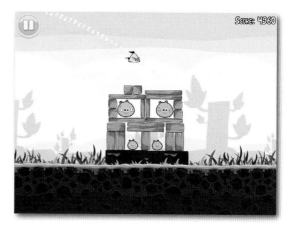 angle and trajectory at which to catapult the avenging avians and knock down a series of increasingly complex structures the pigs try to hide in.

- **Mirror's Edge.** This action game has been around for years and was previously released for the Xbox 360 and PlayStation 3. The $13 iPad version re-creates the tale of Faith, who lives under a totalitarian regime and works as a covert courier. As a "runner," she gallops across rooftops and clambers  up walls on a mission to deliver messages and avoid government surveillance. The game's Hollywood action-picture soundtrack and bright visuals bring to mind the rooftop scene in *The Matrix*—another story about communication and rebellion in an oppressive society.

- **The Pinball HD.** This trio of themed tables (The Deep, Wild West, and Jungle Style) aim to entertain pinball wizards. The $3 app (a revamped version of the company's pinball simulator for the iPhone), can be played in portrait or landscape view, but most players favor the flippers in the wider landscape mode. The game features its own soundtrack and lets you enjoy the spirit of pinball without having to track down a machine in a bowling alley or bus station.

- **Plants vs. Zombies HD.** One of the first iPad titles available from PopCap Games (maker of Bejeweled, Peggle, and several other multiplatform casual games), this $10 app has you protect your home against an invading zombie army by sowing flowers and other plants that attack the badly dressed undead as they advance across your lush green lawn.

- **The Solitaire.** Need something free and familiar? Look no further. This particular version finally added an automatic three-card draw, and, well, the price is right. As you can imagine, though, there's more than one version of solitaire in the App Store to search out.

10

Get Productive with iWork

When you think of the iPad, word processing, spreadsheets, and presentations probably *aren't* the first things that come to mind—unless they're the first things that come to your mind on any topic. After you've used the iPad for longer than two hours, it becomes apparent that it's a great little device for consuming stuff (videos, eBooks, web pages), but not so much for *creating* stuff, like, well, word-processing documents, spreadsheets, and presentations.

Apple's iWork suite for the iPad attempts to change your way of thinking. For many years, iWork—comprised of the Pages, Numbers, and Keynote programs—lived on some Macs in the giant, looming shadow of Microsoft Office. After all, Microsoft Word, Excel, and PowerPoint are the de facto industry standards for documents, spreadsheets, and presentations, from corporate offices to college campuses.

If you're considering buying Apple's iWork suite (or have it already and don't know where to start), this chapter is for you. iWork is not a do-all, be-all desktop suite, but neither does it take up gigabytes of hard drive space for files and features you'll never use. It can, however, keep you productive—even if you'd rather use your iPad to watch episodes of *The Office* rather than work on a spreadsheet *for* the office.

Meet iWork

If you've never heard of iWork, you're not alone. It's oldest component, the Keynote presentation program, has only been around since 2003, with Pages and Numbers arriving on the scene a few years later. Also, all the programs are Mac-only, which means that more than 90 percent of the computing population has never heard of iWork or doesn't care because darn it, there's new antivirus software to install!

Apple created this trio of programs to cover much of the same ground as do Microsoft Office, Corel WordPerfect Office, OpenOffice.org, StarOffice, Google Docs, and any other software suite that contains the holy trinity of business productivity: a word-processing program, a spreadsheet program, and a presentation/slideshow program.

Apple transformed the point-and-click desktop version of iWork into tap-and-drag iPad software, and it isn't just a half-baked copy of an overstuffed office suite, either. Who wants a screen clogged full of toolbars, menus, and floating palettes when your screen *is* your workspace? Apple's iWork re-engineering takes this into account, tucking your formatting, function, and design controls neatly into tappable buttons that deliver toolbars only when you need them—leaving most of the screen free and clear. And those iPad finger moves—zooming and pinching on-screen elements—work here, too.

You can buy the iWork programs in the App Store—just tap the Categories button and look in the Productivity area (circled). Apple sells each program separately, and they cost $10 apiece. This is convenient if, say, you just need to compose memos and wouldn't know a GPA calculator if it bit you—you don't have to buy the whole suite. And if you *do* buy the whole suite, it'll set you back just 30 bucks—a bargain compared to desktop suites that cost $80 or more.

> **Note** The App Store doesn't sell the whole iWork suite as one big app download—you have to buy each $9.99 program separately. But all three apps show up if you search for "iWork" in the App Store search box.

Here's the iWork lineup:

- **Pages.** Pre-stocked with 16 templates for all kinds of documents (résumés, letters, flyers—and even a *blank* page!), the iPad version of Pages aims to make word-processing as efficient as possible. Granted, it's no Microsoft Word in the features department, but it's versatile enough to let you do more than just type words. You can add photos, charts, and tables to documents, and format text with features like bullets and numbered lists. And here's one way Pages trumps Word: As with all the iWork apps, Pages automatically saves your file at least twice a minute.

- **Numbers.** A spreadsheet-making alternative to Microsoft Excel, Numbers also has its own collection of templates so you can create things like budgets and travel planners. It lets you convert a table into a form for speedy data input and can create formulas with more than 250 functions (for those who really like to rock a spreadsheet). Numbers isn't all about numbers, though; it can tap into the iPad's Photos app to jazz up those files with pictures, too.

- **Keynote.** With 20 different slideshow transitions and 12 themes to choose from, Keynote was made for crafting slick presentations for audiences of any size. Although it's not as powerful as Microsoft PowerPoint, Keynote is a nimble app, designed for making shows on the go. And once you get done designing your presentation on the iPad, you can *run* the presentation on the iPad by hooking it up to a projector with Apple's $29 Dock Connector to VGA Adapter.

You may be wondering at this point, "It's all well and good that the iWork can do all this stuff, but does it really matter if nobody besides iPad owners can *open* these files?" Here's the answer: iWork can export files in PDF format, the *lingua franca* of the computer world whose files everyone with the free Adobe Reader can open. Makes it all a little more appealing, eh?

Get Started with iWork

As with any word-processing, spreadsheet, or presentation application, the first step in using the program is to create or open a document so you have a place to process those words, numbers, and slides. Start by tapping open the app's icon on the iPad's Home screen. If this is the first time you're using the program, you land on the My Documents screen; it's called My Spreadsheets in Numbers and My Presentations in Keynote. (All the iWork apps are organized the same way; Pages is used here for explanatory purposes.)

The My Documents screen, shown below, is fairly sparse. It serves as a "folder" for your files as well as a starting point for new documents. With minimal icons, it's also not the most intuitive thing Apple has ever designed. Here's how to interpret the My Documents/My Spreadsheets/My Presentations screens:

❶ **New Document.** Tap here to create a new file from one of iWork's prefab templates.

❷ **Import Document.** If you've synced a file over to your iPad via iTunes, it lands in this folder. Tap the folder to locate and open your imported file. (Flip to the end of the chapter for import/export instructions between iTunes and the iPad.)

❸ **Send Document.** When you're ready to pass the selected file along, tap 🖻 to append it as an email attachment, export it back to iTunes when you sync up, or upload it to iWork.com, Apple's online document-sharing site a few people use (page 161).

❹ **New/Duplicate Document.** Tap here to either create a new document or duplicate the one currently selected.

❺ **Trash.** Don't need the selected file anymore? Tap 🗑 to delete it.

To make a fresh file in any of the apps, tap the New Document button in the top-left corner of the screen. Now you get to choose a template from a screen full of them. To create a specific type of document, like a résumé or that flyer for the school bake sale, flick across the template catalog and tap the page style you need. If you want to start from scratch or just want to type a quick note, choose the Blank page option.

Need to switch to another file or start a brand-new one while you're working on a document? Tap the My Documents button up in the left corner of the screen. The iPad saves your work and returns you to your "folder," which has your previously created files and the helpful New Document button. To select an older file, flick through them until it's in the center of the screen and undimmed (middle right), and then tap the file to open it and get back to work.

Want to rename an existing file? Go to My Documents, select the document, press the generic name underneath the preview ("Visual Report" or whatever template

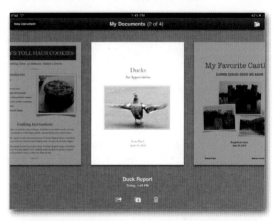

you picked) until the Rename Document screen pops up (above). Here, you can change the name to a more personalized one ("Duck Report"). Tap the document when you're done to go back to the My Documents screen.

Create Documents in Pages

Unless you started with the Zen of a blank page, you'll notice that the Pages templates all use dummy type and stock photos intended as placeholders until you put in your own text and pictures. In its simplest form, Pages lets you craft your documents by just tapping the fake text in the template and typing in your own words; Pages adds new pages as you need them. Tap the corner of the template's placeholder picture and replace it with one of your own from the Photos box that pops.

When you tap into a text field (as opposed to a picture box), a formatting toolbar appears at the top of the screen. It includes a ruler for tab stops and margins, plus text-formatting buttons you can click to do things like add a headline, make characters boldface, and change the text alignment. (Tap the ⊗ on the end if you want to slide the toolbar out of the way.)

A simple set of four icons in the top right corner of the screen contains all the program's other formatting tools. With these, you can:

❶ **Style text.** Select some text on-screen and tap here to open a three-tabbed box labelled Style, List, and Layout. The Style menu has pre-configured type styles for Title, Subtitle, and so on, along with bold, italic, underline, and strikethrough buttons. Tap the List tab if you want to make the selected text a bulleted or numbered list. Tap the Layout tab to change the text alignment (centered, flush right, and so on), change the number of columns on the page, or adjust the space between lines.

❷ **Add images and graphics.** Use this four-tabbed box to add visual elements to your documents. Tap the Media tab to insert a photo from the iPad's Photos app. Tap the Tables tab to stick in an adjustable text table, and tap the Charts tab to insert bar charts, pie charts, and other infographics. Tap the Shapes tab to add geometric forms and arrows to a document. Hate the colors of all these stock graphics charts? Swipe the box with your finger—there are six mini-pages of each type to choose from, as indicated by the dots at the bottom.

❸ Change settings. Tap the Wrench icon to get to the blueprint-y Document Setup screen so you can change the file's headers, footers, and margins. The Find option helps you search documents, and the very helpful Help guide shortcut takes you to the full Pages manual online. The Tools box lets you turn on built-in guides for aligning text and photos, and you can start up Pages' spell-checker here, too.

❹ Go to fullscreen view. Tap these arrows to lose the toolbar and expand your document full-screen.

You can use Pages in either portrait or landscape view, but you'll only see the toolbar and other controls in portrait mode. Want to jump to a different page in a document? Press your finger down on the right side of the screen to see the Page Navigator preview tool, then slide the Navigator up or down and let go when you find the page you want.

Tips for Working with Text and Photos

Pages may have a ton of templates, but you're not locked into having every document look the same. If you want, you can use text-formatting tools to change the type's size, style, and even color (tap ❶→Style→Text Options→Color) to make it look like *you* want it to look.

And you're not locked into rigid photo sizes or placement, either. After you import your own pictures or choose stock graphics, tap the element to get a slider bar so you can resize the image in the frame, or use the blue handles to resize the whole image itself. Drag a selected photo around the page to reposition it. You can even delete photo boxes you don't want.

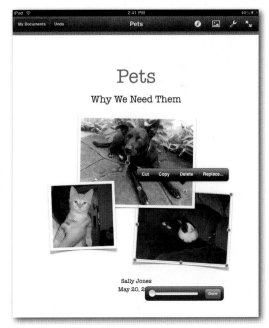

Miss those Ctrl-Z and Ctrl-S lifesavers? If you mess something up, don't worry. Pages, like all the iWork programs, has a handy Undo button on the top-left corner of every screen. And it automatically saves your document every 30 seconds as you work along.

Create Spreadsheets in Numbers

When one thinks of the iPad, one tends to think of shredding a game or cruising around on Safari, not wading deep into a spreadsheet. But if you can't be all play and need to get a little work done on your trusty tablet, the Numbers app can graph your data, crunch your digits, and handle other nerdy tasks.

As with Pages, Numbers offers a collection of 16 pre-fabricated templates for the most popular types of spreadsheets: a mortgage calculator, personal budget tracker, travel planner, weight-loss log, expense report, and more. There's also a Blank template with an empty grid of cells waiting for you. Tap a template to select it. Tap the fake text and numbers in the cells to overwrite them with your own facts and figures. To add new sheets or forms to the spreadsheet, tap the + button on the tab at the top of the screen.

As with Pages, the four icons hanging out in the top-right corner of the screen hold the formatting tools for text and graphics. With a tap, you can:

❶ **Style text, rows, and cells.** You get different options here depending on whether you've selected text or tables. For text, you get a box with Style, Text, and Arrange tabs. Here, you can choose typefaces, colors and effects (like opacity and shadows), and flip objects. When you have a table selected, the ❶ menu becomes a four-tabbed box for changing the color and style of the table. Tabs for Headers and Cells hold the controls for tweaking those elements, and the Format tab lets you pick the number configuration, like currency or a percentage. When you have a chart selected, the ❶ menu gives you color and style options for the chart's text and type (pie chart, area chart, and so on). In short, if you need to format anything on this sheet, the ❶ has it.

❷ **Add images and graphics.** Just as in Pages, this menu holds the tabs (Media, Tables, Charts, and Shapes) to all the photos, tables, charts, geometric shapes you may want to add to your spreadsheet. For example, you can press and hold a pie chart on the page until the Delete button appears, zap the pie chart off the screen, and drag a bar chart out of the menu and onto the sheet to replace it. Then tap or drag a table to add its data to the chart.

❸ Change settings. Tap here to open the Tools menu. The Find option at the top of the menu lets you search for keywords within the file, but it's the second menu item that should find you answers to your Numbers questions. That's the link to the online Help guide, where Apple's detailed manual for using Numbers (and all its formulas and functions) hangs out. The other two items on the Tools menu are Off/On switches for the on-screen Edge Guides that appear to help you align elements as you finger-drag them around the screen, as well as the program's spell-checker to help catch typos in your charts.

❹ Go to fullscreen view. Tap here to dismiss the toolbar for an uncluttered full-screen look at your sheet. Tap the top of the screen to get it back.

You can pull and push pretty much every element in a Numbers template into a different size to accommodate your data set. Need to expand the standard chart by a few rows or columns? Tap the chart and, when the gray bar appears, tap the circular handle on either the horizontal or vertical bar

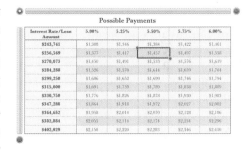

and drag it in the direction you need to add (or delete) rows and columns. Don't like where a table or chart is on the template? Tap it so the same gray adjustment bars appear, press the dotted circle in the top-left corner and drag the table to a new location on the page.

Need to edit the data the chart references? Give it the old double-tap and when the ❈ icon appears at the top of the screen, tap it and choose Plot Rows as Series or Plot Columns as Series.

It wouldn't be a spreadsheet program if it didn't do sums and calculations. Double-tap any cell you want to execute an automatic calculation and the Numbers keypad for punching in math and logic arguments appears. It offers more than 250 formulas and functions in several mathematical specialties, including engineering and statistics for a value-calculating good time.

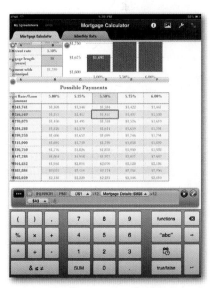

Create Presentations in Keynote

If there's an app in the iWork trio that shows off the iPad's looks best, it's Keynote—it shines when it displays slides and snazzy animated transitions as your presentation plays on the high-resolution screen. Made to let you show off photos, graphics, and short bits of bullet-pointed text, Keynote is the most intuitive of the three apps to use.

Keynote comes with 12 templates, some of them extremely plain for your more serious talks about how the company' missed its financial goals for Q4, and some fancier for middle-school book reports and vacation essays. Once you pick a template, your next task is to fill it up with your own pictures and text. (You have to do it horizontally—Keynote doesn't do portrait mode.)

During your presentation, you don't have to progress statically from slide to slide. Keynote comes with several animated transitions. You can spin, twirl, pop, flip, dissolve, or zoom to get you from one slide to the next—and you can apply a different transition for some or every slide in the presentation.

Keynote gives you control over the text on your slides, building in animated effects that have your titles disappear in a hail of flash bulbs, for instance. Here's a tour of the Keynote toolbar:

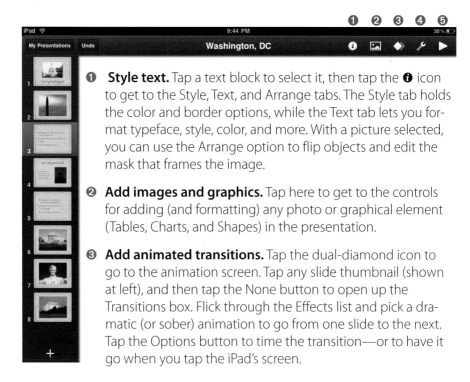

❶ **Style text.** Tap a text block to select it, then tap the ❶ icon to get to the Style, Text, and Arrange tabs. The Style tab holds the color and border options, while the Text tab lets you format typeface, style, color, and more. With a picture selected, you can use the Arrange option to flip objects and edit the mask that frames the image.

❷ **Add images and graphics.** Tap here to get to the controls for adding (and formatting) any photo or graphical element (Tables, Charts, and Shapes) in the presentation.

❸ **Add animated transitions.** Tap the dual-diamond icon to go to the animation screen. Tap any slide thumbnail (shown at left), and then tap the None button to open up the Transitions box. Flick through the Effects list and pick a dramatic (or sober) animation to go from one slide to the next. Tap the Options button to time the transition—or to have it go when you tap the iPad's screen.

❹ Change settings. Tap here to see the Tools menu. As in Pages and Numbers, this is the menu to visit if you want to use the Find feature to search for certain words in your presentation. Tap the "Go to Help..." option to switch over to Safari and browse through Apple's in-depth, online manual for all things Keynote. The rest of the Tools menu consists of On/Off switches for the built-in Edge Guides (for aligning the elements on a slide as you drag them around the screen), the display of each slide's number, and the embarrassment-saving spell-checker to catch giant typos in slide titles and text.

❺ Play. Tap the familiar ▶ icon to start your presentation. If you set your transitions to advance automatically, sit back and enjoy the show. If you opted to manually advance each slide (if your presentation is part of a live talk and you need to time the slides with your narration), tap or swipe the iPad's screen to march through the show.

❻ Add Slide. Tap the **+** at the bottom of the vertical column of slides to call up a box full of slide styles (shown at right) to add new ones to the show. Some slide templates are just text blocks, some are photo-only, and some have both text and photos. If you don't see quite what you want, pick the one closest to your vision and use the text and object formatting controls described on the opposite page to get that slide more to your liking.

To animate text or images on or off a slide, tap the element and then tap the toolbar's dual-diamond icon. Tap Build In (to move the item in) or Built Out (to move it off the slide), and then select an effect from the menu (shown at right). It's good fun.

For an even cooler way to grab your audience's attention during presentation playback, press and hold your finger on a slide for a second or two. A red laser pointer dot appears on-screen and follows your fingertip around as you drag it to point out something...important.

Import, Export, and Share iWork Files

So what good is all this work (and iWork) if you can't share your files with the people who need to see them? And what can you, as an industrious iPad user, do with your fancy iWork suite if you can't view, open, and edit files that people send you—especially if your correspondents don't even *have* iWork and cling to old Microsoft Office for all their business software needs? No problem. Here's why:

- All the programs in the iWork suite can *import*, open, and edit files created in Microsoft Word, Excel, and PowerPoint.

- All the programs in the iWork suite can *export* files as PDF documents. Alternatively, iWork apps can export files in their native iWork formats in case you have the desktop version of iWork and want to do some more editing on your MacBook or iMac. The one bummer here is that although Pages can export to the native Microsoft Word *.doc* format, Numbers and Keynote can't export their contents as Microsoft Excel or PowerPoint files. Yet, anyway.

You can move files on and off your iPad multiple ways—by email, by iTunes, or by a document-sharing site of Apple's called iWork.com.

You can also copy your iWork files to your MobileMe account or to a WebDAV server (the latter so you can work collaboratively).

iWork by Email

How do you normally get most of the files people send you? If the answer is email, you're in luck. If you get an attached Word, Excel, PowerPoint, .csv (comma-separated values) file, or a Numbers, Pages, or Keynote file, you can save it in the corresponding iWork for iPad program. Just press and hold the file attachment icon in the message until the "Open in Numbers" (or whatever) option pops up. Just tapping once opens the attachment as a Quick Look preview for reading, but not editing, though the Quick Look preview does give you a button (in the top-right corner) to open the file in the appropriate app.

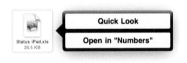

Likewise, you can export iWork files by email from the iPad. Just select the file and tap the  icon to see the menu to the right, then tap the Send via Mail button. In Numbers and Keynote, you can send a file as a PDF document, or as a native Numbers or Keynote file for the Mac desktop editions of iWork. In the case of the more versatile Pages, though,

you get a third option, shown here: a
Word .doc file. Tap your choice to convert
and attach the iWork file to an outgoing
message.

iWork by iTunes Sync

File too big to email? You can also use the
File Sharing option built into iTunes and
sync files back and forth between your computer and iPad. To *import* a file to
the tablet, connect the iPad, click its icon in the iTunes window, and click the
Apps tab. Scroll to the file transfer settings area at the bottom of the screen.

In the Apps column, click the program
whose file you want to share (Pages
and so on), click the Add button, and
navigate to the file you want to transfer. Once you choose it, sync the iPad
to copy the file over. On the iPad, tap the small folder in the upper-right corner
of the My Documents /Spreadsheets/Presentations screen. In the box (shown
here) tap open the transferred file to import it into your chosen iWork app.

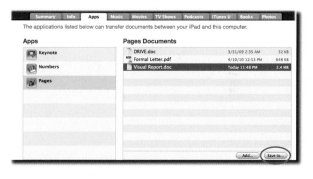

To *export* a file from
the iPad to iTunes (and
then to your com-
puter), tap the icon
and choose Export.
Then tap a format
for the exported file.
Connect the iPad to
your computer, select
it in iTunes, and then
click on the Apps tab. Once the iPad and iTunes sync up, the file appears in
the shared files list. Select it and click the "Save to..." button (circled) to copy
it to a folder on your computer, where you can open it in Word or whatnot.

iWork by iWork.com

To share a file so others can see it on Apple's work-in-progress *www.iwork.com*
site, you need an Apple ID (like a MobileMe or iTunes account). When you
choose the Share via iWork.com option after tapping the iPad's icon, the
file uploads to the Web and you can send email invitations for colleagues to
go look and comment on it from their web browsers.

11

Organize and Sync Media Files with iTunes

With iTunes, you get a program that does many things. It serves as a database for all the audio, video, book, and podcast files in your media library. It converts tracks from compact discs into digital files for iPads, iPods, and iPhones. And it even has its own online mall that you can pop into any time of day or night to buy the latest Stephen King audiobook, grab a copy of the new U2 album, or rent a digital download of *Julie & Julia* for the evening.

Another cool feature of iTunes? It syncs any or all of the items in its library to your iPad. You may have already dabbled in a bit of this in Chapter 7 with the iTunes App Store, or in Chapter 8 when you read up on the iBookstore. This chapter, though, focuses on the basics of iTunes: downloading iTunes Store purchases to your computer—and then getting what you want over to your iPad. (For more on mastering the art of iTunes, see Chapter 12.)

So if you're thinking of syncing, flip the page.

The iTunes Window

iTunes is your iPad's best friend. You can do just about everything with your digital music here—convert songs on a CD into iPad-ready music files, buy music, listen to Internet radio stations, watch video—and more.

Here's a quick tour of the main iTunes window and what all the buttons, controls, and sliders do.

The light-blue Source panel on the left side of iTunes displays all the audio, books, and video you can tap into at the moment. Click an item to display its contents in the main window, like so:

❶ Click any icon in the Library group to see the contents of your media libraries. As you add movies, music, and other stuff to iTunes, click the appropriate icon to find what you're looking for—a song, a TV show, a podcast, and so on. Software you buy through your computer to sync with the iPad lands here under Apps. Want to change the items you see listed? Press Ctrl+comma (⌘-comma) to call up iTunes' Preferences menu, and then click the General tab. In the "Show:" area, turn on (or off) the checkboxes for, say, Ringtones or iTunes U, as you see fit.

❷ In the Store area, click the shopping-bag icon to shop for new stuff. Other icons (some shown on page 193) that may appear include the green Purchased playlist to see what you already bought and a Purchased on iPad playlist. The Downloads icon shows items you're downloading, or subscription files, like TV episodes, waiting or arriving in iTunes.

❸ If you have a music CD in your computer's drive, it shows up in the Devices area, as will a connected iPad. Click the gray Eject icon next to the gadget's name to safely pop out a disc or disconnect an iPad.

❹ In the Shared area, browse the media libraries of other iTunes fans on your network. You can stream music if you see a blue stacked playlist, or copy music and videos between machines with the Home Sharing feature turned on. (See page 171 to learn how you can share libraries.)

❺ iTunes keeps all your custom song lists—whether the iTunes Genius automatically generated them or you lovingly handcrafted them—in the Genius and Playlists sections. The iTunes DJ feature, which quickly whips up randomly selected party mixes, lives here too.

❻ When you click an icon in the Source list—for Music, in this case—iTunes' main window displays all the items in that category. Three columns sitting above the main song list let you browse your collection by genre, artist, and album. Naturally, this part of the window is called the Column Browser. You see it here in the top position, but you can display it as a series of vertical columns on the left side of the iTunes window by choosing View→Column Browser→On Left.

The outer edges of the iTunes window are full of buttons and controls:

❼ Play and pause your current song or video—or jump to the next or previous track. The volume slider adjusts the sound.

❽ The center of the upper pane shows you what song's currently playing. To the right of that you have handy buttons to change views in the center part of the iTunes window and a search box to find songs fast.

❾ At the bottom-left corner are shortcut buttons for (from left to right) creating a new playlist, shuffling or repeating a playlist, and displaying album artwork or videos.

❿ The lower-right corner of iTunes is where the Genius controls hang out. When you have a song selected, click the whizzy electron-shaped icon to create an iTunes-generated Genius playlist based on that song. The boxed-arrow icon toggles the Ping Sidebar panel on (It's intended to get you talking about—and buying—music), and off (to leave you in peace).

How iTunes Organizes Your Content

As mentioned a couple of pages ago, iTunes groups your media files into their own categories in the Library area of the Source list. Music, videos, applications, and other content you download from the iTunes Store land in their respective Source list libraries—songs in the Music library, *30 Rock* episodes in TV Shows, and so on. Those paid-for music and videos also live on the Purchased playlist in the Source list, a one-click trip to see where all your spare cash went.

But say you add files that *don't* come from the iTunes Store, like videos you download from the Internet Archive (a great source of free public-domain material, including eBooks, old movies, and years' worth of Grateful Dead live concert recordings at *www.archive.org*). If one of these files ends up in the wrong part of the iTunes Library, you can fix it so it lands in the proper place— movies in Movies, podcasts in Podcasts, and so on. Click the file you want to change in the iTunes window and choose File→Get Info (or press Ctrl-I or ⌘-I) to call up the Info box. Click the Options tab and, next to the label Media Kind, select your choice from the pop-up menu, and then click OK.

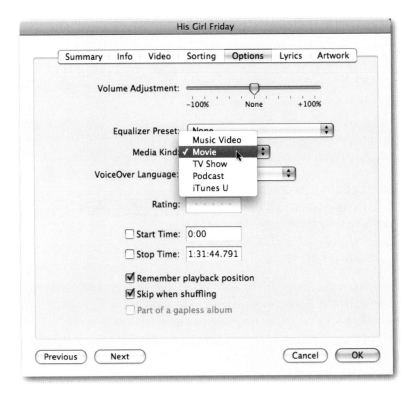

Where iTunes Stores Your Files

Behind its steely silver-framed window, iTunes has a very precise system for storing your music, movies, and everything else you add. Inside its own iTunes folder on your hard drive (which, unless you moved it, is in Music→iTunes [Home→Music→iTunes]), the program keeps all your files and song information. (If you're running Windows 7 or Vista, your iTunes folder is at User→<user name>→Music→iTunes, and Windows XP users can find it at My Documents→My Music→iTunes.)

Your iTunes Library file, a database that contains the names of all the songs, playlists, videos, and other content you've added to iTunes, sits inside the iTunes folder. Be careful not to move or delete this file if you happen to be poking around in the iTunes folder. If iTunes can't find it, it gives a little sigh and creates a new one—a new one that doesn't have a record of all your songs and other media goodies.

If you *do* accidentally delete the Library file, your music is still on your computer—even if iTunes doesn't know it. That's because all the song files are actually stored in the iTunes *Music* folder (or *Media* folder, as explained in the Tip below), which is also inside the main iTunes folder. You may lose your custom playlist if your Library file goes missing, but you can always add your music files back to iTunes (File→Add to Library) to recreate your library.

> **Tip** If your current version of iTunes is an update from an older version of the program, your iTunes Music folder may actually be an iTunes Media folder. If you have a Media folder, iTunes neatly groups things like Games, Music, TV Shows, Movies, and other content in their own subfolders, making it much easier to find your downloaded episodes of *Mad Men* among all the song files. If you want to reorganize, media-style, choose File→Library→Organize Library and choose "Upgrade to iTunes Media organization."

The iTunes Store

Click the iTunes Store icon in the iTunes Source list and you land in iTunes' virtual aisles. The Store is jam-packed with digital merchandise, all neatly filed by category across the top of the main window: Music, Movies, TV Shows, and so on (but not iBooks; remember, Apple's iBookstore is only available through the iPad's iBooks app). Click a tab to go to a store section. You can also hover over a tab and click the triangle that appears; a pop-up menu lets you jump to a subcategory within the section (Blues, Pop, and so on for Music, for example).

The main part of the iTunes Store window—that big piece of real estate smack in the center of your browser—highlights iTunes' latest audio and video releases and specials. Free song downloads and other offers appear here, too. This window is usually stuffed full of digital goodies, so scroll down the page to see featured movies, TV shows, apps, and freebies.

If you're looking for a specific item, use the Search box in the upper-right corner to hunt your quarry; enter titles, artist names, or other searchable info.

Preview songs by double-clicking the track's title. The Buy button is there waiting for your impulse purchase, making it extremely easy to run up your credit-card tab.

If your iPad is in range of a wireless or 3G network connection, you have a third way to get to the Store: over the airwaves, as explained on the next page.

The Wireless iTunes Store

If you have an iPad, you don't even *need* your stodgy old computer to shop the iTunes Store—you can tap your way right into the iTunes inventory over a wireless Internet or AT&T 3G connection. Many Wi-Fi–enabled Starbucks coffee shops also let you tap into the iTunes Store to browse and buy, including whatever music track is currently playing right there at Starbucks.

Now, to buy stuff when you're out and about—and in the mood to shop:

❶ Tap the purple iTunes icon on the iPad's Home screen. Make sure you have a 'Net connection; see Chapter 3 for guidance on making that happen.

❷ The Store appears on-screen. It opens on the Music page the first time out, but remembers your last open page if you've been here before. If you want to buy music, tap your way through the categories like "New Releases" until you find an album or song you like. (Tap an album to see all its songs.)

❸ Tap a title for a 30-second preview.

❹ For other purchases, tap an icon (Music, Video, TV Shows, and so on) at the bottom of the window, or use the Search box at the top to enter search terms. (Want programs? Hit the Home screen's App Store icon.)

❺ To buy and download music, videos, and audiobooks, tap the price, and then tap Buy Now. For free items like podcasts, tap the Free button.

❻ Type in your iTunes Store password and let the download begin. You can check the status of your purchase-in-progress by tapping the Downloads button, which also lets you pause your download if you need to. If you don't have an account, tap the Create New Account button on the Sign In screen and follow the steps. You can sign in and out of your account with a link at the bottom of the Store screen.

When the download's done, you have some brand-new material ready to play on your iPad—the new tracks appear in the Purchased playlist.

To get these fresh songs or videos back into the iTunes library on your computer, sync up the iPad when you get home. The tracks appear in a new playlist called "Purchased on PadMan" (or whatever you called your tablet this week).

Check for Downloads

It's bound to happen sometime: You're breathlessly downloading a hot new book or movie from iTunes and the computer freezes, crashes, or your Internet connection goes on the fritz. Or you and your Wi-Fi iPad were in the middle of snagging an album from the wireless iTunes Store, and the rest of the gang decided it was time to leave the coffee shop.

If this happens, don't worry. Even if your computer crashes or you get knocked offline while you're downloading your purchases, iTunes is designed to pick up where it left off. Just restart the program and reconnect to the Internet.

If, for some reason, iTunes doesn't go back to whatever it was downloading before The Incident, choose Store→Check for Available Downloads to resume your downloading business.

You can check for available purchases any time you think you might have something waiting, like a new episode from a TV Show Season Pass.

Authorize Computers for iTunes Files

Apple's usage agreement lets you play Store purchases on up to five computers: PCs, Macs, or any combination. Although iTunes Plus songs and those sold after April 2009 don't have password-demanding copy-restrictions built in, music tracks purchased before 2009 and most videos still do.

For protected content, you must type in your Apple user name and password on each computer to authorize it to play any songs, videos, or audio books purchased with that account. Each computer must have an Internet connection to relay the information back to Store headquarters. (You don't have to authorize each and every purchase; you authorize the computer once.)

You authorized your first machine when you initially signed up for an Apple Account. To authorize another computer, choose Store→Authorize Computer.

You can also share media among the computers on your home network, using the Home Sharing feature built into iTunes 9 and later.

❶ In the iTunes Source list, click the Home Sharing icon. On the screen that appears, type in an iTunes account name and password. (If you don't see the cute little house-shaped Home Sharing icon in the Source list, choose Advanced→Turn On Home Sharing. If you get told to authorize the computer for that iTunes account, choose Store→Authorize Computer.)

❷ Click the Create Home Share button.

❸ Repeat these steps for every computer you want to share with on the network (up to four others).

Once you set up all the computers, each of their iTunes libraries appears in everyone's Source list. Click the triangle beside the House icon for the library you want to explore. Click on a file to stream it to your own machine over the network. If you must have this file on your computer, select it and click the Import button in the bottom right corner of the iTunes Window. Click the Settings button next to it if you want to automatically share certain types of files, like Music, among these machines—and your iPad.

Deauthorize Your Computer

Unless these are iTunes Plus tracks, you won't be able to play protected pur-chased books or video on a sixth computer if you try to authorize it. Apple's authorization system will see five other computers already on its list and deny your request. That's a drag, but copy protection is copy protection.

To play protected files on Computer Number 6, you have to deauthorize another computer. Choose Store→Deauthorize Computer from the computer about to get the boot, and then type in your Apple Account user name and password. The updated information zips back to Apple.

Are you thinking of putting that older computer up for sale? Before wiping the drive clean and sending it on its way, be sure to deauthorize it, so your new machine will be able to play copy-protected files. Erasing a hard drive, by itself, doesn't de-authorize a computer.

If you forget to deauthorize a machine before getting rid of it, you can still knock it off your List of Five, but you have to reauthorize every machine in your iTunes arsenal all over again. To make it so, in the iTunes window, click the triangle next to your account name and choose Account. Type in your password. On the account information page where it lists the number of computers you've authorized, click the Deauthorize All button. On the Apple Account Information page, click the Deauthorize All button.

Automatically Sync the iPad

As with every iPod model that's come before it, the iPad offers the simple and effective *Autosync* feature. Autosyncing automatically puts a copy of every song, podcast, and video in your iTunes library right onto your player. In fact, the first time you connect your iPad to your computer, the Setup Assistant offers to copy all the music in your iTunes library over to your new tablet. If you opt to do that, your iPad is already set for autosync.

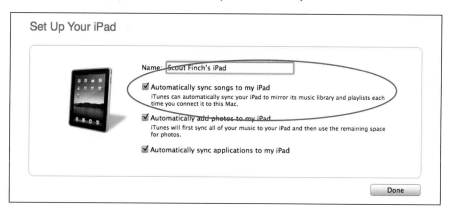

If you added more music to iTunes since that first encounter, the steps for loading the new goods onto your iPad couldn't be easier:

❶ Plug the small end of the USB cable into your Windows PC or Macintosh.

❷ Plug the cable's flat Dock Connector end into the bottom of the iPad.

❸ Sit back and let iTunes leap into action, syncing away and doing all that heavy lifting for you.

You can tell the sync magic is working because iTunes gives you a progress report at the top of its window that says "Syncing iPad..." (or whatever you've named your tablet). When iTunes tells you the iPad's update is complete, you're free to unplug the cable and take off.

Autosync is a beautiful thing, but it's not for everyone—especially if you have more than 16, 32, or 64 gigabytes worth of stuff in your iTunes library. (That may sound like a lot of room for music, but once you start adding hefty video files, that space disappears fast.) If that's the case, iTunes fits what it can on the iPad.

If autosync isn't for you, jump over to the next page to read about more selective ways to load up your 'Pad.

Manually Sync to Your iPad

If you opt out of autosyncing your iPad, you now need to go ahead and choose some songs or videos for it. Until you do, the iPad just sits there empty and forlorn in your iTunes window, waiting for you to give it something to play with.

Manual Method #1

❶ Click the iPad icon on the left side of the iTunes window. This opens up a world of syncing preferences for getting stuff on your iPad.

❷ Click the Music tab, then turn on the "Sync Music" checkbox.

❸ Click the button next to "Selected playlists, artists, and genres" and check off the items you want to copy to your iPad. (No playlists yet? See Chapter 12.)

❹ Click the Apply button at the bottom of the iTunes window. (As the rest of the chapter explains, the steps are similar for Movies, TV Shows, podcasts, and more.

Manual Method #2

❶ This one's for those into fine-grained picking and choosing: Click the Summary tab and turn on "Manually manage music and videos." Now you can click the songs, albums, or videos you want and drag them to the iPad icon in the iTunes Source pane.

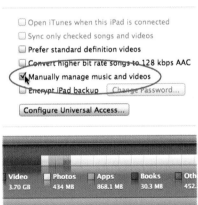

Manual Method #3

❶ Every item in your iTunes library has a checkmark next to its name when you first import it. Clear that checkmark next to whatever you *don't* want on the iPad. (If you have a big library, hold down the Control [⌘] key while clicking any title; that performs the nifty trick of removing *all* checkmarks. Then go and check the stuff you *do* want.)

❷ Click the iPad icon under Devices in the Source list, and then click the Summary tab.

❸ At the bottom of the Summary screen, turn on the checkbox next to "Sync only checked songs and videos" and then click the Sync button.

Sync Music

Once your iPad's connected and showing up in iTunes, you can modify all the settings that control what goes on (and comes off of) your tablet. Thanks to iTunes 9's long, scrollable screen full of checkboxes and lists in most categories, it's easier than ever to get precisely what you want on your 'Pad.

If you want to sync up all or just some of your music, click the Music tab.

In addition to synchronizing all your songs and playlists by title, you can sync them by artist and genre as well. Just turn on the checkboxes next to the items you want to transfer to the iPad, click the Apply button, and then the Sync button to move your music.

Chapter 13 has more on playing music on the iPad.

Sync Video

In iTunes, videos fall into two main classifications: Movies and TV Shows. Each type has its own tab in iTunes. (Podcasts, which can be either audio or video files, stay together in the Podcasts part of the iTunes Library.)

Full-length movies are huge space hogs and can take up a gigabyte or more of precious drive space—which is a significant chunk of a 16-gigabyte iPad. Serious movie-watchers tend to move films on and off portable devices. So iTunes gives you the option to load all, selected, or even just unwatched films. To change up what's playing at your portable cineplex, click the Movies tab when your iPad's connected to your computer and turn on the checkboxes next to your selections.

Since the iTunes Store sells TV shows by season or individual episode, iTunes lets you sync TV shows in several ways: by show, by selected episodes, by the number of unwatched episodes, and so on. Click the TV Shows tab with your iPad connected and make your choices.

Once you decide what movies and TV shows you want to port over to the tablet, click the Apply button and then Sync. Chapter 14 has more on using video on the iPad.

Sync Photos

The iPad, in case you haven't noticed yet, makes a handsome electronic picture frame. To get your pictures on there, you can sync photos from your computer's existing photo-management programs, like Adobe Photoshop Elements—or even a folder of photos. (Chapter 15 has more on displaying photos and making slideshows on the iPad.)

To tell iTunes which pictures you want to take along on the iPad, click the Photos tab. Here, you can select the photo program or folder you want to pull the pictures from, and then turn on checkboxes next to the photo albums you want on the iPad. If you use iPhoto '09 on the Mac, you also have the options to pull over specific iPhoto events, as well as Faces and Places (iPhoto's way of grouping your photos by either what's in them or where they were taken). When you've picked your pictures, click the Apply tab and then Sync.

Sync Info

As you may remember from Chapter 6, the iPad can also carry around a copy of the same personal contact list that you keep on your computer. Even just having the email addresses of everyone you know is handy to have around when you're relaxing in the backyard hammock catching up on your Inbox. Through iTunes, you can grab contacts from a number of popular programs, including Microsoft Outlook 2003 and later, Windows Address Book, Outlook Express, and Windows Contacts. Macs can tap into contact files stored in the Mac OS X Address Book and Entourage 2004 and later. You can also import addresses from Yahoo and Gmail accounts as long as you have an Internet connection.

To copy contacts over to a connected iPad, click the Info tab and use the pop-up menu to choose the program you keep them in. And scroll down the Info screen to see all the other personal data you can sync up on the Info tab:

- **Calendar appoint-ments**—you can put your schedule on the iPad by turning on the checkboxes for your Outlook or iCal calendars.

- **Notes** from Microsoft Outlook or the Mac's Mail program

- **Bookmarks** from Internet Explorer or the desktop Safari web browser get shuttled over to the iPad's copy of Safari.

- **Email account settings** (but not the actual messages) get ported over to save you from having to muck around in the iPad's mail settings.

Make your choices, click the Appy button, and then Sync to move your life farther onto the iPad.

 To get iTunes syncing with Entourage, you need to have it dump your information into iCal. To make that happen, choose Entourage→Preferences→Sync→Services and turn on the checkboxes for syncing Entourage data with Address Book and iCal.

Sync Podcasts

One of the coolest features of the iTunes Store (page 168) is the Podcasts section. Podcasts are like radio and TV shows you can download on a regular basis—for free. Every major media outlet has some sort of audio or video podcast available now alongside more low-budget creations.

For example, you can get the whole video from each week's edition of *Meet the Press* from NBC, *Slate* magazine's audio critique of released movies, or your favorite shows from National Public Radio. To sign up for podcasts, click the Podcasts link on the main iTunes Store page, and browse until you find something you like. Then click Subscribe.

Once you subscribe to a show, iTunes automatically deposits the latest episode of it to your computer as soon as it appears online. Since you may not want to fill up your iPad with tons of podcasts, you can tell iTunes which ones (and how many) to copy over each time you sync up. With the iPad connected, click the Podcasts tab and turn on the checkboxes for the shows you want to sync regularly. Use the pop-up menus to get the number of episodes you want to carry around for each podcast as well. Click Apply and Sync.

 Note Electronic textbooks are one way to get an education on the iPad, but you can also download free lectures and tutorials from a huge number of universities around the world. Just click the iTunes U link on the iTunes Store. To sync the files to the iPad, connect it and click the iTunes U tab to selectively sync up all the content you want to take with you. It's academic!

Sync Books

If you're a big audiobook fan and have been hunting around in vain trying to find an Audiobooks tab in iTunes, don't worry, you're not missing it. The controls for syncing audiobooks to the iPad are actually on the Books tab, shoved way down on the screen where you may have missed it. Scroll down, turn on the checkbox next to Audiobooks (circled), and sync away. You can sync all or selected audiobooks.

You sync text-based eBooks (iBooks and books in the ePub format) the same way, as you can see below. Chapter 8 has all the details on buying and managing eBooks. Note that, in iTunes, you can only *back up* your iBooks, you can't *read* them on your computer screen. If you have the iBooks app on your iPhone or iPod Touch, you can sync books there as well—and PDF files, too (see page 128).

You can listen to audiobooks anywhere, and here's the cool part: When you sync your iTunes-purchased audiobooks back and forth between your iPad and iTunes, they get bookmarked, so you can always pick up listening in the part of the recording where you left off on either your iPad or in iTunes.

Sync Apps and Games

It's easy to download apps and games directly on the iPad over its Wi-Fi or 3G connection. You can also buy, download, and install new iPad programs from the big comfortable shopping window of iTunes—and then sync them all over to your connected iPad later. This sort of thing can be helpful if, say, you want a 300-megabyte birdwatching app that can take a while to download on your iPad—besides, Apple currently limits individual App Store downloads to 20 megabytes over a 3G connection.

Syncing apps through iTunes has several other advantages. First, you get a backup copy of the app on your computer (and even your computer's backup program) instead of having it on the iPad only until you sync up again. Second, it's easier to rearrange your apps when you have your iPad connected; iTunes displays all your iPad app screens at once, so you can click and drag the apps around in relation to other apps and screens. When you rearrange apps from the iPad itself, you have to blindly drag them across each screen.

And third, if you have a bunch of hefty space-hogging apps and an iPad with a small drive, you can sync the apps on and off the tablet as you need them. Turn on the checkboxes next to the apps and games you want to copy over and click Apply or Sync (or one, then the other if you've been tinkering).

Troubleshoot Syncing Problems

Apple has tried to make the whole getting-stuff-on-your-iPad process as simple and flexible as possible. Every once in awhile, though, minor hardware or software issues may trip up that smooth syncing experience and make you wonder what's making the iPad so unfriendly toward your files. These next couple of pages explain some of the more common issues—and how you can fix them.

• **iPad doesn't show up in iTunes.** The first step to syncing is getting the iPad to appear in the iTunes Source list. If it's not there, check a few simple things. First, make sure you have the latest version of both iTunes and the iPad firmware installed (page 274). If so, check to see that the USB cable is firmly plugged in on both ends. If that doesn't help, try plugging the smaller end into a different USB 2.0 port on your PC or Mac. Also, make sure the iPad has a decent battery charge. Still no luck? Restart the iPad (page 270) and while you're at it, restart the computer as well. Antivirus software may be hindering the communication between your iPad and iTunes, so check your security settings or temporarily turn off the program to see if that's the problem. If nothing else has worked, Apple recommends reinstalling iTunes (page 272).

• **Weird error messages while syncing.** You may see iTunes toss up an alert box saying something like "Error 13019" and suddenly stop syncing. If that happens, try turning off the checkbox for Sync Music, click Apply, and then click Sync. After iTunes gets done syncing, go back to the preferences and turn on the Sync Music checkbox again. Then try to freshly sync all those tunes again.

If you're syncing contacts, calendars, notes, and other items from the Info tab, you may see the Sync Alert box pop up if, say, you have two different versions of someone's contact file between  your computer and iPad (usually from editing it on both machines between sync sessions), or if more than five percent of the information

> **Tip** A bad or damaged cable may be the reason your syncing is stinking. If you have another Apple USB cable from an iPod or iPhone, try swapping it in. If your cable is noticeably damaged, you can get a replacement for $19 at *store.apple.com*. It's called the Dock Connector to USB Cable and you can find it in the Accessories area.

will get changed on the computer during the sync session. Click the Show Details button to see the different versions and pick the one you want to go with. You can also cancel the Info part of the sync session in case you want to check out your data on both computer and iPad—but don't have time to deal with it now.

- **Some items didn't sync to the iPad.** The two most common reasons for an incomplete sync are fullness and formats. If the iPad's drive is close to overflowing, you simply can't fit any more content on its bulging drive. And if some of the files you try to sync are in incompatible formats, the iPad won't sync them. (This is often the case with video files—there are many formats around the Web, but the iPad only works with a few of them: *.mp4*, *.m4v*, and *.mov*.) In either case, iTunes probably gave you a message about the situation. The solutions are simple: delete some other files from the iPad to make room for the new things you want to sync, and convert files in incompatible formats to ones that work on the iPad. (Apple's $30 QuickTime Pro software at *www.apple.com/quicktime* is one of the many software options here.)

12

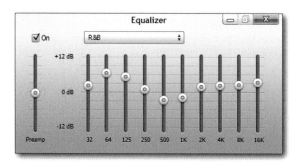

Mastering iTunes

As you can tell from the last chapter, iTunes is an important part of your iPad experience, because it brokers the transfer of data between your tablet and computer. In addition, it keeps copies of your purchases and helps you organize your growing media collection.

If you've never had an iPod or iPhone before you got your iPad, you may not know what a powerful media jukebox program iTunes is in its own right. As this chapter explains, you can customize iTunes' look, make playlists in all kinds of ways, change a song's file format, adjusting each song's equalizer settings, and even back up your entire iTunes library contents to a set of discs for safekeeping.

So when it comes time to charge the iPad for a few hours, take a spin through iTunes, especially if you've never spent much time with the program except to sync data. You'll find it's got a lot to offer.

Change the Look of the iTunes Window

Don't be misled by the brushed-aluminum look of iTunes. You can push and pull various window parts like salt-water taffy.

- You can adjust how much of the iTunes Browser—the three-paned quick-browse area—by dragging the tiny dot at the top of the song list window up or down. The Ctrl+B (⌘-B) keyboard short-cut toggles the Browser off and on. (You can also put the Browser on the left; see page 165.)

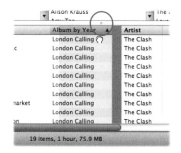

- iTunes divides the main song list into columns you can sort or re-arrange. Click a column title (like Name or Album) to sort the list alphabetically. Click the column title again to reverse the sort order. Change the order of the columns themselves by grabbing them by the header and reordering them to your liking.

- To adjust a column's width, drag the right-hand vertical divider line (right). You may need to grab the line in the column title bar.

- To resize all the columns so their contents fit precisely, right-click (Control-click) any column header and choose Auto Size All Columns.

- To add (or delete) columns, right-click (Control-click) any column title. From the pop-up list of column categories (Bit Rate, Date Added, and so on), choose the column name you want to add or remove. Checkmarks indicate currently visible columns.

- Click the black triangle in the first column to display or hide album covers alongside song titles. If you don't have any artwork for the song, iTunes displays the generic gray Musical Note icon. If you find life has too many gray areas already, the next chapter tells you how to add album art to your files. (In iTunes 10 and later, this album art appears in the Album List view.)

Change the Size of the iTunes Window

Lovely as iTunes is, it takes up a heck of a lot of screen real estate. When you're working on other things, you can shrink it down. In fact, iTunes can run in three sizes: small, medium, or large:

❶ *Large.* This is what you get the first time you open iTunes. (Hate the music hard-sell from the Ping Sidebar on the right? Close the panel by clicking the square button in the lower-right corner.)

❷ *Medium.* Switch back and forth between large and medium by pressing Ctrl+M (Shift-⌘-M) or choosing View→Switch to Mini Player.

❸ *Small.* To really scrunch things down, start with the medium-size window. Then drag the resize handle (the diagonal lines in the lower-right corner) leftward. To expand it, just reverse the process.

Tired of losing your mini-iTunes window among the vast stack of open windows on your screen? Make the iTunes mini-player *always* visible on top of other open documents, windows, and assorted screen detritus. Open iTunes Preferences window (Ctrl+comma [⌘-comma]), click the Advanced tab, and then turn on the checkbox next to "Keep Mini Player on top of all other windows." Now you won't have to click frantically around the screen trying to find iTunes if you get caught listening to your bubblegum-pop playlist.

Change Import Settings for Better Audio Quality

iPads can play several different digital audio formats: AAC, MP3, WAV, AIFF, and a format called Apple Lossless. If you find the audio quality lacking, you can change the way iTunes encodes, or *converts*, songs when it copies tracks from your CDs. iTunes gives you two main options in its import settings box . Go to Edit (iTunes)→Preferences→General, and then click the Import Settings button to get there. They are:

- **Audio format (use the drop-down menu beside "Import Using").** Some formats tightly compress audio data to save space. The tradeoff: lost sound quality. Highly compressed formats include AAC (iTunes' default setting) and MP3. Formats that use little or no compression include WAV and AIFF, sound better, but take up more space. Apple Lossless splits the difference: Better sound quality than AAC and MP3, but not as hefty as WAV or AIFF.

- **Bit rate (beside "Setting").** The higher the number of bits listed, the greater the amount of data contained in the file (in other words, your files take up more storage space). The advantage? Better sound quality.

To see a song's format and other technical information, click its title in iTunes, press Ctrl+I (⌘-I), and then click the Summary tab in the Get Info box.

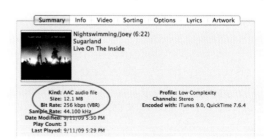

Four Ways to Browse Your Collection

Instead of just presenting you with boring lists, iTunes gives you four options for browsing your media collection—some of them more visual than others. Click the View button at the top of iTunes to switch among views.

- **List View** is the all-text display; you can see a sample of it on page 187. Press Ctrl+B (⌘-B) to toggle on and off the browser that shows vertical (or horizontal) panes that group your music by genre, artist, and album. Press Ctrl+Alt+3 (Option-⌘-3) to jump back to List View from another view.

- **Album List View** shows an album cover in the first column if you have five or more tracks from an album. (Choose View→Always Show Artwork to override the five-track minimum.) Press Ctrl+Alt+4 (Option-⌘-4) to jump to Album List View.

- **Grid View** presents your collection in a nifty array of album covers and other artwork. There's a lot you can do in Grid View, so flip the page for more. Press Ctrl+Alt+5 (Option-⌘-5) to switch to the Grid.

- **Cover Flow.** If you *really* like album art, this view's for you. Ctrl+Alt+6 (Option-⌘-6) is the shortcut. Your collection appears as a stream of album covers. To browse them, press the left- and right-arrow keys on the keyboard or drag the scroll bar underneath the albums. Click the little Full Screen button by the slider bar to turn your whole screen into Cover View, complete with playback controls.

Get a Birds-Eye Look at Your Collection with Grid View

Although it's been around since iTunes 8, Grid View is still probably the most eye-catching way to see your media library. It's like laying out all your albums on the living room floor—great for seeing everything you've got without the hassle of having to pick it all back up. More picturesque than List View and not quite as moving as Cover Flow, Grid View is the middle road to discovering (or rediscovering) what's in your iTunes library.

iTunes groups your music collection into four categories: album, artist, genre, and composer. Click each named tab to see the music sorted by that category. (If you don't see the tabs, choose View→Grid View→Show Header.) Here's how to work the Grid:

- Hover your mouse over any tile on the grid to get a clickable Play icon that lets you start listening to the music.

- Double-click a cover in Albums view to display both the cover and song titles in List View.

- If you have mutliple albums under the Artists, Genres, or Composers tabs, hover your mouse over each tile to rotate through the album covers. If you want to represent the group using a particular album cover or piece of art, right-click it and choose Set Default Grid Artwork. You can do the opposite for art you *don't* want to see: right-click it and choose Clear Deafult Grid Artwork.

- Adjust the size of the covers and art by dragging the slider at the top of the window.

One thing about Grid View, though: It's pretty darn depressing unless you have artwork on just about everything in your collection. (If you don't, and you see far too many generic musical-note icons there, Chapter 13 shows you how to art things up.) And if you hate Grid View, don't use it—iTunes just defaults to whatever view you were using the last time you quit the program.

Search for Songs in iTunes

You can call up a list of all the songs with a specific word in their title, album name, or artist attribution just by clicking the Source pane's Music icon (under Library) and typing a few letters into the Search box in iTunes' upper-right corner. With each letter you type, iTunes shortens the list of songs it displays, showing you only tracks that match what you type.

For example, typing *train* brings up a list of everything in your music collection that has the word "train" somewhere in the song's information—maybe the song's title ("Mystery Train"), the band name (Wire Train), or the Steve Earle album (*Train A Comin'*). Click the other Library icons, like Movies or Audiobooks, to comb those collections for titles that match a search term.

You can also search for specific titles using the iTunes Browser mentioned earlier in this chapter. If you can't see the browser pane, press Ctrl+B (⌘-B) to summon it. Depending on how you configured it in View→Column Browser, the browser reveals your music collection grouped by genre, artist, and album. Hit the same keys again (Ctrl+B [⌘-B]) to close the browser.

> **Tip** If you're searching for music in general, why not see what your pals are listening to? Ping, Apple's new social-networking service in iTunes 10, lets you create profile pages, follow your friends' musical tastes, and more; click the Ping icon under Store in the Source list or check out *www.apple.com/itunes/ping* for more info.

You're the Critic: Rate Your Music

Although there's no way to give a song two thumbs up in iTunes, you *can* assign an album or each song in your collection a one- to five-star rating. Then you can use the ratings to produce nothing but playlists of the greatest hits on your hard drive.

If you assign an album a single rating, *all* the songs on the album get the same number of stars. If you rate just a few tracks on an album but not all of them, the album rating reflects the average of the *rated* songs—so an album with two five-star songs and a bunch of unrated tracks gets a five-star rating.

❶ To add ratings, first make sure you turn on the Album Rating and/or Rating columns in the iTunes View Options box (Ctrl+J [⌘-J]).

❷ Click on the song you want to rate to highlight it. iTunes displays five dots in the Rating column (in the iTunes main window). When you click a dot, iTunes turns it into a star. Now either drag the mouse across the column to create one to five stars, or click one of the dots itself to apply a rating (click the third dot, for example, and iTunes gives the song three stars).

❸ Once you assign ratings, you can sort your song list by star rating (click the Album Rating or Rating column title), create a Smart Playlist of only your personal favorites (File→New Smart Playlist; choose Album Rating or Rating from the first drop-down menu), and so on.

You can even rate songs on your iPad, and iTunes records the ratings the next time you sync up.

To rate a song on your iPad, start playing it and tap the small album cover in the Now Playing corner to switch to the full-screen Now Playing window. Tap the screen to get the hidden playback controls to appear, then tap the ▤ icon on the bottom right corner. The album cover spins around to reveal the track listing. Swipe your finger along the row of dots above the song list to transform those empty dots into critical stars for the track that's currently playing.

Listen to Internet Radio

Not satisfied with being a mere virtual jukebox, iTunes also serves as an international radio—without the shortwave static. You can tune in everything from mystical Celtic melodies to Zambian hip hop. Computers with high-speed Internet connections have a smoother streaming experience, but the vast and eclectic mix of music is well worth checking out—even with a dial-up modem. Just click the Radio icon in iTunes' Source list to see a list of stations.

If you find your radio streams constantly stuttering and stopping, summon iTunes' Preferences box (Ctrl+comma [⌘-comma]). Click the Advanced icon or tab on the right side of the box. Then, from the Streaming Buffer Size pop-up menu, choose Large. Click OK. You may have to wait a little longer for the music to start, but iTunes will pre-load enough data to reduce the stutters.

Once you listen to all the stations listed in iTunes, hit the Internet. You can find more radio stations at *www.shoutcast.com*. Windows 7 and Mac OS X users can play them through iTunes by clicking the yellow Tune In button. (If this is your first time at Shoutcast, a prompt asks how you want to hear the stream—click the button for iTunes.) XP users, save the offered *.pls* file to your desktop and then drag and drop it on "Playlists". Click the resulting "tunein-station" playlist.

Change a Song's File Format

Sometimes you've got a song in iTunes whose format you want to change—you might need to convert an AIFF file before loading it onto your iPad, for example. First, head over to Edit→Preferences (iTunes→Preferences), click the General tab, and then the Import Settings button. From the Import Using pop-up menu, pick the format you want to convert *to* and then click OK.

Now, in your iTunes library, select the song you want to convert and choose Advanced→Create MP3 Version (or AIFF, or whatever format you just picked).

If you have a whole folder or disk full of potential converts, hold down the Shift (Option) key as you choose Advanced→"Convert to AAC" (or your chosen encoding format). A window pops up, which you can use to navigate to the folder or disk holding the files you want to convert. The only files that don't get converted are protected ones: Audible.com tracks and older tracks from the iTunes Store that still have copy-protection built in. If you bought a song after April 2009, though, odds are you are delightfully free of such restrictions, since that's when Apple stopped copy-protecting music.

The song or songs in the original format, as well as the freshly converted tracks, are now in your library.

> **Tip** Although you have intentionally created a duplicate of a song here, you may have other unintended dupes from home sharing, ripping the same album twice, or other accidental copying. To find these duplicates—and recover a little hard drive space—choose File→Display Duplicates. iTunes dutifully rounds up all the dupes in one window for you to inspect and possibly delete. Just make sure they are true duplicates, not, say, a studio and a live version of the same song. (To search for exact duplicates, hold down the Shift [Option] key and choose File→Display→ Exact Duplicates.) Click the Show All button to return the window to your full collection.

Change a Song's Start and Stop Times

Got a song with a bunch of onstage chitchat before it starts, or after the music ends? Fortunately, you don't have to sit there and listen while your iPad's battery burns down. You can change a song's start and stop times so you hear only the juicy middle part.

To change a track's stop time, play the song and observe the iTunes status display window. Watch for the point in the timeline where you get bored. Then:

❶ Click the track you want to adjust.

❷ Choose File→Get Info (Ctrl+I [⌘-I]) to call up the song's information box.

❸ Click the Options tab and take a look at the Stop Time box, which shows the full duration of the song.

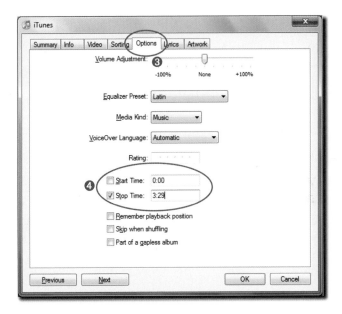

❹ Enter the new stopping point for the song, as you noted earlier.

You can perform the exact same trick at the beginning of a song by adjusting the number in the Start Time box. The shortened version plays in iTunes and on your iPad, but the additional recorded material isn't really lost. If you ever change your mind, go back to the song's Options box and return the song to its full length.

Improve Your Tunes with the Graphic Equalizer

If you'd like to improve the way your songs sound, you can use iTunes' graphic equalizer (EQ) to adjust various frequencies in certain types of music. You might want to boost the bass tones in dance tracks to emphasize the booming rhythm, for example.

To get the equalizer front and center, choose View (Window)→Equalizer and unleash some of your new EQ powers.

❶ Drag the sliders (bass on the left, treble on the right) to accommodate your listening tastes (or the strengths and weaknesses of your speakers or headphones). You can drag the Preamp slider up or down to compensate for songs that sound too loud or too soft. To create your own presets, click the pop-up menu and select Make Preset.

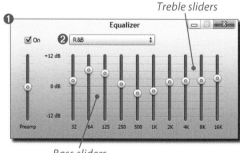

Treble sliders

Bass sliders

❷ Use the pop-up menu to choose one of the canned presets for different types of music (Classical, Dance, Jazz, and so on).

You can apply equalizer settings to an entire album or to individual songs.

❸ To apply settings to a whole album, select the album's name (either in Grid View or in the iTunes browser pane). Then press Ctrl+I (⌘-I) and click "Yes" if iTunes asks whether you're sure you want to edit multiple items. In the box that pops up, click the Options tab and choose your preferred setting from the Equalizer Preset pull-down menu.

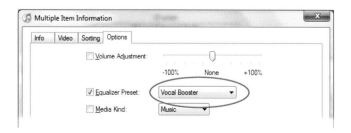

Equalization is the art of adjusting the frequency response of an audio signal. An equalizer emphasizes, or boosts, some of the signal's frequencies while lowering others. In the range of audible sound, *bass* frequency is the low rumbly noise; *treble* is at the opposite end of the sound spectrum, with high, even shrill, notes; and *midrange* is, of course, in the middle, and it's the most audible to human ears.

❹ You can apply equalizer pre-sets to specific songs as well. Instead of selecting the album name in the iTunes window, click the song name, and then press Ctrl+I (⌘+I). Click the Options tab and choose a set-ting from the Equalizer Preset menu.

❺ Finally, you can change the EQ settings right from your song lists by adding an Equalizer column. Choose View→View Options and turn on the Equalizer checkbox. A new column appears in your track lists, where you can select EQ settings.

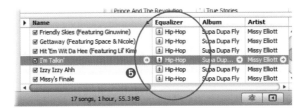

 The iPad itself has more than 20 equalizer presets you can use on the go. To set your iPad's Equalizer to a setting designed for a specific type of music, tap Settings→iPod→EQ. Flick down the list of presets until you find one that matches your music style, and then tap to select it. Your iPad now lists the preset's name next to "EQ" on the Settings menu and your music, hopefully, sounds better.

Edit Song Information

Tired of seeing so many tunes named *Untitled*? You can change song titles in iTunes—to enter a song's real name, for example, or to fix a typo—a couple of ways.

In the song list, click the text you want to change, wait a moment, and then click again. The title now appears highlighted and you can edit the text—just like when you change file names on a desktop computer.

Another way to change a song's title, artist name, or other information is to click the song in the iTunes window and press Ctrl+I (⌘-I) to summon the Get Info box. (Choose File→Get Info if you forget the keyboard shortcut.) Click the Info tab and type in the new track information.

Too much work? You can always try Advanced→Get CD Track Names and see what comes up, although the Gracenote database iTunes uses may not know the title, either, if it's something deeply obscure or homemade.

Tip Once you've got a song's Get Info box on-screen, use the Previous and Next buttons to navigate to other tracks grouped with it in the iTunes song list window. That way, you can rapidly edit all the track information in the same playlist, on the same album, and so on, without closing and opening boxes the whole time.

Edit Album Information and Song Gaps

You don't have to adjust your track information on a song-by-song basis. You can edit an entire album's worth of tracks simultaneously by clicking the Album name in the iTunes col-

umn browser (or on its cover in Grid View) and pressing Ctrl+I (⌘-I) to bring up the Get Info box.

Ever careful, iTunes flashes an alert box asking if you really want to change the info for a bunch of things all at once. Click Yes.

You can make all sorts of changes to an album in the four-tabbed box that pops up. Here are just a few examples:

❶ Fix a typo or mistake in the Album or Artist name boxes.

❷ Manually add an album cover or photo of your choice to the whole album by dragging it into the Artwork box.

❸ Click the Options tab and change the Equalizer preset for all the songs.

❹ Have iTunes skip the album when you shuffle music—great for keeping winter holiday music out of your summer barbecue rotation.

❺ Tell iTunes to play back the album without those two-second gaps between tracks by choosing the "Gapless album" option. (Perfect for opera and *Abbey Road*!)

Make a New Playlist in iTunes

To create a playlist, press Ctrl+N (⌘-N). You can also choose File→New Playlist or click the + button at the bottom-left of the iTunes window.

All freshly minted playlists start out with the impersonal name "untitled playlist." Fortunately, this generic name is highlighted and ready for editing—just type in a better name: Cardio Workout, Hits of the Highland Lute, or whatever you want to call it. As you add playlists, iTunes alphabetizes them in the Playlists area.

Once you create and name a spanking-new playlist, you're ready to add your songs or videos. You can do this in several ways, so choose the method you like best.

Playlist-Making Method #1

❶ If this is your first playlist, double-click the new playlist's icon in the Source list. You get your full music library in one window, and your empty playlist in the other. (iTunes may pop up an intro screen. Ignore it and go to Step 2.)

❷ Go back to the main iTunes window and drag the song titles you want from your library over to the new playlist window. (Make sure you click the Music icon in the Source list to see all your songs.) Drag songs one at a time, or grab a bunch by selecting tracks as you go: just Ctrl+click (⌘-click) each title.

Playlist-Making Method #2

❶ Some folks don't like multiple windows. No problem. You can add songs to a playlist by highlighting them and dragging the tunes to the playlist's icon right from the main iTunes window.

❷ Tip: If you create lots of playlists, you may need to scroll down to get to your new one.

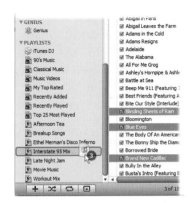

Playlist-Making Method #3

❶ You can also pick and choose songs in your library and then create a playlist out of the highlighted songs. Select tracks by Ctrl+clicking (⌘-clicking) the titles.

❷ Then choose File→New Playlist From Selection, or press Ctrl+Shift+N (⌘+Shift+N). The songs you selected appear in a brand-new playlist. If all of them came from the same album, iTunes names the playlist after the album (but it also highlights the title box so you can rename it).

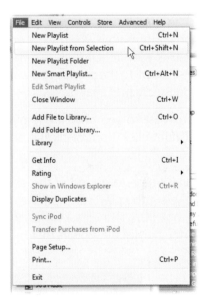

Don't worry about clogging up your hard drive. When you drag a song title onto a playlist, you don't *copy* the song, you just tell iTunes where it can find the file. In essence, you're creating a *shortcut* to the track. That means you can have the same song on several playlists, but only one copy of it on your PC.

That nice iTunes even gives you some playlists of its own devising, like "Top 25 Most Played" and "Purchased" (a convenient place to find all your iTunes Store goodies listed in one place—and one to *definitely* back up to a CD or DVD).

Change or Delete an Existing Playlist

If you change your mind about a playlist's tune order, drag the song titles up or down within the playlist window. Just make sure to sort the playlist by song order first (click the top of the  first column, the one with the numbers listed in front of the song titles).

You can always drag more songs into a playlist, and you can delete titles if you your playlist needs pruning. Click the song in the playlist window and then hit Delete or Backspace. When iTunes asks you to confirm your decision, click Yes. Remember, deleting a song from a playlist doesn't delete it from your music library—it just removes the title from that particular playlist. (You can get rid of a song for good only by pressing Delete or Backspace from within the iTunes library; select the Music icon under "Library" to get there.)

You can quickly add a song to an existing playlist right from the main iTunes window, no matter which view you happen to be using: Select the song, right-click (Control-click) it, and then, in the pop-up menu, choose "Add to Playlist". Scroll to the playlist you want to use and then click the mouse button to add the track to that playlist.

If you want to see how many playlists contain a certain song, select the track, right-click (Control-click) it, and choose "Show in Playlist" in the pop-up menu.

When it's time to get rid of the playlist once and for all because the party's over, select the playlist icon iTunes and press the Delete key. You see a message box from iTunes asking to confirm your decision. If you autosync the iPad, the playlist disappears there, too.

iTunes DJ: Get the Party Started

The standard iTunes song-shuffle feature can be inspiring or embarrassing, depending on which songs the program happens to play. The iTunes DJ feature lets *you* control which songs iTunes selects when it shuffles at your next wingding. It also shows you what's already been played and what's coming up in the mix, so you know what to expect.

❶ Click the iTunes DJ icon in the Playlists area of the iTunes Source list. Now you see a new pane at the very bottom of iTunes.

❷ Use the Source pop-up menu to select a music source for the mix. You can use either an existing playlist, the Genius, or your whole library.

❸ If you don't like the song list that iTunes proposes, click the Refresh button at the bottom-right of the iTunes window. iTunes generates a new list of songs for your consideration.

❹ Click the Settings button at the bottom of the window. In the Settings box, you can change the number of recently played and upcoming songs that iTunes displays. If iTunes is DJ'ing your interactive music party, the Settings box also has a place to put a Welcome message for guests changing up your music with the Remote program on their iPhones, iPod Touches, and iPads. (To get it, visit the App Store and download *Remote*.)

❺ Arrange the songs if you feel like it. Back on the playlist, you can manually add songs, delete them from the playlist, or rearrange the playing order. To add songs, click the Source list's Music icon and then drag your selected tunes onto the iTunes DJ icon.

❻ Click the Play button. And let the music play on.

Make a Genius Playlist in iTunes

Playlists are fun to make, but occasionally you just don't have the time or energy. If that's the case, call in the expert—the iTunes Genius. With the Genius feature, you click any song you're in the mood for and iTunes crafts a playlist of 25 to 100 songs that it thinks go well with the one you picked.

The first time you use it, Genius asks permission to go through your music collection and gather song information. Then it uploads that data to Apple. When your information has been analyzed (by software) and anonymously added to a big giant database of everybody else's song info (to improve the Genius's suggestions), the Genius is ready for duty. Here's the procedure:

❶ Click a song title in your library.

❷ Click the Genius button ⬚❅⬚ at the bottom-right of iTunes. If you're playing the song, click the Genius icon in the iTunes display window.

❸ iTunes presents you with your new playlist in a flash.

❹ Use the buttons at the top of the Genius window to adjust the number of songs in the playlist, refresh it with new songs if you want a different mix, and—best of all—save the playlist permanently.

The Genius doesn't work if it doesn't have enough information about a song—or if there aren't enough similar songs available to match your kick-off song. In that case, pick another tune. If you frequently add new music to your library and want to get it in the mix, inform the Genius at Store→Update Genius.

And if you happen to have the Genius Sidebar panel open in your iTunes window, the Genius cheerfully presents you with a list of other songs that you can buy right there to round out your listening experience.

 If you declined iTunes' initial offer to activate the Genius, you can summon it again by choosing Store→"Turn On Genius". And if you're regretting your choice to invite the Genius into your iTunes home, kick him out for good by visiting the same menu and choosing "Turn Off Genius".

Genius Mixes in iTunes

Yes, the iTunes Genius feature takes almost all the effort out of making a playlist—all you do is click the Genius button. But if even a one-button click seems like too much effort, iTunes 9 makes computerized playlist creation even *easier*. Welcome to Genius Mixes.

The Genius Mix feature works like this: iTunes takes it upon itself to search your entire music library and then automatically compose (depending on the size of your library), up to 12 different types of song collections. Unlike a Genius playlist of tunes calculated to go well together, a Genius Mix is more like a radio station or cable-TV music channel based on *genre*. Depending on what's in your iTunes library, the Genius could present you with a hip hop mix, a country mix, a classical mix, and so on. In addition, the Genius Mix creates up to 12 playlists at once, all saved and ready to play, unlike the Genius's single mix that you have to save to preserve.

If you don't already see a square purple Genius Mix icon in your iTunes Source list, choose Store→Update Genius. Once activated, the Genius quietly stirs up its sonic concoctions from your music library.

To play a Genius Mix, click the Genius Mix icon in the Source list. The iTunes window reverts to Grid View and displays the different mixes it's created. Each is represented by a quartet of album covers from tracks in the mix. Pass the mouse cursor over the album squares to see the name of the mix or click the squares to start playing music.

Like most traditional radio stations, you don't get to see a playlist of what's actually in a particular Genius Mix—it's all a surprise. If you don't care for a particular song the Genius has included, you can always hit the forward button or tap the right-arrow key on the computer's keyboard to skip to the next track.

Genius Mixes can be another great way to effortlessly toss on some background music at a party, and you may even hear songs you haven't played in forever. Want to take the Genius Mix with you? Sync it to your iPad (page 175).

Smart Playlists: Another Way for iTunes to Assemble Playlists

As cool as the Genius is, sometimes you want a little more manual control over what goes into your automatically generated music mixes. That's where Smart Playlists rise to the occasion.

Once you give it some guidelines, a *Smart Playlist* can go sniffing through your music library and come up with its own mix. A Smart Playlist even keeps tabs on the music that comes and goes from your library and adjusts itself based on that.

You might tell one Smart Playlist to assemble 45 minutes' worth of songs that you've rated higher than four stars but rarely listen to, and another to play your most-often-played songs from the 1980s. The Smart Playlists you create are limited only by your imagination.

❶ To start a Smart Playlist, press Ctrl+Alt+N (Option-⌘-N) or choose File→New Smart Playlist. A Smart Playlist box opens: It sports a purple gear-shaped icon next to its name in the Source list (a regular playlist has a blue icon with a music note icon in it).

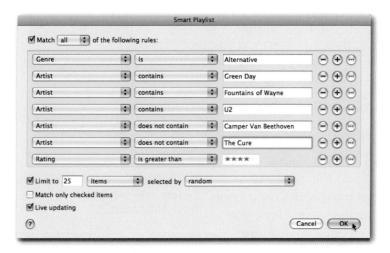

❷ Give iTunes detailed instructions about what you want to hear. You can select a few artists you like and have iTunes leave off the ones you're not in the mood for, pluck songs that only fall within a certain genre or year, and so on. To add multiple, cumulative criteria, click the plus (+) button.

❸ Turn on the "Live updating" checkbox. This tells iTunes to keep the playlist updated as your collection, ratings, and play count change. (The play count tells iTunes how many times you play a track, a good indicator of how much you like a song.)

❹ To edit an existing Smart Playlist, right-click (Ctrl-click) the playlist's name. Then choose Edit Smart Playlist.

A Smart Playlist is a dialogue between you and iTunes: You tell it what you want in as much detail as you want, and the program whips up a playlist according to your instructions.

You can even instruct a Smart Playlist to pull tracks from your current Genius playlist. Just click the + button to add a preference, choose Playlist as another criteria, and select Genius from the list of available playlists.

> **Tip** When you press Shift (Option), the + button at the bottom of the iTunes window turns into a gear icon (✿). Click this gear button to quickly launch the Smart Playlist creation box.

Set Up Multiple iTunes Libraries

There's Home Sharing and then there's home, sharing. Many families have just one computer. If everyone's using the same copy of iTunes, you soon get the Wiggles bumping up against Wu-Tang Clan if you have iTunes shuffling the music tracks, or when you autosync multiple iPads. Wouldn't it be great if everyone had a *personal* iTunes library to have and to hold, to sync and to shuffle—separately? Absolutely.

To use multiple iTunes libraries, follow these steps:

❶ Quit iTunes.

❷ Hold down the Shift (Option) key on your PC or Mac keyboard and launch iTunes. In the box that pops up, click Create Library. Give it a name, like "Tiffany's Music" or "Songs My Wife Hates."

❸ iTunes opens up, but with an empty library. If you have a bunch of music in your main library that you want to move over to this one, choose File→"Add to Library".

❹ Navigate to the music you want and add it. If the songs are in your original library, they're probably in Music→iTunes→iTunes Media→Music (Home→Music→iTunes→iTunes Media→Music), in folders sorted by artist name. Choose the files you want to add.

To switch between libraries, hold down the Shift (Option) key when you start iTunes, and you'll get a box that lets you pick the library you want. (If you don't choose a library, iTunes opens the last one used.) Tracks from CDs you copy go into whatever library's open. And now that you have those songs in this library, you can switch back to the other one and get rid of them there.

> **Tip** Multiple libraries can be a real help if you have a huge video collection that you want to store on an external hard drive to save space on your main computer.

Three Kinds of Discs You Can Create with iTunes

If you want to record a certain playlist on a CD for posterity—or for the Mr. Shower CD player in the bathroom—iTunes gives you the power to burn, burn more, or back up. The program can create any of three kinds of discs when you choose File→Library→Burn Playlist to Disc:

- **Standard audio CDs.** This is the best option: If your computer has a CD burner, it can serve as your own private record label. iTunes can record selected sets of songs, no matter what the original sources, onto a blank CD. When it's all over, you can play the burned CD on  any standard CD player, just like the ones from Best Buy—but this time, you hear only the songs you like, in the order you like, with all the annoying ones eliminated. You can also burn a selected playlist to a CD by clicking the Burn Disc button on the bottom-right corner of the iTunes window.

- **MP3 CDs.** A standard audio CD contains high-quality, enormous song files in the AIFF format. An *MP3* compact disc, however, is a data CD that contains music files in the MP3 format. Because MP3 songs are much smaller than AIFF files, many more of them fit in the standard 650 or 700 MB of space on a recordable CD. The bottom line? Instead of 74 or 80 minutes of music, a CD full of MP3 files can store *10 to 12 hours* of tunes. The downside? Older CD players may not be able to play these CDs.

- **Backup CDs or DVDs.** If your computer can play and record both CDs and/or DVDs, you have another option: iTunes can back up your entire library, playlists and all, by copying it to a CD or DVD. (The disc won't play in any kind of player, of course; it's just a glorified backup disk for restoration when something goes wrong with your hard drive.) Flip to the end of this chapter to learn how to use these data discs to back up your iTunes library.

To see if your disc drive is compatible with iTunes, select a playlist and click the Burn Disc button on the iTunes window to get the Burn Settings box. If your drive name is listed next to "CD Burner," iTunes recognizes it.

See Your iTunes Purchase History and Get iTunes Store Help

Ever notice songs on playlists or in the iTunes library that you don't remember buying? Good thing the iTunes Store keeps track of what you buy and when you buy it. If you suspect that one of the kids knows your password and is sneaking in forbidden downloads or maybe that your credit card was wrongly charged, you can contact the Store or check your account's purchase history page to see what's been downloaded in your name.

To do the latter, in the iTunes window, click the triangle next to your account name and choose Account from the menu, then type in your password and click Purchase History.. Your latest purchase appears at the top of the page, and you can scroll farther down to see a list of previous acquisitions. Everything billed to your account over the months and years is here, including gift-certificate purchases. If you see something wrong, click the "Report a Problem" link and say something.

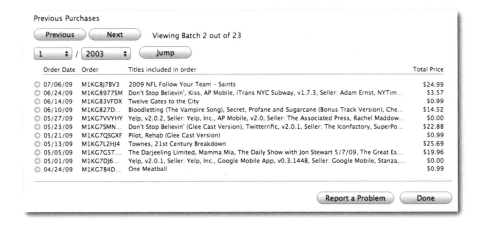

If you have other issues with your account or want to submit a specific query or comment, the online help center awaits. From the iTunes Store's main page, click the Support link. Your Web browser presents you with the main iTunes service and support page; click the link that best describes what you want to learn or complain about. For billing or credit card issues, check out the iTunes Account and Billing Support link on that same Web page.

Buy Songs from Other Music Stores

There are many online music services out there and every one of 'em wants to sell you a song. But due to copy-protection, some of these merchants' songs don't work on the iPad. Some of them do, though. Thanks to recent moves by many stores to strip out the digital-rights management (DRM) protection on song files, their music has been liberated into the friendly MP3 play-anywhere format. Vive la musique!

Buying songs from somewhere other than the iTunes Store is as easy as supplying a credit card number and downloading the file using a Web browser. Once you have the file on your computer, use iTunes' File→Add to Library command to add it to your collection. Here are some of the online music services that now work with the iPad, iPod, and iPhone:

- **Napster.** You don't get the full Napster software and services, but Windows and Mac users can download and save MP3 files to your iTunes folder through the Napster Web site. (*www.napster.com*)

- **eMusic.** Geared toward indie bands, eMusic offers several subscription plans based on quantity: 16 bucks a month, for example, gets you 35 songs of your choice to download. (*www.emusic.com*)

- **Amazon MP3 Downloads.** From the main page, click Digital Downloads and then choose MP3 Downloads. Amazon has a free piece of software called the Amazon MP3 Downloader that takes half a minute to install and automatically tosses your purchases into iTunes for you. Click the link (circled below) at the top of the Amazon MP3 page to snag the Downloader program. (*www.amazon.com*)

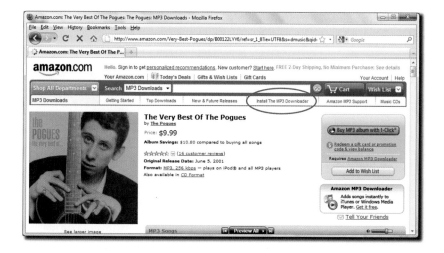

Move the iTunes Music/Media Folder to an External Drive

Media libraries grow large, and hard drives can seem to shrink, as you add thousands of songs and hundreds of videos to iTunes. You may, in fact, think about using a big external drive for iTunes storage (and more iPad video). That's just dandy, but you need to make sure that iTunes knows what you intend to do.

If you rudely drag your iTunes Music (or Media) folder to a different place without telling iTunes, it thinks the songs and videos in your collection are gone. The next time you start the program, you'll find a newly created, empty Music folder. (While iTunes remains empty but calm, *you* may be having heart palpitations as you picture your media collection vanishing in a puff of bytes.)

To move the Music folder to a new drive, just let iTunes know where you're putting it. Before you start, make sure iTunes has been putting all your songs and videos in the iTunes Music folder by opening the Preferences box (Ctrl+comma [⌘-comma]) and confirming the folder location. Then:

❶ Click the Advanced tab and turn on the checkbox next to "Keep iTunes Music folder organized."

❷ Click the Change button in the iTunes Music folder location area and navigate to the external hard drive.

❸ Click the New Folder button in the window, type in a name for the iTunes library, and click the Create button.

❹ Back in the Change Music Folder Location box, click the Open button.

❺ Click OK to close the iTunes Preferences box.

❻ Choose File→Library→Organize Library and then check "Consolidate files".

Ignore the ominous warnings from iTunes (*"This cannot be undone"*) and let iTunes heave a complete copy of your iTunes folder to the external drive. Once you confirm that everything is in the new library, trash your old iTunes Media folder and empty the Trash or Recycle Bin to get all those gigs of space back.

Back Up Your iTunes Files to Disc

If your hard drive dies and takes your whole iTunes folder with it, you lose your music and movies—and your iPad will be lonely. This can be especially painful if you paid for lots of songs and videos from the iTunes Store, because Apple won't let you re-download new copies unless it's an app or an iBook. Luckily, iTunes gives you a super simple way to back up your files onto a CD or DVD.

❶ In iTunes, choose File→Library→"Back Up to Disc".

❷ In the box that pops up, choose what you want to back up—everything, or just items you paid for in the iTunes Store. Later, after you've backed up for the first time, you can turn on a checkbox to back up only the stuff you added since the last backup.

❸ Have a stack of discs ready to feed into your computer's disc drive. Depending on the size of your library, you may need several CDs (which store up to 700 megabytes of data each) or DVDs (which pack in at least 4.7 gigabytes of files per disc). You'll get nagged by iTunes to feed it a new disc once it fills up the current one.

If you ever need to use your backup copies, open iTunes and put in one of those discs to start restoring your files. Remember, there's nothing really exciting about file backups—until you have to use them to save the day.

Play Music and Other Audio

When the iPad was announced in January 2010, many technology critics quickly dismissed it as "a giant iPod Touch" before going back to complaining about other things they hadn't actually experienced. Although that particular response was snarky, it was also correct. Among many other things, the iPad *is* a giant iPod Touch. And what a handsome flat-screen jukebox it is.

Thanks to its larger size, the iPad makes playing music, audiobooks, and podcasts a more visually exciting experience. It's much easier to see cover art more clearly, find the tracks you want to hear, create your own playlists, and control your music on the bigger screen.

Granted, the iPad is a bit bulky to haul to the gym or schlep along for the morning jog, but it's a great music machine for other situations—like when you have a stack of email to get through and you want to bliss out to a little Yo-Yo Ma.

No matter whether you want your music in the background or front-and-center on the screen, this chapter shows you how to get your iPad singing.

Get Music and Audio for Your iPad

Have absolutely no music or audio files on your computer? Here are a few ways to get some tracks on your iPad. (If you've had an iPod for years and have the music-collection thing down cold, feel free to skip ahead to the next page to see how the iPad organizes your music once you get it on there.)

Import a CD

You can use iTunes to convert tracks from your existing audio CDs into iPad-ready digital music files. Start up iTunes and stick a CD in your computer's disc drive. The program asks if you want to import the CD into iTunes. (If it doesn't ask, click the Import CD button at the bottom-right of the iTunes window.) If you're connected to the Internet, iTunes automatically downloads song titles and artist information for the CD. (Yes, strange as it may seem, music managers like iTunes don't get information about an album from the album itself, they search for it in a huge database on the Web.)

Once you tell it to import music, iTunes gets to work and begins adding the songs to your library. You can import all the tracks from a CD, but if you don't want every song, turn off the checkbox next to the titles you want iTunes to skip. Eject the CD when iTunes is done converting the files.

Import Existing Songs into iTunes

If you've had a computer for longer than a few years, odds are you already have some songs in the popular MP3 format on your hard drive. When you start iTunes for the first time, the program asks if you'd like to search your PC or Mac for music and add it to iTunes. Click "Yes" and iTunes will go fetch.

Buy Music in the iTunes Store

Another way to get music for your iTunes library and iPad is to buy it from the iTunes Store (page 168). Once you have an iTunes account, (page 108) you can buy and download audio files directly on the iPad (page 169) or via iTunes on your desktop computer. To shop the Store from the PC or Mac side, click the iTunes Store icon in the list on the left side of the iTunes window and browse until you find something you like.

Unless you buy music and audiobooks on the iPad itself, you need to add it to the iPad by syncing your 'Pad with iTunes (page 175). If you already have music on your iPad, read on to see how to organize and control it.

Explore the iPod Menu

The iPad has a Photos icon and a Videos icon. If you're looking for a Music icon—because that would make some *sense*—don't bother. Apple has chosen to put all of the iPad's music functions in the iPod menu, so tap the iPod icon on the Home screen:

The iPad divvies up the iPod screen into four distinct areas:

❶ **Controls & Search bar.** Located at the very top of the screen are all the audio playback controls, like volume, next/previous buttons for moving between songs or audio-book chapters, and the time counter for the track that's playing. The Search box is also there, in the top-right corner, if you need to find a tune fast.

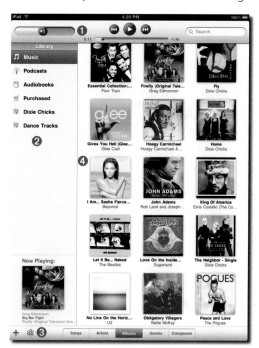

❷ **Library.** As in iTunes, your music, podcast, and audiobook tracks are all grouped under tappable sub-menus, as are any playlists (page 200) you've added. The Now Playing pane in the bottom-left corner shows the cover of the current selection; tap it to get to the giant Now Playing screen (page 220).

❸ **Bottom bar.** The lower edge of the iPod window is further concerned with music organization. Click the ✚ icon to create a playlist with the songs you choose. Click the atom-shaped Genius icon to have the iPad *automatically* generate a playlist based on songs like the one currently selected. In the center of the bar, click the appropriate button to display your music collection by Songs, Artists, Albums (shown here), Genres, or Composers.

❹ **Main window.** No matter which media collection you choose to see— music, podcasts, audiobooks, or playlists—the iPad displays track names in the center of the screen. Most views show cover art in one size or another, except for Songs, which shows a text list of tracks, and Genre, which shows themed art depicting "Folk," "R&B," and so on.

Play Music

To play a song, just tap its title on the screen. If you sorted your music collection by album, tap the album cover to spin it around and reveal its list of songs, and then tap a title to hear it play. Use the playback controls at the top of the screen to adjust the volume, to play and pause songs, and to jump between tracks.

To switch to the full-screen version of the album cover and the Now Playing screen's controls (page 220), tap the artwork in the Now Playing corner.

If you have a playlist on the iPad that you'd like to hear, tap the name of it in the Library list and tap the title of its first song to kick it off. Should the iPad screen go to sleep while you're rocking out, the album cover of the current song appears on your Lock screen when you wake it back up. (Don't have any album art, just a big gray musical note? See page 222.)

Tip The iPad lets you keep playing music even as you move on to other things, like Safari browsing or writing. If you need to call up the iPod controls in a hurry while you're on another screen, you can program the iPad to summon them with a double-click of the Home button. Page 6 has instructions.

Play Audiobooks and Podcasts

Spoken-word tracks, like audiobooks and podcasts, have some special controls that regular music tracks don't have. To get to these controls, tap the Now Playing artwork corner of the main iPod screen, then tap the larger full-screen version of the artwork that appears. Once you tap on the full-screen art, all the controls appear. The usual playback buttons and sliders are at the very top of the screen, and you can drag the slider to any point in the recording to jump around within it. But now you can do other things like:

❶ Tap the envelope icon to email a link to the podcast to a friend.

❷ Speed up or slow down the narrator's voice. Tap the 1x button for normal speed, 2x for double-time (if the person is talking too slowly), and ½x for half-speed (in case the person talks too fast for you).

❸ Tap here to see other chapters in the audiobook or other episodes in the podcast series on your iPad.

❹ Tap this button to replay the last 30 seconds of the recording, in case you spaced out and missed something.

❺ Tap the arrow button in the bottom-left corner to leave the Now Playing screen and go back to the iPod list of audio files.

Control the Now Playing Screen

On the full-size Now Playing screen, a few controls await your fingertip—some obvious and some not so obvious. First, the obvious ones:

- **Volume.** Drag the round ◀)) icon forward or backward on the slider bar to increase or decrease the iPad's volume. (You can also use the Volume rocker on the right side of the iPad.)

- **Play/Pause (▶/II) button.** The Pause button looks like this II when you have music playing. If you press that button to pause a song, it turns into the Play button (▶).

- **Previous, Next (I◀◀, ▶▶I).** These buttons work exactly as they do on any other iPod. That is, tap I◀◀ to skip to the beginning of a song (or, if you're already at the beginning, to skip to the previous song). Tap ▶▶I to skip to the next song.

If you hold down one of these buttons instead of tapping, you rewind or fast-forward through a song. It's rather cool, actually—you hear the music speed by as you keep your finger down, without turning the singer into a chipmunk. The rewinding or fast-forwarding accelerates if you keep holding down the button.

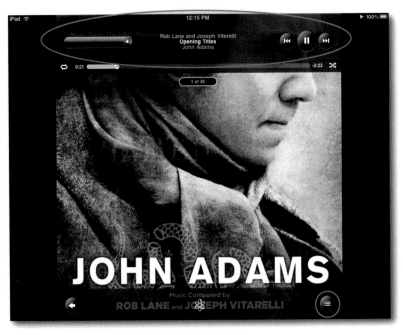

To see a list of all the tracks on an album, tap the button in the lower-right corner, circled above. The cover spins around to reveal the list.

So those are the obvious controls. Then there are the ones that look like iPad hieroglyphics, numbered here for your illumination.

❶ **Loop button.** If you *really* love a certain album or playlist, you can command the iPod to play it over and over again, beginning to end. Just tap the Loop button (⟳) so that it turns blue (⟳).

❷ **Scroll slider.** This slider (top of the screen) controls your position in a track and reveals three useful statistics: how much of the song you've heard in "minutes:seconds" format (at the left end), how much time remains (at the right end), and which slot this song occupies in the current playlist or album. To operate the slider, drag the tiny round handle.

❸ **Shuffle button.** Ordinarily, the iPad plays the songs on an album sequentially, from beginning to end. But if you love surprises, tap the ⤬ button so it turns blue. Now you'll hear the songs in random order.

❹ **Genius playlist.** Tap the ✳ icon to make a Genius playlist based on this song. Page 204 has details.

To rate a song by assigning a one- to five-star ranking, swipe the series of dots below the scroll slider to convert dots into stars. Tap the album icon in the bottom-right corner to return to the full-screen album art. Tap the arrow in the bottom-left corner to return to the full list of audio files on the iPad.

Get Album Art in iTunes

Are you plagued with gray musical note icons mixed in with regular album cover art on your iPad's screen? Do you long for a fully arted album collection? While songs purchased from the iTunes Store include album-cover artwork, tracks you ripped from your own CDs don't. But you have options here.

Automatically Add Art

You can ask iTunes to head to the Internet and find as many album covers for you as it can. You need a (free) iTunes Store account to make this work, so if you haven't signed up yet, flip back to page 108 to learn how. To make iTunes go fetch, choose Advanced→Get Album Artwork.

Since Apple has to root around in your library to figure out what covers you need, you get an alert box warning you that the company will be getting (and then dumping) personal information from you. Click OK and let iTunes get to work—which may take a while. When iTunes finishes, though, you should have a healthy dose of album art filling up the iTunes window.

Manually Add Art

Despite its best intentions, sometimes iTunes can't find an album cover (or retrieves the wrong one). If that happens, take matters into your own hands by manually adding your own album artwork—or a photo of your choice. If Pachelbel's *Canon in D* makes you think of puppies, you can have a baby dachshund photo appear every time you play that song.

❶ To add your own art to a song, pick a photo or image—JPEG files are the most common.

❷ If you found the cover on Amazon (*hint*: a great source!), save a copy of it by dragging it off the web page and onto your desktop or by right-clicking (Ctrl-clicking) it and choosing "Save Image" in your browser.

❸ With your image near the iTunes window, select the song and click the Show Artwork button in the bottom-left corner of the iTunes window.

❹ Drag the image into the iTunes Artwork pane to add it to the song file.

No matter which method you choose, the art rides along when you sync the songs over to the iPad.

Add Lyrics in iTunes

You can save lyrics with a song file just as you do album art. To add lyrics, select a song in iTunes and press Ctrl+I (⌘-I) to call up the Get Info box. Then click the Lyrics tab.

Here, you can either meticulously type in a song's verses or look them up on one of the hundreds of web-sites devoted to lyrics. Once you find your words, getting them into iTunes is a mere cut 'n' paste job. If you want to add lyrics to all the songs on an album, or have several to add on the same playlist, click the Next button (circled). That advances you to the next song, thereby saving yourself repeated keystrokes invoking the Get Info command.

Now that you've spent all that time grooming your song files, sync them to the iPad to get the fruits of your labor on the tablet's screen.

When you're listening to a song on the iPad's Now Playing screen, just tap the album cover to see the lyrics.

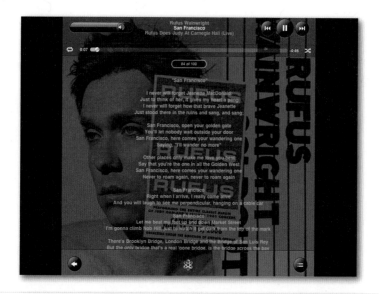

Tip Don't see any lyrics when you tap? Jump to the Home screen to Settings→iPod and make sure the button next to Lyrics & Podcast info is set to On.

Make Playlists

You have a few ways to make *playlists*—those personalized song sets made up of tunes you think go great together. You can make them in iTunes and sync them over to the iPad (page 200), you can make them on the iPad, or you can have the iPad make them for you.

In iTunes, one way to make a new playlist is to choose File→New Playlist. When the Untitled Playlist icon appears in the iTunes Source list, click once to select it—so you can type in a better name—and then drag songs from your library onto the playlist name. You can also select a bunch of tracks in the library (hold down the Control key while clicking), and choose File→New Playlist From Selection. Sync the new playlist to the iPad (page 175).

You can also make a playlist on the iPad from tracks in its music collection:

❶ On the main iPod screen, tap the ✚ button at the bottom of the Library column. In the box that pops up, give the resulting blank playlist a memorable new name and tap Save.

❷ A list of all your songs pops up. Each time you see one worth adding, tap its name (or the ⊕ button). You can also tap one of the icons at the bottom of the screen, like Artists or Albums, to find the stuff you want—or tap the Sources button at the top of the screen.

❸ When you finish, tap Done. Your playlist is ready to play.

To change a playlist, tap its name and tap the blue Edit button. You can put more tracks in the mix by tapping the Add Songs button.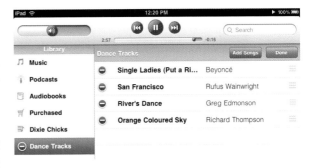

Note the "grip strip" at the right edge of the screen (≡). With your finger, drag these handles up or down to rearrange the order of songs in your playlist. When you finish, tap Done. You also see the universal iPad Delete symbol (⊖). Tap it, and then tap the Delete confirmation button on the right side, to remove a song from the playlist—but not from the iPad. Note the ⊖ next to the playlist name in the Library list. Tap it to whack the whole playlist.

Make Genius Playlists on the iPad

Apple's *Genius* feature in iTunes and on the iPad analyzes your music collection and automatically generates Genius Playlists and Genius Mixes for you. These are sets of songs (or in the case of the Mixes, entire musical genres) that are supposed to sound good together.

The iPad automatically generates Genius Mixes; they appear in the Library list when you have enough music to collect into genres. Click the Genius Mixes icon to see them. Genius Playlists are a little more personalized, because they require you to choose the first song, which inspires the Genius to select other songs that go with it.

❶ Tap the ✸ icon at the bottom of the iPod window. When the Songs list appears, tap the track you want to use as the playlist foundation.

❷ The Genius whips together a song set. If you don't like the resulting mix, tap the Refresh button atop the screen to get new tunes.

❸ If you love the work of the Genius, select or tap the Save option at the top of the screen. Tap New to start over again.

To delete a Genius playlist, select it in the Library list and tap Delete. As in iTunes, Genius playlists are named after the song you chose as the foundation for your mix. When you sync the iPad with iTunes, the Genius playlists get copied back over to iTunes. You can't delete them from the iPad after they sync with iTunes; you have to trash them from the iTunes side of the USB cable and resync computer to tablet to get them off the iPad.

 Tip If your currently playing song is totally the vibe you want for a playlist, you can summon the Genius from the Now Playing screen (page 220). Just tap the screen to call up the playback controls; then tap the electron-shaped Genius icon in the lower-middle part of the screen.

14

Watch Videos

Apple started putting video-playback powers on its iPods back in 2005. Over the past five years, the devices' screen sizes have gradually increased from 2.5 inches on that very first video iPod to the iPad's majestic 9.7 inches of high-resolution, backlit real estate. It's perfect for immersing yourself in the movie in your hand—or watching it inflight with your spouse on a shared pair of headphones while crammed into a couple of knee-knocking coach seats.

You and your iPad can get video in all sorts of ways. You can use iTunes to buy, rent, or stream movies, TV shows, music videos, and video podcasts; download iPad apps from the App Store; tap websites via Safari, and load the iPad's built-in YouTube application (discussed back in Chapter 6).

And if the whole family wants to watch a video, you can connect your iPad to your TV and move to an even bigger screen.

From getting video content onto your tablet to sharing it once it's there, this chapter guides you through one of the most fun parts of the iPad experience.

Get Video on Your iPad

Depending on what you want to watch and where you want to watch it, you can get movies moving on your iPad screen in a variety of ways. Here are the common methods of video acquisition:

- **The iTunes Store, desktop edition.** You can shop the iTunes Store in your computer's window, browsing through the hundreds of movies, TV shows, video podcasts, and music videos offered for sale or rent (page 168 gives you an overview). When you click to buy or rent a video, iTunes downloads the file to your computer. Plug in the iPad and transfer the video with a quick sync (page 176).

- **The iTunes Store, iPad edition.** You can also buy video directly from your iPad. Tap the purple iTunes icon on the iPad's Home screen, browse until you find what you want, and click to buy or rent the video. (Video podcasts and iTunes U content are free). The file downloads to your iPad, where you can find it by tapping the Videos icon on the Home screen. Video files you buy on the iPad (except for rented videos) get synced back to the iTunes library the next time you plug in the iPad.

- **Video-streaming apps.** With a speedy and steady Internet connection, you can skip the iPad-drive bloat and stream video with apps like the free ABC Player (shown at right). Here, you can watch recent episodes of the network's popular prime-time shows—with commercials, alas. The App Store also hosts the iPad version of Netflix. The ubiquitous movie-rental company streams full-length theatrical films to the iPad with a paid monthly membership of $9 to $17 (go to *www.netflix.com*).

- **Video-streaming websites.** While many videos on the YouTube website (*not* the iPad's YouTube app) use Flash and so won't work on the iPad, other sites use QuickTime for video clips (page 60), and they will. And as the Internet switches to new web-page coding technology, sites using the new HTML5 standard will have iPad-compatible video streams, too.

Your video options will only increase as the iTunes Store adds more stuff, video apps continue to pop up in the App Store, and more sites move to HTML5.

Transfer Video from iTunes to iPad

Chapter 11 gives you the lowdown on moving all kinds of files between iTunes and your trusty iPad. If you don't feel like flipping back, here's a quick summary:

- **Synchronization.** Connect your iPad to your computer and click its icon under Devices in iTunes. Click the Movies tab and turn on the "Sync movies" checkbox. You can also choose to sync only certain movies to your tablet. If you have TV programs in your iTunes library, click the TV Shows tab and adjust your syncing preferences there. Ditto for video podcasts on the Podcasts tab.

- **Manual management.** Click the appropriate library in iTunes' Source list (Movies, TV Shows, Podcasts, etc.), and then drag the files you want from the main iTunes window onto your connected iPad's icon.

The iTunes Store is chock-full of videos, but sometimes you want to add your own flicks to your iTunes library. No problem, just drag the file from your desktop and drop it anywhere in iTunes' main window, or choose File→"Add to Library" to locate and import your files. Once you get videos into iTunes, you can play them there or copy them to your iPad.

Another way to add files to iTunes is to drag them into the Automatically Add to iTunes folder. This clever folder analyzes what you put inside it, and—based on the file extension—shelves it in the right spot for you.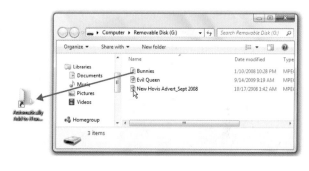
You find the auto-folder not through iTunes, but by navigating your system files. In Windows, it's usually in C:/Music→iTunes→iTunes Media→Automatically Add to iTunes (Home→Music→iTunes→iTunes Media→Automatically Add to iTunes). If iTunes can't match a file, it dumps it into a Not Added subfolder.

> **Tip** The iPad can play video in razor-sharp high-definition formats, but as members of the AV Club know, a few different resolutions are considered "HD video." The iPad can play only HD video at a resolution known as 720p. While many movie lovers have digital video files in higher resolutions, like 1080p, iTunes won't transfer those files to the iPad unless you convert them to the lower 720p resolution. So how do you do that? See page 234 for a list of video-conversion programs. And if you find all these numbers confusing, see *http://www.geek.com/hdtv-buyers-guide/resolution/* for more on HDTV screen resolutions.

Find and Play Videos on the iPad

To play a video on the iPad, tap open the Home screen's Videos icon. On the Videos screen, tap the type of video you want to watch: Movies, TV Shows, or Podcasts. On the next screen, find the movie or  episode you want to watch and tap the title or Play button to start the show.

But how do you run the show on an iPad that has no physical controls? Easy; the playback buttons are *on the screen*.

When you watch video, *anything* else on the screen distracts you, so Apple hides these controls. Tap the screen once to make them appear, and again to make them disappear. Here's what they do:

- **Done.** Tap this blue button, in the top-left corner, to stop playback and return to your master list of videos.

- **Scroll slider.** This progress indicator at the top of the screen displays the elapsed time, the remaining time, and a little white, round handle that you can drag to jump forward or backward in a video.

- **Widescreen/Full Screen.** See the little ⬓ or ⬚ button in the top-right corner of the screen? Tap it to adjust the zoom level of the video, as described below.

- **Play/Pause (▶/‖).** These buttons do the same thing during video playback as they do during music playback: they alternate between playing and pausing your media.

- **Previous, Next (◀◀, ▶▶).** Hold down your finger to rewind or fast-forward the video. The longer you hold, the faster the zipping. (When you fast-forward, you even get to hear the sped-up audio for a few seconds.)

  If you're watching a movie you bought from the iTunes Store, you may be surprised to discover that it comes with predefined chapter markers, just like DVDs do. Internally, your movie is divided into scenes. Tap the ◀◀ or ▶▶ buttons to skip to the previous or next chapter marker.

- **Volume.** You can drag the round, white handle of this scroll bar (bottom of the screen) to adjust playback volume.

 And if you're watching a video that has multiple audio tracks, subtitles, or closed captioning, tap the playback control icon shown at the left to get to the settings for those extra features.

Zoom/Unzoom Video

The iPad's screen is bright, vibrant, and stunningly sharp. (It's got 1,024×768 pixels, crammed so tightly together that there are 132 of them per inch.) It's okay for old-fashioned TV shows with the squarish 4:3 ratio, but the screen is not the right proportion for widescreen movies and HDTV shows. So when you watch movies, you wind up with *horizontal* letterbox bars above and below the picture.

Some people can't stand these bars. You're already watching a comparatively small screen, so why sacrifice precious real estate to black bars?

Fortunately, the iPad gives you a choice. If you double-tap the video as it plays, you zoom in, magnifying the image so that it fills the entire screen. If the playback controls are visible, you can also tap ⬓ or ⬚ .

Truth is, part of the image is now off the screen; you're not seeing the entire composition as originally created. You lose the top and bottom of TV scenes, and the left and right edges of movie scenes. If this effect winds up chopping off something important—say some text on the screen—restoring the original letterbox view is just a double-tap away.

Play iPad Videos on Your TV

Movies on the iPad are great, but watching them on a bigger screen is often even more gratifying—especially if everyone in the house wants to watch, too. In case you were wondering, you *can* put all those movies and videos up on your TV screen— you just need to connect your iPad to your television set. *What* you connect them with depends on the hardware involved.

Modern TV sets, (and those fancy AV receivers that connect all the components in your entertainment center) usually offer a few types of video ports for connecting new gear. The ports your iPad works with include component and composite connections, as well as VGA, which you can connect to a TV or a projector. But to output the iPad's video signal to the big screen, you need to buy a cable that connects to the iPad's Dock Connector port. (Make sure the cable is intended for the iPad.)

The easiest place to find these cables is the Apple Store (*store.apple.com*). Here, you can find the Apple Composite AV Cable for TVs with older video inputs. You can also find the Apple Component AV Cable, made for high-end TVs and widescreen sets that can handle higher-quality video and audio connections. Both versions of the cable cost about $50, but that includes an integrated AC adapter to make sure your iPad is powered for a whole-weekend movie marathon.

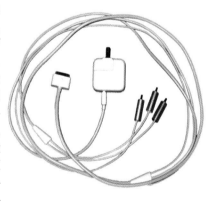

Apple's Dock Connector-to-VGA adapter sells for $29. And if you want to perch your 'Pad on a stand, the iPad Dock has a port for these AV cables; it sells for $29 as well. Third-party docks and cables are also out there.

 Tip What your video to remember its position when you pause or stop it? Easy. On the iPad, just tap the Home screen, then the Settings icon. On the Settings screen, tap Video and next to Start Playing, select Where Left Off.

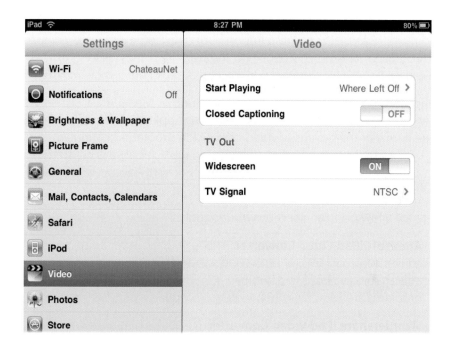

The iPad senses when it's connected to a TV set and automatically pipes the video feed to the big screen, but there are some settings you can adjust at Home→Settings→Video. You can turn on closed captioning subtitles for videos that include text descriptions on the screen. You can also flip the On button next to Widescreen if you don't want your widescreen movies squashed into the 4:3 aspect ratio for older TV sets. And if you travel internationally, pick your TV Signal. Choose NTSC if you live in the U.S. or Japan, pick PAL if you're connecting to a European or Australian TV set.

Once you get the iPad hooked up to play movies, be sure to select the alternate video source on your television set, just as you would to play a DVD or game. Then call up the video from the iPad's library, press the Play button, pop up the corn, and enjoy the show from big screen to bigger screen.

 Tip When watching shows on the iPad, you'll notice it displays the video whether you're holding it it landscape or portrait mode. The horizontal landscape view is better for high-quality video, but if you've got some blurrier, low-quality clips in your collection, watching it in portrait mode makes it look a little better since it's not getting blown up to the wider screen size.

Video Formats That Work on the iPad

As described in Chapter 11, the iTunes Store now sells movies, TV shows, and music videos. You can also import your own home movies, downloaded movie trailers, and other videos into the iPad via iTunes, as long as the files have one of these file extensions at the end of their name: *.mov*, *.m4v*, or *.mp4*.

Other common video formats, like *.avi* or Windows Media Video (*.wmv*), won't play in iTunes, but you can convert them with Apple's $30 QuickTime Pro software or any of the dozens of video-conversion programs floating around the Web. (If you're unsure whether a file's compatible, it's always worth trying to drag it into iTunes' main window and then choosing Advanced→"Create iPad or Apple TV Version".)

Here are a few popular video-conversion tools:

- **Aneesoft iPad Video Converter**. Aneesoft offers several video and DVD conversion programs for both Windows and Mac OS X systems. Free trial editions are available to download from the site and full versions of the programs are $30 or less. (*www.aneesoft.com*)

- **Wondershare iPad Video Converter.** Based in China, Wondershare offers two separate $30 conversion programs for Windows: one for DVDs and one for other types of video files. (*www.wondershare.com*)

- **HandBrake.** Available in versions for Windows and Mac OS X, this easy-to-use bit of freeware converts DVD movies and other files for everything from iPods to the Apple TV. (When converting for the iPad, go for the higher-quality settings for bigger  screens—using the iPod setting may lead to a fuzzy picture when blown up to iPad size.) You can get HandBrake at *http://handbrake.fr*.

> **Tip** Movies and TV shows get their own libraries in the iTunes Source list. If you import a video yourself and it's in the wrong place in the Source list, you may need to tweak the file's labeling info. Open the file's Get Info box (Ctrl+I [⌘-I]), click the Options tab, and then assign it a video format from the Video Kind drop-down menu: Music Video, Movie, TV Show, Podcast, or iTunes U file.

Delete Videos

Having a personal movie library with you at all times is great, but if there's one thing about high-quality video files, it's that they're *huge*. Sure, movie rentals from iTunes delete themselves when they expire, but what about your regular collection? A long movie can take almost up to two gigabytes of your limited iPad drive space. And if you're traveling with a full iPad and want to download a fresh flick for the plane, what do you do?

Fortunately, you *can* delete video files directly off the tablet—without having to link the iPad to the computer and turn off checkboxes to "unsync" files by way of iTunes. (However, removing the files this way is another way to regain some space, with the added advantage that the video files stay safely in your computer's iTunes library, ready for you to sync to your iPad again should you want it back.)

When you're ready to lose a movie or two, go to the iPad's Videos area and tap open the category for the relevant file. Press your finger down on the icon until the ❸ appears on the corner (circled). Tap the ❸ and in the box that pops up, tap Delete (or Cancel, if you have second thoughts). The selected video goes *poof!* off the iPad. If you synced it from your computer through iTunes, a copy is still there and you can sync it back to the iPad later if you miss it.

 Pay attention to what you're deleting. If you accidentally delete an unwatched or unfinished movie-rental download on the iPad, it's gone for good. You have to rent the whole thing all over again if you want to see it. And remember, you can rent movies in iTunes on the computer and transfer them to the iPad, but you can't sync a movie you rented on the iPad back to iTunes.

15

View and Manage Photos

With its big glossy screen and wide black border, you could easily mistake the iPad for one of those digital picture frames designed to sit on the mantle and let proud parents show off an ever-running slideshow of their kids and pets. The iPad is no imposter here—it *can* serve as a digital picture frame when you want it to. But it can also do so much more.

The thin little iPad can replace stacks and stacks of paper-based photo albums. It can show your photos on a map, based on where you shot them. It lets you email your favorite snaps to friends. And with the right kind of audio-video cable, it can even play your pictures on the big screen for the whole room—making it the Kodak Carousel of the 21st century.

A picture may be worth a thousand words, but when your friends see what you can do with photos on the iPad, you may hear a few thousand more.

Get Pictures onto Your iPad

The iPad can display your handsome photographs in most of the file formats digital cameras use, including JPEG, PNG, TIFF, GIF, and even those large, uncompressed RAW files favored by serious photographers who don't want to squish a pixel of precious image data. But to show them off on the iPad, you have to first get them *on* the iPad. There are several ways you can do that.

Transfer Photos with iTunes

If you keep your digital photo collection organized in programs like Adobe Photoshop Elements, iPhoto, or Aperture—or even loose in a folder on your hard drive—you can sling them onto the iPad with an iTunes syncing session. Chapter 11 has general information on using and syncing iPad content using iTunes, but here's what you need to do for photos:

❶ Connect your iPad to your PC or Mac with the iPad's USB cable.

❷ Once the iPad shows up in the iTunes Source list, click its icon to select it.

❸ In the iTunes tabs for your iPad, click the one for Photos, the last tab over.

❹ Turn on the checkbox next to "Sync photos from" and then choose your photo program or photo-storage folder; that lets iTunes know where to find your pix. You can copy everything over or just the *albums* (sets of pictures) you select. If you don't use any of the programs that the "Sync photos from" menu lists and you just want to copy over a folder of random photos from your hard drive, select

"Choose folder" from the menu and then navigate to the desired folder.

❺ Click Sync (or Apply, if this is your first time syncing photos) after you make your selections.

Once you start the sync, iTunes "optimizes" your photos. This has nothing to do with your photographic skills and everything to do with storage space. If necessary, iTunes down-samples your pix to "TV quality" so they take up less room on your 'Pad but still display in high-res format on your tablet or TV screen.

> You can only sync photos from one computer to the iPad. If you try to sync with another machine's photo library, iTunes erases all the pix from the first computer.

Transfer Photos from Mail Messages

Do you have a bunch of photos someone sent you as file attachments to an email message? Or do you see an image on a web page you want to add to your collection? To add these pictures to your iPad's Photos program, press your finger on the photo when the iPad displays it. Wait for a box to pop up with a Save Image button. Tap Save Image to store a copy of the picture in the Photos→Saved Photos

album, where you can admire it. If you have multiple photos attached to an email message, the iPad asks if you want to save them all.

Transfer Photos with the iPad Camera Connection Kit

The iPad can slurp pictures directly off of your digital camera, but there's a catch: you first have to plunk down $29 for Apple's iPad Camera Connection Kit at *store.apple.com* or other fine retail establishments.

The kit contains two white plastic adapters for the iPad's Dock Connector port. One has a jack for your camera's USB cable and the other has a slot for Secure Digital memory cards full of pictures—in case you don't have your camera's USB cable. (While the USB adapter only *officially* works with cameras, some USB keyboards and headsets have been known to *unofficially* work.)

Once you plug an adapter into the iPad and connect the camera via USB cable —or insert the memory card—wait for the Photos app to open, and then:

❶ Tap Import All to grab all the pictures, or tap individual shots to check-mark them before you tap the Import button.

❷ When the iPad asks, decide if you want to *keep* or *delete* the photos on the camera or memory card after you import them.

❸ To see the new arrivals on your iPad, tap Photos→Last Import.

Unplug the iPad camera connector and put it in a safe place. When you get back to your computer, you can sync these pictures back to iPhoto or Adobe Photoshop Elements by connecting the iPad and using your picture program's command to import the new photos.

> **Tip** You can also import photos to your iPad from your iPhone. Connect the iPad to the phone with that familiar USB-to-Dock Connector cable and follow the steps above.

Find Pictures on Your iPad

Now that you've copied some pictures onto your iPad, it's time to locate them on that big, shiny Slab of Joy. Go to the Home screen and tap the Photos icon.

The iPad organizes your picture collection in up to five ways—if you happen to use all the features of iPhoto '09 on the Mac. After you open the iPad's Photos app, tap the buttons at the top of the window (circled) to see the ways you can sort your photos:

- **Photos.** This view displays thumbnails of all your pictures lumped together one place. If you didn't group your images into albums before you transferred them, they show up all together here.

- **Albums.** If you did tick off boxes for individual albums in the iTunes window, tap the Albums button to see those picture sets grouped under the same names as they were in your PC or Mac photo program.

- **Events.** Mac folks using recent versions of iPhoto or Aperture can also sort photos into Events. (Events are a way iPhoto automatically organizes images, like pictures taken on the same day.) Tap the Events button on the iPad to see any of these sets synced from the Mac.

- **Faces.** Apple introduced a face-recognition feature in iPhoto '09 that automatically groups photos based on the people in them. If you use this feature on the Mac, iTunes gives you the option to sync entire albums of just one person. Then you can find your Cate or Zachary photo sets when you tap the Faces button on the iPad.

- **Places.** If you geo-tag your photos—by shooting them with a GPS-enabled camera or by manually placing them on a map with tools in iPhoto '09—your pictures appear in the Places area based on their geographic coordinates. Tap Places to see your photo sets stuck to a world map with virtual red push-pins.

In album form, your picture sets look like a stack of loose photographs clumped in a sloppy pile. Tap one of the piles with a fingertip and the photos disperse and snap into grid where you can see each one as a small thumbnail image. If you're not quite sure what photo is in which album pile, pinch and spread your fingers over a pile to see a quick animated preview of its contents without opening the album all the way.

Tip Want to take a snap of some cool thing on your iPad's screen? Hold down the Home button and press the Sleep/Wake button as thought it were a camera shutter. The resulting screenshot lands in Photos→Saved Photos. You can transfer it back to your computer the next time you sync. In fact, if your computer has a program that senses when you connect a digital camera, it will likely leap up and offer to pull in the iPad's screenshots just as it would regular photos.

View Pictures on Your iPad

To see the pictures you synced from your computer, tap the Photos icon on the iPad's Home screen. Then tap the Photos button at the top of the screen to see your pictures in thumbnail view, filling the iPad screen in a grid. If you chose to copy over specific photo albums, tap the name of the album you want to look at. Mac syncers can also tap the Events, Faces, or Places button to see photos sorted in those categories, as page 240 explains.

On the thumbnails screen, you can do several things:

- Tap a photo thumbnail to see it full-size on the iPad screen.

- Double-tap an open photo to magnify it.

- Spread and pinch your fingers on-screen (those fancy moves described in Chapter 2) to zoom in and out of a photo. Drag your finger around on-screen to pan through a zoomed-in photo.

- Flick your finger horizontally across the screen in either direction to scroll through your pictures at high speeds. You can show off your vacation photos really fast this way (your friends will thank you).

- Rotate the iPad to have horizontal photos fill the width of the screen or to have vertical photos fill its height.

- With a photo open, tap the iPad's glass to display a strip of itsy-bitsy thumbnails of all the photos in the current album at the bottom of the screen. Tap or slide to a thumbnail to jump to a particular picture.

When you tap the ⤴ icon in the menu bar, you can set a photo as wallpaper (page 248), assign a picture to your iPad's Contact's program (page 91), send a pic to MobileMe (page 254), or start a photo slideshow (page 244).

To get back to your library, tap the Photos or album-name button at the top of the screen.

Email Photos

If you want to share your photographic joy, you can email one or a bunch of pictures right from the Photos program:

- **One photo.** To email the photo currently on-screen, tap the iPad's glass to make the photo controls appear, and then tap the ✉ icon in the upper-right corner. Tap the Email Photo button. The mail program attaches the photo to a new message, ready for you to address.

- **Multiple photos.** To email a bunch of pictures at once, tap open the album containing the photos. Tap the ✉ icon in the top-right corner and then tap the pictures you want to send (blue checkmarks appear in the corner of the thumbnails to show you've selected them). Tap the Email button to attach them to a new message. If you have a draft message in progress, tap the Copy button, then switch to the mail program, open your message, and hold down your finger until the Paste button appears. Tap it to paste in the pictures.

Delete Photos

You have two ways to delete photos from your iPad. If you synced photo albums from iTunes, connect the iPad to the computer, open iTunes, hit the Photos tab, and turn off the checkboxes by those albums. Click Apply and then Sync to "unsync," or remove, those pix from the iPad's gallery.

If you have pictures in your Saved Photos album you want to ditch, you can delete a currently open picture by tapping the 🗑 icon and then tapping the Delete Photo button. To delete multiple pictures from the Saved Photos thumbnail view, tap the ✉ icon, then tap the unwanted pictures to assign the Blue Checkmarks of Selection. Tap the small red Delete button on the top-left side of the menu bar. There's a blue Cancel button on the other side of the menu bar if you change your mind.

Play Slideshows on Your iPad

A photo slideshow takes all the photo tap-and-drag work out of your hands, freeing you up to sit back and admire your pictures without distraction. To run a slideshow on an iPad, you need to set up a few things, like how long each photo appears on-screen and what music accompanies your photo parade.

The iPad keeps its slideshow settings in two different places. All of the timing and ordering options are in the iPad's general Settings area. To get there, tap Settings→Photos. Here, you can choose:

- **Play Each Slide For...** Pick the amount of time you want a picture to stay on the screen. You can choose 2, 3, 5, 10, or 20 seconds (for those photography buffs with really long attention spans).

- **Repeat.** Tap this setting to On if you want the slideshow to keep looping, starting over after it plays through the first time.

- **Shuffle.** If you want to randomly mix up the order of the pictures in an album, tap the On button next to "Shuffle".

Now that you have these matters worked out, go back to the Photos app and tap open the album you want to present as a slideshow. On the upper-right side of the menu bar, tap the Slideshow button. As you can see from the illustration above, the Slideshow Options box unfolds. Here, you can choose:

- **Music.** If you want to set your show to music, tap the On button next to Play Music. Next, tap Music and in the box that appears, select a song from any of the tunes you've synced to the iPad.

- **The transition effect between photos.** Dissolves, wipes, and all the usual razzle-dazzle styles are here.

Once you make all your selections, you're ready for showtime. Tap the Start Slideshow button. To stop the show, tap the iPad screen.

 If you plan to do a lot of slideshows, consider getting an iPad dock or a folding case that lets you prop the Pad up at a nice hands-free viewing angle.

Play Slideshows on Your TV

Flip back to the previous chapter if you need help connecting your iPad to a television set so you can view your digital goodies on the big screen.

Once you make the iPad-TV link, you're almost ready to start the show. You need to adjust a few more things on the iPad.

❶ Tap Settings→Video. When you connect an Apple-approved AV cable to the iPad, your slideshow automatically appears on your TV set instead of on your tablet. In the TV Out section here, you can toggle Widescreen On or Off, depending on the type of TV screen you have.

❷ In the TV Signal area, select your local television broadcast standard. If you're in North America or Japan, choose NTSC. If you're in Europe or Australia, choose PAL.

> **Tip** If you wrangle your picture collection in iPhoto '09 on the Mac, you can export your intricately crafted and scored iPhoto slideshows as little movies sized up just for the iPad—and put them right into iTunes. Select a slideshow in iPhoto and click the Export button. In the "Export your slideshow" box that appears, turn on the checkbox for Medium or Large (the preferred settings for iPad viewing) and make sure you turn on the checkbox next to "Automatically send slideshow to iTunes". Click the Export button. To actually complete the transfer, connect your iPad to your computer and click the Movies tab on the iPad preferences screen in iTunes. Select the slideshow and sync away.

❸ Turn on your TV and select the video input source for the iPad. You select the input for the iPad's signal the same way you tell your TV to display the signal from a DVD player or videogame console. Typically, you press the Input or Display button on your TV's remote to change from the live TV signal to the new video source.

❹ On the iPad, navigate to the album you want.
Press the Slideshow button in the menu bar at the top of the screen, tap the Start Slideshow button, and the show begins.

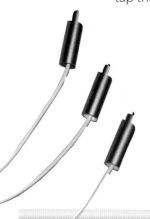

Tip Apple sells its own AV cables (shown at left) for either component or composite video connections between the iPad and the input jacks on your TV or AV receiver. The cables are $49 each at *store.apple.com*. If you want to hook up the iPad to a TV, computer monitor, or projector that uses a VGA connection, you need the $29 Dock Connector to VGA Adapter—also conveniently available in Apple's stores.

Change the iPad's Wallpaper

The iPad comes pre-stocked with several gorgeous high-resolution photos—mostly of nature scenes and textured patterns to use as background images for both the Lock and Home screens. (In case you're wondering what the difference is, the Lock screen is the one you see when you first turn on the iPad, and the Home screen has all your app icons scattered about.)

If you want to change these background images to spice things up, you can assign new photos in two ways.

The first is to go to the Home screen and tap Settings→Brightness & Wallpaper. Tap the appropriate Wallpaper icon (circled). On the next screen, choose a photo from any of your photo albums, or tap Wallpaper to pick a new Apple stock shot. Tap the photo you want to use. You can drag the image around and finger-pinch and spread to shrink or enlarge the parts of the picture you want to display.

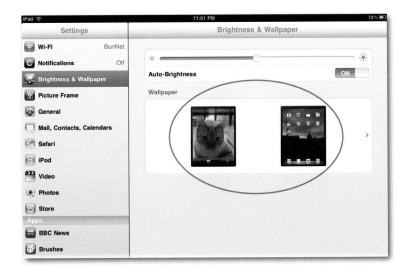

When you're done, tap the appropriate button at the top. You have your choice of Set Lock Screen, Set Home Screen, or Set Both. You can also bail out with a Cancel button in the left corner.

The second way to wallpaper your 'Pad is to pick a picture out of one of the iPad's photo albums and tap the 🖼 at the top of the screen, then tap the Save as Wallpaper option. Here, you can size and save the photo with the methods mentioned above. No matter which way you choose to change it, there's nothing like fresh new wallpaper to personalize your iPad—and show off your own photography.

Turn the iPad into a Picture Frame

As mentioned at the beginning of this chapter, the iPad does resemble a digital picture frame. And if you really *want* one of those, you can turn its Lock screen into a 10-inch window that displays your photo collection, a pleasant diversion as the iPad recharges from a wall outlet.

❶ Go to the Home screen and tap Settings→Picture Frame.

❷ Pick the type of transition between photos you want to use—either the traditional Hollywood-style "Dissolve" or Apple's new foldy-paper "Origami" animation.

❸ At the bottom of the Settings screen, choose the album of images you want to use—or just let the iPad grab all the photos you added to it.

 To test out your framed slideshow, press the Sleep/Wake button to turn off the iPad screen and press it again to get back to the Lock screen. Tap the small flower icon next to the lock slider to start the slideshow. If you want to pause the pictures, tap the iPad's screen. You can either swipe the slider to unlock the iPad and go back to work, or tap the flower icon again to resume the show.

Note If you're a Mac user with iPhoto '09 and you've used the Faces feature to identify and tag the kissers in your pictures, the Picture Frame program will zoom in to show off those faces in close-up shots. It only works with the traditional "Dissolve" transition, though.

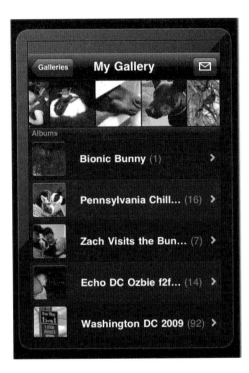

Sync Up with MobileMe

E ven though your iPad is a cool personal media center, under the hood, it's a computer (a sleek one, yes, but a computer nonetheless). Odds are, you have another one or two computers in your life—at work, at home, or both. You may have an iPhone, too. Each of these devices can send and receive email, store contact information, keep track of your appointments, and save website bookmarks. Wouldn't it be great if all these gadgets could share the same information, and you could keep them constantly up-to-date?

That's where Apple's MobileMe service comes in. For an annual subscription fee of $100, MobileMe keeps your personal information in sync across all your gadgets: iPad, iPhone, iPod Touch, PC, and Mac—or any combination thereof. If you update a phone number in the iPad's Contacts program, MobileMe pushes that change out to your iPhone and Windows computer at home—saving you the trouble of both *remembering* to do it then actually doing it. Pretty nifty, eh?

But that's not all MobileMe does. You also get an email account, a photo-sharing service, and a bunch of remote storage. Turn the page to get the details.

Sign Up for MobileMe

First, a little bit more about MobileMe. For one, it's not an Internet service provider that gives you Internet access—you still have to pay your cable or DSL company for that. Instead, it's an Internet *service* that syncs your email, contacts, calendars, and bookmarks to keep your info up-to-date on all your devices in the programs you use to manage mail and personal information.

On the PC side, MobileMe works with Outlook 2007 and 2003, Outlook Express, and Windows Mail, and you can bookmark sites from Internet Explorer or Safari. On the Mac side, you can sync data from the Mac OS X Address Book, iCal, and Safari.

When you sign up, you get an *@me.com* email address. MobileMe automatically keeps all your me.com mailboxes current across your iPad, iPhone, and computers, no matter whether you read them on the Web or in your dedicated mail program. (MobileMe can also receive mail from other POP-based mail accounts and deposit them in their own folder so you can read them and know which account they came from—but it doesn't synchronize these non-Me accounts across all your devices.)

You also get an online photo and video gallery, and a chunk of space on Apple's servers called an iDisk, where you can back up or share large files. You start out with 20 gigabytes of room, but Apple will gladly sell you more—doubling that to 40 gigabytes, for example, costs another $49 a year.

So how do you get started with MobileMe? Easy. Connect your iPad to your computer and click the Info tab in iTunes. In the MobileMe area, click the Learn More button (Windows) or Set Up Now (Mac).

iTunes whisks you away to MobileMe's sign-up area, where you supply your credit-card number, pick out a user name and password, and download any necessary software, like the MobileMe control panel for Windows. (You can also sign up and road-test it for free for 60 days at *www.apple.com/mobileme*).

Once you're all signed up and have that software installed, it's time to set up your computer and then your iPad. The next page explains how to do both.

Set Up MobileMe on a PC or Mac

Now that you have a MobileMe account to sync data between your machines, you have to tell MobileMe *what* you want to sync.

❶ In Windows, choose Start→Control Panel→Network and Internet→ MobileMe. On a Mac, choose →System Preferences→MobileMe.

❷ Click the Account tab and sign in with your user name and password.

❸ Click the Sync tab. Turn on the checkbox next to "Sync with MobileMe" and choose how often you want your MobileMe data pushed out to your iPad (and any other computer you plan to use with the service). Most people choose the "Automatically" option.

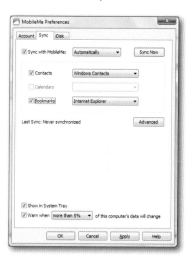

❹ Next, choose the info on your computer, like email, contacts, appointments, and bookmarks, that you want to sync to your iPad (and other devices) .

❺ Click The Sync Now button to upload the info on your computer to Apple's servers.

Click OK to close the box. All right, that part's done. Now you need to set up the iPad to accept all the data that MobileMe will send it.

Set Up MobileMe on the iPad

❶ On the iPad, choose Settings→Mail, Contacts, Calendars.

❷ Tap Fetch New Data. On the next screen, make sure you set the Push option to On.

❸ In the line above Fetch New Data, tap Add Account, choose MobileMe, and fill in your MobileMe user name and password.

❹ Turn on Mail, Contacts, Calendars, and Bookmarks. You can even activate Find My iPad—which maps the location of a lost or stolen tablet on *www.me.com* if it's within range of a 3G or known Wi-Fi network.

Use the MobileMe Gallery

The life-synchronization function is just one of MobileMe's features. Subscribers also get an elegantly designed online gallery to showcase their favorite digital photos and videos, with easy, built-in tools for uploading new media.

From your Windows PC or Mac, you can post your favorite snaps and clips on MobileMe for all to see. That way, you save your relatives tons of time and hard drive space by *not* having to download huge email attachments. (And if these are personal family photos, you can even password-protect them.)

Creating an album in the Gallery and filling it with images is easy. Here's how:

❶ Find some photos or videos on your computer you'd like to share.

❷ Log into your MobileMe account on the Web at *www.me.com.*

❸ Click on the Gallery icon (it looks like a perky sunflower).

❹ When the Gallery page appears, click the little plus (+) button at the bottom of the column on the left side (circled) to add a new photo album. The Album settings screen appears, asking you to name the album and to set up permissions for what viewers can do there, like download your photos or upload theirs (which is useful when everybody at the family reunion brought their own camera).

❺ Click the Create button to add the new album to the Gallery.

❻ On the next screen, click the green arrow. In the box that pops up, click the Choose button and navigate to the photos on your computer. Click the names of photos you want to add to the new album. Hold down the Ctrl (or ⌘) keys to grab multiple files as you click.

❼ Click the Select button to start the upload. You can upload images in the JPEG, GIF, or PNG formats and video in the MOV format, but nothing bigger than one gigabyte in size. For on-screen display, MobileMe resizes images larger than 6 megapixels, but this doesn't affect the originals.

Another advantage of putting your photos and videos on MobileMe is that you can view them on your iPad over its Internet connection, which is especially handy if you have a lot of photos and, say, a 16-gigabyte iPad. Why devote some of that precious space to photos and videos when you can store them online and look at them *there*, through the iPad's Web connection? You'll end up with more room on your iPad for music, movies, and apps.

And speaking of apps, you can download a Gallery app from the iTunes App Store to make it even easier to see your pictures and videos. Rather than fire up Safari and jump to your MobileMe page through the Web all the time, use an app right on your iPad to view and share your online media.

To get the Gallery app, tap the App Store icon on the iPad's Home screen. Then tap the Search button and look for *Gallery*. It's free for MobileMe subscribers. When the app appears, tap it and tap the Free button, and then the Install button. (When the iPad debuted, Gallery was still a runty-screen iPhone app and may be still, depending on Apple.)

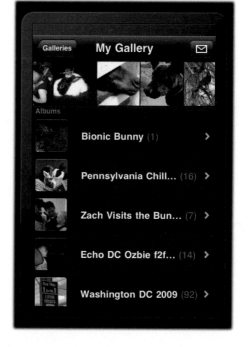

Once you install the app, tap it open and type in your MobileMe account name and password. You'll see all your uploaded albums and videos listed. Samples from your collection crawl across the top of the screen.

You can share Gallery items with friends by tapping the envelope icon in the top-right corner of the screen. This opens a Mail message with a link to your Gallery or a particular album, ready for your pals' email addresses.

Tip If you use iPhoto '08 and iMovie '08 (or later), you can publish photos and videos right to your MobileMe Gallery from within either program. When it comes time to show off your stuff, select the photos, album, or movie you want and choose Share→MobileMe Gallery to start the trip to the Web.

Use iDisk

In addition to photo- and video-sharing online, MobileMe gives you a personal Internet-based file server called an iDisk. Need to back up some Microsoft Word files but don't have a flash drive handy? Want to make sure you can always get to a set of important PDF documents, whether you're at home or in a London hotel room? With iDisk, you get a set of private folders to hold your files that any Web-connected computer can retrieve.

From your computer, you can tap into your iDisk in a couple of ways:

- Open your browser and log in to *www.me.com*, and then click on the blue iDisk icon in the MobileMe toolbar.

- On a Mac, double-click the iDisk icon in the Finder sidebar.

- In Windows, you can add the iDisk as a network drive. In Windows XP, choose Start→Network→My Network Places and choose "Add a network place" in the next box. As the Add a Network Place wizard opens, go with "Choose another network connection" and when asked for a URL, type in *http://idisk.me.com/YourAccount/*, and then enter your MobileMe name and password.

   For Windows 7 and Vista, choose Start→Computer→Map a Network Drive. In the next box, pick a drive letter and in the Folder field, type in *http://idisk.me.com/YourAccount*. Turn on the checkbox for "Connect using different credentials/user name." Click Finish and type in your MobileMe name and password when prompted.

No matter how you get to your iDisk, you'll find a series of folders there with names like Documents, Pictures, and Public. You can upload and download files from these folders. From the Web, click the MobileMe toolbar button that looks like an upward-pointing arrow to upload files. You'll also see a button to download files.

If you have an iDisk icon in the Mac's Finder or Windows Explorer, just drag files on and off the iDisk from the desktop. For files too huge to email, put them in the iDisk's Public folder, click the Share File button, and send a clickable link to your friends so they can download the files.

The iDisk App on Your iPad

So yeah, MobileMe is great for the computer and all, but just what does it do for you on the iPad? Just as you can get a native iPad program for the MobileMe Gallery, so you can get a free iDisk app from the iTunes App Store. It gives you access to all the files you store online. Need to double-check something in an Excel spreadsheet or refer to a PDF manual? Tap the iDisk icon on the iPad's Home screen and browse your way through your MobileMe drive. This is especially helpful if you need to view a Microsoft Office file and don't have iWork (Chapter 10) installed on your iPad.

Away from your main computer but need to send that giant Word document to a colleague? The iDisk app, like its desktop counterpart, lets you share files. Open the file you want to send and tap the Share Files icon at the bottom of the screen (it looks like a dot with radio waves). The iPad's Mail program opens with a link to the file embedded in the body of the message, ready for your recipient's address.

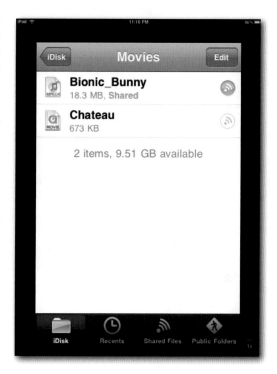

To stop sharing a file after you've sent out links, open the shared folder, tap the green Share icon on the right side, and then choose Stop Sharing from the menu that slides up.

 Tip By default, MobileMe's 20 gigabytes is split 50-50 between your @me.com email account and file storage for your gallery and iDisk. If you don't use the mail account much but really like to share photos, you can change this allocation to, say, 15 gigs for photos and 5 gigs for mail. Log into your account at *www.me.com*, click the Settings icon in the MobileMe toolbar, retype your password (for security), click the Settings button next to Mail and iDisk storage, and change the allocation.

iPad Settings

Despite its slim good looks, the iPad is still a computer. And like most computers, you can customize its settings to suit your needs. Need to tone down the screen brightness, turn on Bluetooth, or add a new email account? You do it all right in the iPad's Settings area. In fact, unless you go in there and poke around for a bit, you may have no idea how much of the iPad you can actually fiddle with—and that's what this chapter is for.

In addition to allowing you to tweak the way your iPad works, the Settings area also has *re*setting options you can use when the iPad isn't working so great (Appendix B has more on troubleshooting, by the way). So if you want to see where to find the controls for adjusting the iPad's date and time, turning off Location Services, or powering down the cellular chip in your Wi-Fi + 3G when the flight attendant tells you to, turn the page to start the Settings tour.

Tour the iPad Settings

To get to any of the Settings on the iPad, start on the Home screen and tap the Settings icon. The column on the left lists all the categories of stuff you can change, grouped under headings like Brightness & Wallpaper and Safari.

Tap an item name in the list to see all its preferences and settings on the right side of the screen. Then tap the relevant button, link, or label to get to the setting you want to change. To return to the main Settings area, tap the arrow button underneath the iPad's on-screen clock (circled).

Wi-Fi

Tap Wi-Fi on the Settings column to turn the iPad's wireless networking chip on or off. If you're outside a Wi-Fi zone, turning it off saves power and preserves battery life. If you're in a Wi-Fi zone with Wi-Fi set to On, the iPad sniffs around for your usual set of airwaves. If it can't find them, it lists any hot spots it does find and asks if you want to join one. Tap the name of a network to join it, or tap the ◉ to see the network's settings—or to Forget this Network entirely (remove it from your list of networks). To turn off the message bugging you to join a new network, choose Settings→Wi-Fi→Ask to Join Networks→Off.

Notifications

Certain applications, mainly social-networking programs, can *push* notifications to your iPad, even when you're not actively using the program. This basically means that they nag you with a sound or text alert when someone does something like post a comment on your Facebook wall. You might also see a *badge* alert notification—that number in a little red circle on an app's Home screen icon.

Push notifications can help keep you up-to-date, but all that notifying can run down the iPad's battery more quickly. The type of notification available depends on the app, but to use them, tap Settings→Notifications→On, then tap the name of the application and choose how you want it to notify you, usually by Sound, Alert, or Badge.

 Note The settings for the Wi-Fi and the Wi-Fi + 3G iPads differ slightly. If you see a setting listed here that you don't see on your iPad screen, odds are you either have the other type of iPad or an iPad system software update has changed things.

Airplane Mode (Wi-Fi + 3G iPads Only)

Anybody who's been on a commercial flight in the past 10 years knows the drill: just before the plane takes off, the cabin crew asks all the passengers to turn off their cellphones and electronic devices to avoid interfering with the airplane's own instruments. Yes, you have to turn the iPad off, including its cellular 3G chip that connects you to the Internet (and make sure your tray table is in the upright and locked position). So choose Settings→Airplane Mode→On to comply with the captain's orders. A tiny airplane icon at the top of the iPad's screen lets you know Airplane Mode is on.

Switching Airplane Mode to On turns *off* your iPad's link to the Internet and its GPS functions. However, you can still use the device to read downloaded iBooks, listen to music, type up Notes and documents, and do other non-Net activities—once the cabin crew says it's OK to turn on your electronics.

"But wait," you say, "many flights now have Wi-Fi on the plane. What about that??" If the plane offers onboard Wi-Fi from Gogo Inflight or a similar flying Internet service, you can go back to Settings→Wi-Fi→On and turn on just the Wi-Fi so you can join the network and get online in the air. When the aircraft lands and you're free to move about the cabin and off the plane, don't forget to choose Settings→Airplane Mode→Off.

Cellular Data (Wi-Fi + 3G iPads Only)

With a Wi-Fi + 3G iPad, you can get on the Internet by using your own wireless network (Wi-Fi), just as Wi-Fi iPad owners can, or you can tap in via AT&T's nationwide data network (3G). To use AT&T's network, you have to pay a monthly fee. The company sells two plans (page 38), one that gets you a limited 250 megabytes of data transfer for about $15 a month, and a $30-a-month plan that offers unlimited data coursing through your iPad's connection.

The Unlimited Plan people paid twice as much as the 250 Meg folks just so they don't have to worry about counting bits and bytes, but Settings→Cellular Data (shown on page 41) has something for everyone.For one, you can add a PIN code number to lock down the iPad's micro-SIM card so others can't mess with your iPad; just tap SIM PIN and pick a number.

Within the Cellular Data settings, you can turn the 3G network on or off, which is helpful for Limited Plan people close to that 250-megabyte limit. If you're on an international trip, you can turn off Data Roaming; leaving it on could mean your iPad starts grabbing data over pricier international data networks. And finally, to see how much data you've used, upgrade your plan, add an international plan, or edit your payment information, tap the View Account button.

Brightness & Wallpaper

You really get no surprises here. Tapping Settings→Brightness & Wallpaper takes you to the place where you can A.) use a virtual slider to make the screen dimmer or brighter so it's more comfortable for your eyes, and B.) select a new image to appear as the background wallpaper for both your iPad's Lock Screen (the one you see when you wake the iPad up but before you swipe the unlock slider) and its Home Screen (the screen where all your app icons live).

Tap the Wallpaper icon here to select new background images from either Apple's own stock shots or from a photo collection you added to the tablet (see Chapter 15 for the details on how to do that). Tap a thumbnail photo to select it and see a preview, then tap the button of your choice: Set Lock Screen, Set Home Screen, Set Both, or Cancel.

Picture Frame

The iPad's built-in Picture Frame feature (page 249) lets you show off your photo collection when you're not using the tablet for other things. Tap Settings→Picture Frame to tell the iPad how to play the slideshow. Here, you can choose the type of transition between images (the standard Dissolve or the fancier, animated Origami), if you want the Picture Frame to zoom in on people's faces, and if you want the photos shuffled out of the order in which they appear in their original photo album. Finally, you can pick *which* photos you want to appear. (Hint: It might be a good idea to *not* pick those Las Vegas bachelorette party photos if you know your mother is coming over for tea this afternoon.) To set up a reguar photo-album slideshow, see page 244.

General

This collection of General settings mostly concerns the overall iPad itself—and not so much a specific app or function, like Photos or 3G-network connectivity. When you tap Settings→General, you see a whole screen full of menus for changing the way the iPad behaves. These include:

- **About.** Tap here to see your iPad's vital statistics: its total drive capacity, amount of space available, system software version, model number, Wi-Fi and Bluetooth network addresses, and serial number. You can also see how many songs, videos, photos, and apps live on the iPad. And as a special bonus for the extremely bored or insomnia-afflicted, you can tap to read Apple's Legal and Regulatory information about the iPad.

- **Sounds.** Tap Sounds to get a volume slider for adjusting the iPad's audio level. You can also opt to turn Off (or On) alert sounds for New Mail, Sent Mail, Calendar Alerts, Lock Sounds, and the tap-tap-tappy Keyboard Clicks noises.

- **Network.** This is where you tap to see what Wi-Fi network you're currently connected to—or to pick a new network. If your office has given you a connection to its *virtual private network* (VPN) for a more safe and secure link to the Internet, tap VPN. Here, you can turn on the iPad's VPN function and configure your connection based on the information you got from the corporate IT folks.

- **Bluetooth.** To pair up a Bluetooth keyboard (page 29) or headset (page 5), tap Bluetooth to On. Then follow the instructions that came with the keyboard or headset for wirelessly connecting it to the iPad.

- **Location Services.** Tap Location Services to On if you want the iPad to calculate your position on a map or supply information about where you are to certain location-aware applications (like restaurant finders). Tap it to Off if you don't want to be found—or want to save some battery power.

- **Auto-Lock.** Tap this setting to adjust the amount of time the iPad screen stays on before it turns itself off (and displays the Lock Screen when you wake it up). You can choose 2, 5, 10, or 15 minutes—or Never.

- **Passcode Lock.** If you have sensitive information on your Pad (or just want to keep the kids from sneaking in there and messing things up when you're not around), tap Passcode Lock. On the next screen, tap Turn Passcode On. Think up a four-digit number and verify it. To get by the iPad's Lock Screen now, you must type in this code. If you have really sensitive data on the iPad, you can tap Settings→General→Passcode Lock→Erase Data to completely wipe all the information off of the iPad's drive if someone incorrectly enters the passcode more than 10 times. Just make sure you have that top secret info securely tucked away on another computer as a full set of back-up files, since it won't be on the iPad anymore.

- **Restrictions.** Speaking of the kids, tap Settings→General→Restrictions→ Enable Restrictions to set up some rules on the iPad; you need to set up a Passcode Lock for this feature. Once you do, you can block the kiddies from using iTunes, Safari, and YouTube. (The iPad removes the screen icons for these apps until the passcode is entered.) You can also set limits on installing apps or mapping the kids' whereabouts via Location Services. And you can restrict the type of content they can play on the iPad—like, say, *no* music with Explicit lyrics.

- **Home.** Tap here to set up your Home button's double-click powers (page 6), to always display the iPod controls when music is playing, and to choose what iPad apps to include (and in what order) in a Spotlight search (page 28).

- **Date & Time.** Tap here to switch between the 12-hour (AM/PM) clock or the military-style 24-hour clock. Frequent travelers can also pick a time zone and manually set the iPad's date and time.

- **Keyboard.** Within the Keyboard settings area, you can turn on (or off) the Auto-Correction and Auto-Capitalization features that fix your typing, plus turn on the Enable Caps Lock feature. You also go here to turn on the so-called "." *Shortcut* that sticks a period at the end of a sentence, adds a space, and then capitalizes the next letter when you double-tap the keyboard's space bar. Speaking of keyboards, tap International keyboards here to select and add an alternate keyboard in another language like French or German.

- **International.** World travelers can easily set the language the iPad uses for its menus and commands here by tapping Settings→General→International→Language. Tap Settings→General→ International to turn on international keyboards (see Keyboard above) and format dates, times, and phone numbers based on the standards of a particular country.

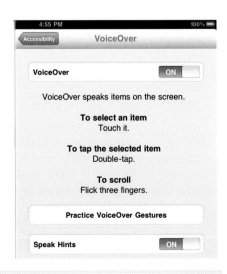

- **Accessibility.** Apple has built in a number of features that make the iPad easier to use for those with visual impairments. When you choose Settings→General→Accessibility, you can turn on the VoiceOver feature that announces menu names and titles out loud.

(VoiceOver has a bit of setup involved and has many special gestures you can use to operate the iPad; for more information, tap Home→Safari and go to *help.apple.com/ipad/mobile/interface* , and then tap Accessibility for in-depth instruction on using this extensive feature.)

The iPad's built-in accessibility settings also include Zoom, for major magnification by double-tapping with three fingers, (although, according to Apple, you can't use it at the same time as the VoiceOver function). For easier reading, tap the high-contrast White on Black function that reverses the screen colors. You can also switch the iPad's audio output from stereo to Mono Audio to let those with hearing impairments hear the entire sound signal at once instead of split into two channels. If you want the iPad's auto-correction function to shout out the typos it's fixing while you're busy looking at the keyboard, choose Settings→General→ Accessibility→Speak Auto-Text→On. And you can set the Home button to toggle VoiceOver or the White on Black screen on or off with a triple-click.

- **Battery Percentage.** What to know exactly what percentage of battery power the iPad has left? Flip this setting to On. Don't care? Choose Off.

- **Reset.** Tap here to get to all the buttons for blanking the iPad's memory. You can reset all its settings (or just the network settings), reset the dictionary that corrects your typing, revert to the Home screen's original layout, and resume getting those little warnings about using your location settings after you've given programs like Maps permission to use them. If you want to erase everything off the iPad, choose Settings→General→Reset→Erase All Content and Settings. But remember, you're nuking everything off your iPad—personal information, music, videos, photos, iBooks—*everything*.

Mail, Contacts, Calendars

Settings for the Mail app hog much of the screen when you tap Settings→Mail, Contacts, Calendars. Still, you're probably going to be adjusting your Mail settings more than Contacts or Calendars.

For example, you come here to add new email accounts to the iPad (or delete them), tell it how often to fetch your new messages, and change the look of the Mail program in general. You can choose the number of messages from your email accounts that you wish to see in the iPad's Inbox (25 to 200 recent messages at a time) and have the inbox reveal more or less of a message (one to five lines, or none at all).

You can change the font size to squint less, choose a default mail account if you have more than one on the iPad, and change your Signature file—the standard bit of text that gets attached to the end of every outgoing message.

You can also make the iPad ask you each time you want to delete messages, show (or hide) remote images from HTML mail, and show the To/Cc label to see if a message was addressed directly to you. Want to send a secret copy of a message to yourself? Turn on the Always Bcc Myself setting.

In the Contacts area, you can specify which way you want the iPad to sort and display people's names—last name *first* and first name *last*, or the first name and then the last name. In the Calendars area, you can turn on your New Invitation Alert to pipe up when someone sends you a meeting invitation, and also select a time zone for your calendar's appointments (useful if you live in New York but telecommute to the main office in San Francisco). Finally, you can pick a default calendar for your appointments if you have multiple calendars synced to the iPad.

Safari

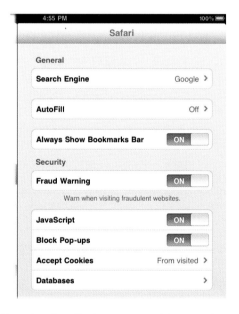

The Settings area for the iPad's Safari browser has many helpful buttons. Here, you can choose if you want your search results to come from Google or Yahoo and opt to have the Autofill feature fill in information automatically in web forms. To see your Bookmarks Bar at all times in the Safari window? Tap Settings→Safari→Always Show Bookmarks Bar→On to make it so. In the Security area of the Safari settings, you can help protect yourself when web surfing by turning on the Fraud Warning (which spots certain phishing sites out to rip off your personal information), enabling or disabling the JavaScript-powered interactive features some websites use (if you're worried about security), blocking pop-up ads, and rejecting cookies from sites you don't personally visit.

Tap Databases to see content Safari stores locally on your iPad (like files from Apple's online iPad help guide). If Safari is acting sluggish or you want to erase your tracks, tap the buttons to clear the browser's history, cookies, and cache files. Are you a web developer who wants to know why your web page is acting wiggy on iPad Safari? Tap Settings→Safari→Developer→Debug Console→On to get some help deciphering those page errors.

iPod

The iPod settings on the iPad include just four options to fiddle with. Here, you can turn on the Sound Check feature, which is intended to smooth out the differing volumes of songs in a playlist into one fairly consistent sound level. Tap EQ to pick a preferred equalizer preset to make your music sound better. If you worry about hearing loss or damage from headphones full of loud music, tap Volume Limit to On and set a maximum audio level. And if you don't want to see song lyrics or podcast info on-screen when listening to the iPad's iPod, choose Settings→iPod→Lyrics & Podcast Info→Off.

Videos

In the Videos settings, you can opt to have the iPad bookmark the spot in a movie or TV show where you stop it so you can pick right up again when you come back to it. Just tap Settings→Videos→Start Playing→Where Left Off; you can also choose From Beginning if you want to always start the whole thing over again. If you have videos with Closed Captioning text descriptions embedded in the files, you can flip the Closed Captioning control On or Off. And when you're funneling movies and TV shows off the iPad and onto the TV screen (page 233), you can flip the Widescreen button On to make sure the picture retains its original aspect ratio. Using the iPad with a TV in another country? Choose the TV Signal standard here: NTSC or PAL (page 246).

Photos

The iPad keeps a few settings for photo slideshows at Settings→Photos. You can choose the amount of time each picture stays on-screen, Repeat the slideshow over and over again automatically, and decide if you want to Shuffle the pictures into a different order from how they appear in your photo album.

Store

Tap the Store icon in the Settings list, then tap the View Account button if you need to see your address and billing information for the iTunes Store or App Store. You can also sign out of your account by tapping the Sign Out button.

App Preferences

Different apps may have application-specific settings as well. The iPad lists the ones that do under Apps in the Settings column. For example, you can change what the iBooks app does when you tap the left margin of the screen—you can go to the previous page or onward to the next page. If you use Skype on the iPad, you can tell it to sign you in automatically (or not) when you turn the iPad on and to stay online even if the iPad's Lock Screen comes on. Each app has different settings—and some don't have any settings at all—but it's worth a tap of the Settings icon to see what you can adjust.

B

iPad Troubleshooting and Care

Like most electronic gadgets, the iPad always works perfectly fine—until it doesn't. Many woes are common and pretty easy to fix—the battery ran all the way down and needs to charge up a bit before iTunes sees it, or the rotation lock is still on and that's why the screen won't reorient itself. Less obvious glitches in the iPad's behavior can be solved by adjusting something in the Settings area, as explained in Appendix A.

But the iPad is a little mini-computer in its own right, and it can exhibit bigger issues that require more than flipping a setting, and may even need the help of a technical expert. Figuring out what your iPad is trying to tell you when it's sick is the first step in getting it back to good health. This chapter explains what to do if your iPad starts acting weird—and where to go if you need more information or can't fix it yourself.

Apple's iPad Troubleshooting Pages

For in-depth advice on a variety of iPad ailments, Apple offers a detailed set of troubleshooting documents at *www.apple.com/support/ipad*. Its support site also addresses issues with iTunes and syncing content to and from the iPad.

If you don't feel like putting this book down to go running off to the Web, here are some common tricks to try if your iPad starts acting up:

- **Restart the iPad.** Like a computer that's behaving badly, sometimes restarting the device clears up a cranky or stalled system. To restart the iPad, hold down the Sleep/Wake (On/Off) button on the top of the tablet until  the red "Slide to Power Off" bar appears. Swipe your finger to shut things down. Then press the Sleep/Wake button again until the Apple logo appears on-screen and the iPad starts back up again.

- **Force Quit a frozen app.** Apps are software, too, and sometimes software gets stuck (just ask anyone who's used a computer for more than a month). To make a cranky app shut down without having to restart the whole iPad, press and hold the Sleep/Wake button down until you see the red "power-off" slider—but don't slide this time. Instead, press and hold the Home button down until the app quits and you find yourself back on the Home screen.

- **Reset the app's settings.** Sometimes an app's personal settings just get a little scrambled, so tap the Settings icon on the Home screen. In the Settings area, check to see if this particular app has its own entry, and tap whatever button is there to reset the app's own settings. Page 118 has more on troubleshooting apps.

- **Reset the iPad.** A reset is a bit more abrupt that a restart, but it can free up a completely frozen tablet. The next page tells you how to execute one (a reset, not a frozen tablet).

If you're having problems even after you fiddle with an app's settings, you can reset the iPad's settings (not the iPad itself; that's covered next). Choose Settings→General→Reset. The Reset screen lets you wipe your custom configurations (like your network info) and take the iPad back to its default settings.

Always check your battery level before going too far—if it's in the red, plug in the iPad for a few hours to recharge.

Reset Your iPad

Restarting the iPad (turning it off and back on again) can solve many problems, but what do you do if the iPad doesn't respond to your gentle touch? If it's stuck and you can't even restart your 'Pad, you can physically *reset* it without losing your files. (Note that resetting the iPad is different from resetting its settings, explained on the previous page.)

To give your iPad the old reset move, follow the steps below:

❶ Plug the iPad into its wall charger if you suspect its battery is running low.

❷ Simultaneously press and hold down the two iPad buttons that are *not* the volume rocker: the Sleep/Wake button on top and the Home button on the front. Let go when you see the Apple logo. You can hold it up or lay it flat on the table to reset it, as long as you hit the buttons properly.

If the technology gods are smiling on you, your iPad will go through its little start-up sequence and then return you to the main menu.

Download and Reinstall iTunes and iTunes Updates

If iTunes is acting up, you may need to download and install a fresh version of the program. The latest version's always waiting at *www.apple.com/itunes/ download*. Your iTunes program itself may also alert you to a new version—or you can make sure it does so in the future:

- If you use iTunes for Windows and installed the Apple Software Update utility when you added iTunes, an alert box appears whenever Apple updates iTunes and offers to install it for you. If you skipped installing the utility, choose Edit→Preferences→General and turn on "Check for updates automatically." If you prefer to check manually, choose Help→"Check for Updates". In either case, you're prompted to snag an update if one's available.

- The Mac's Software Update program is designed to alert you, via a pop-up dialog box, about new updates for iTunes. If you turned Software Update off (in System Preferences), however, you can run it manually by choosing Software Update from the Apple menu.

 Note If you've tried reinstalling iTunes to no avail, fully uninstall the old copy first to clear any lingering problems. One way to do this on a PC is to choose Start→Control Panel→Add/Remove Programs (or choose Start→Control Panel and select "Uninstall a program"). Find iTunes in the list and click the button to uninstall it.

On a Mac OS X system, choose Go→Applications and drag the iTunes application icon to the Trash. Then choose Go→Utilities→Activity Monitor (or go to the Mac's Applications folder and open the Utilities folder to find the Activity Monitor). Find iTunes Helper in the list and click the big red Quit Process button at the top of the window. Finally, choose →System Preferences→Accounts→Login Items. Select iTunes Helper in the list and click the minus button (-) to remove it. Restart the Mac. Apple has more detailed instructions at *support.apple.com/kb/ht1224*.

As with any software update, once you download the software, double-click the installer file's icon and follow along as the program takes you through several screens of upgrade excitement. If the version of iTunes you're installing is newer than the one you've got, you get "Upgrade" as a button option when you run the installer—and it usually takes less time to do the job.

If you're installing the same version of the program, the iTunes installer may politely ask if you want to either *Repair* or even *Remove* the software. Choosing Repair can often fix damaged files that iTunes needs to run properly. It can also be a quicker fix than fully removing the program and reinstalling it again. (See the Note on the opposite page for another uninstall method.)

Reinstalling iTunes doesn't erase all of your music, movies, books, or other items out of your iTunes library. It just gives you a new and hopefully better-working version of the software.

If you open the reinstalled iTunes to an empty library, don't panic. Quit iTunes and go find the iTunes folder, usually in My Documents→My Music→iTunes or Music→iTunes. Drag the iTunes Library file from the iTunes folder onto the computer's desktop. Then go back to the iTunes folder, open the Previous iTunes Libraries folder and find the iTunes Library file stamped with the date you updated the program. Drag this file out into the main iTunes folder and rename it to just iTunes Library without the date in the file name. Now start up iTunes again and see of everything's all better. If not, take a trip to *www.apple.com/support/itunes* for further help.

Update the iPad's Software

Updating the iPad's internal software—which Apple occasionally does to fix bugs and add features—is much easier than it used to be, thanks to iTunes. No matter which iPad, iPod, or iPhone model you have, iTunes 9 and later handles all software updating chores for Apple's devices.

To make sure you have the latest version of the iPad software, follow these steps:

❶ Connect your iPad to the computer and select it in the Source list.

❷ On the Summary tab, click the "Check for Update" button in the Version area (circled below). If your iPad is up to date, iTunes tells you so.

❸ If iTunes finds new iPad software, you'll be prompted to download it. Click the Downloading icon in the Source pane to monitor your download progress. Sometimes iTunes will have already downloaded the new iPad software. In that case, just click the Update button in the iTunes main window.

❹ Follow the instructions on-screen.

You mainly just have to sit there while iTunes handles everything. The iPad usually just sits there quietly with a progress bar and an Apple logo on its screen while it's getting its new system software. Once all that goes away, your iPad screen returns to normal and iTunes displays a message box letting you know the update's complete.

 Note If you bought your iPad before November 2010, iTunes will alert you to the tablet's first major software update: iOS 4.2. The update brings all kinds of fabulous new features to the iPad, including the Game Center app for multiplayer gaming, multitasking to run more than one app at a time, and wireless printing from Safari, Mail, iWork, and other apps. You can also drag wiggling Home screen icons (see the bottom of page 7) on top of each other to create folders of apps. If you got your iPad in December, you're probably already enjoying all these cool new treats, but be sure to check in occasionally for future iOS updates.

Use iPad Backup Files

You may not notice it at the time, but iTunes creates backup files of your iPad's settings and other system information when you sync the tablet to the computer. It also creates backups when you do more serious stuff, like update or restore (page 276) the iPad's system software. Now you may be thinking, "Cool! I don't have to worry if I accidentally destroy my iPad because I can copy all its content onto a replacement!" This, however, is not the case.

That's because iTunes only backs up data from apps, system settings, and that sort of stuff—not your entire music and video collection, nor your contacts and calendars, nor your actual photos, nor your apps. Apple assumes you have all those files on your computer, from syncing the iPad with iTunes to copy data back and forth.

When you restore an iPad from its backup file, though, it remembers your syncing *settings*, so you just have to let iTunes resync all the content to the iPad during the process. This also means you should connect the iPad to iTunes every once in a while so it can sync up and have a record (back-up) of what you currently have on your iPad.

To restore an iPad from its backup file:

❶ Connect the iPad to the computer you usually sync it with and right-click (Control-click) its icon in the iTunes source list.

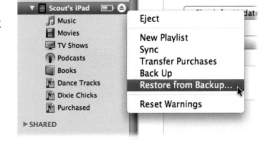

❷ From the pop-up menu, choose Restore from Backup. In the box that appears, choose the backup file you want to use (if you sync more than one iPad to this computer).

❸ Click the Restore button and let iTunes do its thing.

When iTunes is done, your iPad should look pretty much like it did the last time you backed it up.

 Tip If you're worried about security, you can encrypt your iPad backups with a password. Click the iPad's icon in iTunes, click the Summary tab, and turn on the checkbox next to "Encrypt iPad backup." Enter a password—the same password you'll need to complete Step 3 above.

Start Over: Restore Your iPad's Software

Just like the operating system that runs your desktop computer, your iPad has its own software that controls everything it does. *Restoring* the iPad software isn't the same thing as updating it. Restoring is a much more drastic procedure, like reformatting the hard drive on your PC or Mac. For one thing, restoring the software *erases everything on your iPad*.

So, restore with caution, and do so only if you try all the other troubleshooting measures in this chapter. If you decide to take the plunge, first make sure you have the most recent version of iTunes (flip back to page 272 for information on that), then proceed as follows:

❶ Start iTunes, and connect your iPad to your computer with its cable.

❷ When the iPad appears in the iTunes Source list, click its icon to see the Summary information (in the main area of the iTunes window).

❸ In the Summary area, click the Restore button.

 Note Now, just because you've sucked the life out of your iPad doesn't mean that all your songs, videos, and so on are gone from iTunes. That's the beauty of the iPad-iTunes partnership: By storing everything in iTunes, you can always re-load it onto your iPad, as described on the next page.

❹ As mentioned back on page 275, iTunes gives you the chance to back up your iPad's settings—like your preferences for contacts and calendar syncing and other personalized data on your iPad. This means much less work getting your iPad all re-personalized after you reinstall its software. But if you want to wipe every trace of your existence from the iPad, skip the backup.

❺ Because restoring erases everything on your iPad, you get a warning message. If you're sure you want to continue, click Restore again.

❻ If you use a Mac, enter an administrator password; a progress bar appears on your iPad's screen. Leave the iPad connected to your computer to complete the restoration process. You may also see an Apple logo appear on-screen.

After iTunes finishes the restore process, its Setup Assistant window appears asking you to name your iPad and choose your syncing preferences—just like when you connected your iPad for the first time. Let the iPad automatically update your files, or add your songs, photos, and videos back manually and see if this little procedure fixed the tablet's predicament.

Protect Your iPad

The iPad was meant to be held—held up for others to see, held on your lap, held under your arm as you walk down the hall, and so on. But with *holding* sometimes comes *dropping* (and with *that,* cursing), so protecting your iPad with a case or cover might help cushion its fall. Cases and covers also protect the surface of the tablet, (especially that glossy screen) when it's riding around in a purse or backpack.

In addition to protecting the iPad, adding a case shows off a bit of your own personality, from a hot-pink zippered number to a stately leather portfolio. Here are a few of the many places to find the latest in geek chic for your iPad:

- **Apple Store.** The company that makes the iPad also makes sure you have plenty of other stuff to buy to go with it, including cases, covers, docks, keyboards, headphones, and more. If there's no brick-and-mortar Apple Store in your town, visit the online emporium at *store.apple.com*.

- **Belkin.** After years of making computer and mobile accessories, Belkin has added about a dozen different iPad cases to its product line. Prices range from about $30 to $60; the $60 Leather Folio case is shown here. (*www.belkin.com*)

- **Hard Candy Cases.** Made of shock-absorbing rubber, Hard Candy's $40 Sleek Skin case for iPad protects the tablet in brightly colored armor that also shields the screen. (*www.hardcandycases.com*)

- **Griffin Technology.** A long-time maker of iPod and iPhone accessories, Griffin has jumped right in with iPad gear as well. Several iPad-case styles are available here (prices range from about $30 to $50) as is the $25 Screen Care Kit for iPad, which includes a low-glare stick-on screen protector and a cleaning cloth. (*www.griffintechnology.com*)

AppleCare—What It Is and Whether You Need It

You probably have an insurance policy on your house and car, so why not get one for your iPad? That's the logic behind getting the AppleCare Protection Plan for your iPad. The price for this peace of mind? Why, that'd be $99.

When you buy a brand-new iPad, you automatically get free telephone support to fix one problem within your first 90 days of iPad ownership, plus a year-long warranty on the hardware. If the iPad starts acting weird or stops working altogether during this time, Apple will fix it for free or send you a replacement tablet.

If you buy the AppleCare Protection Plan (available in many places where you buy iPads or at *www.apple.com/support/products/ipad.html*), you get:

- Two full years of free telephone support from the date of your iPad purchase

- Two full years of hardware protection from the date of your iPad purchase

If you need a repair or replacement, your iPad's covered, and the plan covers your tablet's battery and cables, too. Paying an extra hundred bucks to get the extended warranty may not appeal to everyone. But if you want a little peace of mind with your new iPad, it's a small price to pay, especially if you want to just relax and have fun with your tablet.

> **Tip** Have more questions about the AppleCare plan? Apple has a Frequently Asked Questions page on the topic at *www.apple.com/support/products/faqs.html*. As noted above, you get a full year of limited warranty on the iPad's hardware in case anything goes wrong with it—aside from user-inflicted damage. You can buy AppleCare any time within that year (dated from iPad purchase date) to extend the warranty. So if you don't feel like popping that extra $100 when you buy your iPad, wait and pony up for AppleCare towards the end of the first year—perhaps after you've paid off the credit card with the original iPad charge on it.

Index

Symbols

½x button (audio) **219**
1x button (audio) **219**
2x button (audio) **219**
2X button (scaling up iPhone apps) **113**
3G **260–262**
  (see also Wi-Fi + 3G)
  turning service on/off **41**
3G (3) icon **40**
(AA) Type icon (iBooks) **132**
± (Add bookmark) button (Safari browser)
  46
" (Back) button (Safari browser) **46**
} (Bookmarks) button (Safari browser) **46,**
  54, 58
(¶) button (Now Playing screen) **221**
(«, ») buttons (Now Playing screen) **220**
(÷/¿) buttons (Now Playing screen) **220**
[button (YouTube) **95**
] button (YouTube) **95**
} button (YouTube) **95**
√ Compose New Message (Mail) **75, 78**
fl button (Now Playing screen) **221**
' (Forward) button (Safari browser) **46**
ƒ (Check Mail) **75**
ƒ (Reload) button (Safari browser) **46**
° (GPRS) icon **40**
± icon (Notes) **93**
¬ icon (Notes) **93**
„ key **21**
= key **21**
≈ (Move to Folder) (Mail) **75, 79**
: (Page Juggler) (Safari browser) **46, 67**
"" shortcut **25**
symbol **21**
% symbol **21**
», «, ¿ video controls **95**
∑ (Wi-Fi) icon **40**

A

A2DP **5**
AAC audio format **188, 194**
About (General settings) **262**
AC adapter **14, 15, 232**
accented characters **24**
Accessibility (General settings) **264**
accessibility software **10**
Account and Billing Support link **210**
Activity Monitor (Macs) **272**
Add bookmark button (Safari browser) **46**
Add CalDAV Account option **89**
adding slides (Keynote) **159**
Add International Plan **43**
Add/Remove Programs **272**
Address bar (Safari browser) **46**
Add to Existing Contact (Mail) **77**
Add to Home Screen **52**
Add to Library **129, 167, 208, 211, 229**
Adobe Photoshop Elements **177, 238, 239**
AIFF audio format , **188, 15**
AIM **65**
Airplane Mode **261**
Album
  editing information and song gaps **199**
album cover art **215, 217, 222**
Album name box **199**
album ratings **192**
Albums **240, 241**
Albums view **190**
alcohol-based cleansers **16**
Alice for iPad **129**
Always Bcc Myself setting **266**
Always (cookies) **69**
Amazon
  album cover art **222**
  Kindle **121, 129**
  MP3 Downloads **211**

H

I

M

Get even more for your money.

Join the O'Reilly Community, and register the O'Reilly books you own. It's free, and you'll get:

- 40% upgrade offer on O'Reilly books
- Membership discounts on books and events
- Free lifetime updates to electronic formats of books
- Multiple ebook formats, DRM FREE
- Participation in the O'Reilly community
- Newsletters
- Account management
- 100% Satisfaction Guarantee

Signing up is easy:

1. Go to: oreilly.com/go/register
2. Create an O'Reilly login.
3. Provide your address.
4. Register your books.

Note: English-language books only

To order books online:

oreilly.com/order_new

For questions about products or an order:

orders@oreilly.com

To sign up to get topic-specific email announcements and/or news about upcoming books, conferences, special offers, and new technologies:

elists@oreilly.com

For technical questions about book content:

booktech@oreilly.com

To submit new book proposals to our editors:

proposals@oreilly.com

Many O'Reilly books are available in PDF and several ebook formats. For more information:

oreilly.com/ebooks

O'REILLY®

Spreading the knowledge of innovators   www.oreilly.com

Buy this book and get access to the online edition for 45 days—for free!

"The Missing Manual series is simply the most intelligent and usable series of guidebooks..."
—KEVIN KELLY, CO-FOUNDER OF WIRED

iPad
the missing manual®
The book that should have been in the box

O'REILLY®   J. D. Biersdorfer

iPad: The Missing Manual

By J. D. Biersdorfer
May 2010, $24.99
ISBN 9781449387846

With Safari Books Online, you can:

Access the contents of thousands of technology and business books

- Quickly search over 7000 books and certification guides
- Download whole books or chapters in PDF format, at no extra cost, to print or read on the go
- Copy and paste code
- Save up to 35% on O'Reilly print books
- **New!** Access mobile-friendly books directly from cell phones and mobile devices

Stay up-to-date on emerging topics before the books are published

- Get on-demand access to evolving manuscripts.
- Interact directly with authors of upcoming books

Explore thousands of hours of video on technology and design topics

- Learn from expert video tutorials
- Watch and replay recorded conference sessions

To try out Safari and the online edition of this book FREE for 45 days,
go to *www.oreilly.com/go/safarienabled* and enter the coupon code MIUZGAA.
To see the complete Safari Library, visit safari.oreilly.com.

Spreading the knowledge of innovators   safari.oreilly.com